Value Optimization for Project and Performance Management

Value Optimization for Project and Performance Management

ROBERT B. STEWART

WILEY

John Wiley & Sons, Inc.

Published by John Wiley & Sons, Inc., Hoboken, New Jersey.
Published simultaneously in Canada.

For general information on our other products and services or for technical support, please contact our Customer Care Department within the United States at (800) 762-2974, outside the United States at (317) 572-3993 or fax (317) 572-4002.

Wiley also publishes its books in a variety of electronic formats. Some content that appears in print may not be available in electronic books. For more information about Wiley products, visit our Web site at www.wiley.com.

Library of Congress Cataloging-in-Publication Data

Stewart, Robert B., 1968–
  Value optimization for project and performance management / Robert B. Stewart.
    p. cm.
  Includes bibliographical references and index.
  ISBN 978-0-470-55114-1 (cloth)
  1. Project management. 2. Value analysis (Cost control) 3. Value. I. Title.
  HD69.P75S746 2010
  658.4′04—dc22
                                         2009051055

Printed in the United States of America

10 9 8 7 6 5 4 3 2 1

Contents

Preface

A wise man named Larry Miles once said, "Poor value is a people problem." If he is right, and I believe he is, then value is ultimately more about communication than things such as financial markets and monetary policy. Value begins when a need is expressed by one person and subsequently fulfilled by another. The communication involved in that exchange is fundamental yet essential in providing a framework for value for both the producer and the consumer.

Sadly, communication is seldom efficient in framing value and yet it is really the only means we have to do so. It begins with the abstract nature of thought, which is subjected to the ambiguity of language and then further diluted by the countless cognitive biases that stand between perception and meaning. One cannot help but marvel that we are able to communicate effectively at all.

This book is first and foremost about framing value. This value framework is built upon its constituent elements: performance, cost, time, and risk. These are in turn communicated through a common language—that of function. If the language of function is the lingua franca, then each of the aforementioned elements possesses its own vernacular. This book attempts to show how fluency in each of these variables is essential to understanding value.

The rise of the professional fields of project and program management has created a kind of renaissance in the managerial sciences. Projects are largely about things, whereas traditional management is mostly about people. The merger of these concepts has created a demand for knowledge in how to best manage both through the synthesis of theory and applied techniques. The management of scope, cost, schedule, communications, quality, and risk are all core knowledge areas within the modern practice of project management. The theories and techniques of Value Methodology provide a means of considering the synergistic effect of all of these components within the context of project management as they relate to project value.

Many management improvement processes and fads have come and gone in the past several decades. Value Methodology, as presented in this book, has withstood the test of time as a proven means of improving value. It is one of a handful of methodologies to have been formally legislated by government bodies at all levels. Value Methodology is scalable to meet the needs of any project. It has been applied to the simplest manufactured items and to unimaginably large and complex infrastructure projects. Value Methodology is reproducible in that it provides a framework and toolset that can be duplicated on project after project. Finally, Value

Methodology is timeless in its relevance. Though it can be elusive, value is the measure of what will make a project a success or a failure.

The primary audience for this book is those involved in the development and delivery of projects and programs. This includes project and program managers, designers, engineers, architects, purchasing agents, cost estimators, schedulers, and risk managers, as well as those seated within upper management who have a vested interest in developing a working fluency with Value Methodology. Management consultants will find this book particularly well suited to their needs. Students will also find this book useful, as it is written in plain English and does not demand any prerequisite skills or experience other than a healthy thirst for knowledge.

This book provides an in-depth survey of both the theory and application of Value Methodology. Examples relevant to design and construction, manufacturing, industrial design, management processes, services, and systems design are presented in a clear and concise manner. Each technique is demonstrated using examples that flow through the entire book so that readers may witness how the process unfolds with each new step of its execution.

Chapter 1: The body of knowledge known as Value Methodology (VM) is introduced. This chapter explores the history and evolution of VM; its relevance to today's economic challenges and the practice of project management; and examples of its current application within the public and private sectors.

Chapter 2: The theory of value is considered and the concept of functional value is presented. The nine most common factors that commonly lead to poor project value are explored. These range from the insidious (preoccupation of internal value rather than customer value) to the banal (habits and attitudes).

Chapter 3: The Value Methodology framework, commonly referred to as the Job Plan, is presented. This chapter provides an overview of the process from start to finish and lays the groundwork for subsequent chapters.

Chapter 4: The first phase of the VM Job Plan is presented: preparation. Topics range from the selection and timing of value studies to the composition of value teams. This chapter also introduces a case study, that of a construction project, that demonstrates each step of the VM Job Plan that is carried through Chapter 11.

Chapter 5: The organization and analysis of project information is the focus of this phase of the VM Job Plan: information. Life cycle costing is discussed, as is the use of cost modeling techniques. The use of schedules and sequence flowcharts are examined and risk analysis techniques are presented. Finally, the unique process of performance and value measurement, called Value Metrics, is discussed at length.

Chapter 6: The powerful concept of functions is introduced in this chapter. The definition, classification, and analysis of functions are discussed in great detail. The technique of FAST diagramming is also presented, as well as methods for dimensioning them with various types of project information to increase their potency.

Chapter 7: Creativity is the focus of this chapter. A variety of creativity techniques are explored with an emphasis on those that will yield the greatest results in the shortest amount of time. The dichotomy of left- versus right-brain thinking is explored and methods for breaking down roadblocks to creative thought are discussed.

Chapter 8: Critical thinking is often taken for granted. This chapter explores the mental shortcuts that are often employed, called heuristics, and how they can often lead our thinking astray. A number of group evaluation techniques are presented that will help improve critical thinking and help teams evaluate ideas more thoroughly and thoughtfully.

Chapter 9: This chapter is about the development of ideas. Good development requires that the information supporting a new idea is synthesized in a way that addresses performance, cost, time, and risk. Techniques for developing alternative concepts are presented and numerous examples are provided to illustrate these principles.

Chapter 10: The best idea in the world is worthless if it falls upon deaf ears. This chapter focuses on techniques for presenting ideas both concisely and effectively. The assembly and presentation of performance, cost, time, and risk information culminate in a simple but elegant expression of value.

Chapter 11: The job isn't finished until all those great ideas are implemented. The critical and final phase of the VM Job Plan, Implementation, is explored. Techniques for implementing change and monitoring its progress are presented.

Chapter 12: Improving value takes leadership. This chapter focuses on the qualities and characteristics of value specialists. The professional aspects of VM are discussed and the nuances between the roles of leader and facilitator are explored.

This book is the culmination of three generations of knowledge and experience in the field of Value Methodology. Throughout history there has always been a desire and need to improve upon the value in our world and our daily lives. It is my hope that the knowledge contained within this book will help address this driving force and can therefore be applied toward the betterment of society, the environment, and the human condition.

Supplements to this book, the author's blog, contact information, useful links, and additional resources, including software, are available at www. valueoptimization.net.

About the Cover

Bo Diddley once said that you can't judge a book by its cover. He may be right, but I figure people, being creatures of habit, will probably do it anyway. So I thought it might be a good idea to select a graphic for the cover that was somehow representative of its contents. This wasn't an easy task for a book like this one. The image of the five figures in five different colors represents the five key concepts of this book: performance, cost, time, risk, and value. Guess which one holds the missing piece?

Acknowledgments

There is a long list of people that I would like to thank in helping me write this book. I would like to first thank my grandfather Robert H. Mitchell, who initially piqued my interest in Value Methodology, took me under his wing, and pointed me in the right direction. Through your example you have shown me what can be accomplished through hard work, persistence, self-confidence, and a wee bit of charm.

Without Terry Hays I would not have been able to write this book. He has been a wonderful friend, business partner, and teacher who has not only given me room to grow but has encouraged it through the years.

In what I would consider the ultimate test of friendship, Eric Trimble devoted countless hours of his time in reviewing and editing this work. What drudgery. His attention to detail has greatly contributed to the value of this book. Thank you.

Special thanks to George Hunter for his help and support in developing Value Metrics during the early years. Thanks also to Dr. Jong-Kwon Lim, my South Korean connection and brother-in-arms. Keep up the fantastic work.

Thanks to Dr. Thomas Saaty and his two dynamic sons, John and Dan, for their groundbreaking work in the creation and continued development of the Analytic Hierarchy Process and Decision Lens. Their contributions to the decision sciences and assistance with this book have been invaluable.

Thanks to Ginger Adams, Jill Woller, and Michael Holt for their contributions to this book.

Thanks to everyone at the Lawrence Delos Miles Value Foundation for their inspirational work and dedication to the proliferation of Value Methodology. You are the keepers of the flame.

I am greatly indebted to those that have contributed to my knowledge and appreciation of Value Methodology: Jerry Kaufmann, Ted Fowler, Art Mudge, and Carlos Fallon. Although I never met Carlos, every time I read his words, it feels like I have. You were way ahead of your time.

Thanks to everyone at VMS. It is an honor to work with such a lovable collection of misfits.

Last year I became a father for the first time. My daughter, Daphne, has developed to the point now where she is getting into everything and, as a result, I find myself saying "No." She just looks at me, smiles blithely, and carries on. It hasn't begun to sink in yet, but soon it will. When it finally does, I will have succeeded in making the first step toward introducing her to critical thinking at the expense of presenting her with her first roadblock to creativity. Alas, life is all about trade-offs. Thanks to you, Daphne, for teaching me this lesson every day.

Finally, thanks to my father, Ken, and my mother, Terri, for instilling in me the values I hold dear. I wouldn't have written this were it not for you. And of course, thanks to my wife Vanessa for her love and support. Without love, what's the point?

Value Optimization for Project and Performance Management

CHAPTER 1

Introduction

© Magixl 2009, www.magixl.com

Poor value is a people problem.

—Larry Miles

Lawrence Delos Miles was born in 1904 to Delos Miles, a public school superintendent, and Vinetta Miles, an elementary school teacher in Harvard, Nebraska. Miles was very bright, and he graduated from high school in three years rather than the usual four. He attended Nebraska Wesleyan University in Lincoln, Nebraska, with a degree in education. In 1925, he was a teacher and high school principal in Winnebago, Nebraska. In 1926, he made a career change and moved into banking. Dissatisfied with this, he returned to college to study engineering. In 1931, Miles graduated from the College of Engineering at the University of Nebraska with a degree in electrical engineering.

In 1932, Miles began a long and productive career at General Electric Co. in Schenectady, New York. His first assignment at GE was that of a design engineer in the Vacuum Tube Engineering Department. Over a six-year period in this position, he earned 12 patents for vacuum tubes and related circuitry. During this time, Miles developed awareness for unnecessary costs and began seeing the need for developing better ways of doing things.

This sensitivity to cost earned him a transfer to GE's purchasing department, and in 1938 he was promoted to the position of purchasing engineer. During this time, Miles worked closely with vendors to reduce costs associated with electronic components, eventually moving on to precision-machined parts. In 1944, Miles was transferred to a subsidiary of GE called Locke Insulator. While at Locke, he began the development of the process that has now evolved into the function-oriented problem solving methodology known today as Value Methodology.

Miles was instrumental in the initial development and spread of Value Methodology. In 1959, he helped create the Society of American Value Engineers and served as its first president between 1960 and 1962. He was the author of the first book on the subject, *Techniques of Value Analysis and Engineering*, which was published in 1961. He taught seminars and lectured extensively throughout the United States and the rest of the world.

Larry Miles received many accolades and awards during his career, but none were greater than the honor bestowed on him by Japan. In 1984, he was post-humously awarded the Third Order of Merit with Cordon of Sacred Treasure by the emperor of Japan. The Japanese bestowed this honor on Miles due to the major impact that the use of Value Methodology had on making Japan an industrial and economic powerhouse. In addition, he received international recognition from Germany and South Africa for his contributions.

The story of Larry Miles is a fitting introduction to this book. Without him, the writing of this book would not have been possible.[1] Larry Miles also exemplified the role that Value Leadership can play in improving the value of products, services, and facilities. While other leaders in business improvement, like Dr. W. Edwards Deming and Phillip Crosby, have received greater notoriety, the work of Larry Miles has created a quiet legacy that endures today.

Today's Challenges

Most people today would agree that long-term profitability is the main objective of private enterprise, while the timely delivery of needed services would describe the goal of public bodies. They would also quickly point out that the products and services these entities produce should be competitively priced and/or efficiently provided while meeting or exceeding the performance expectations of their customers. In order to adapt to an ever-changing environment, organizations are challenged to make better use of their most important resource, their people.

This idea has been demonstrated through the innovations introduced by the quality movement and by the evolution of program and project management that has been experienced in recent years. Executive management has learned that through the emphasis of programs and projects and by ingraining a culture of quality improvement, the effectiveness of an organization can realize significant gains. Despite the benefits of these innovations, they will amount to little unless the organization possesses an active understanding of the value that its customers place on its products and services, and is capable of defining, measuring, and improving it.

In late 2008, the world was confronted with the sudden end to the unbridled growth that the global economy had experienced earlier in the decade. At the heart of our "irrational exuberance"[2] was the delusion that the market could only go up; that growth would be perpetual; that the uncertainty posed by risks could be completely avoided; and that value could be created from nothing. Looking back, it is remarkable to think that at least tacitly, the majority of us held these beliefs to be true. Like the laws of physics, the laws of value cannot be circumvented. Value is grounded in reality. It demands honesty. It does not suffer fools or charlatans.

One need only look at the following recent phenomenon to see how easily we can be led astray when we lack a means to anchor value to reality:

- The overvaluations of Internet companies during the growth of the "dot-com" bubble were fueled by wildly optimistic speculation on fast-growing Internet businesses. One Internet company spent $135 million in capital over its 18-month life span while never once generating a profit.[3] Too great an emphasis was placed on rapid growth and not enough on the actual value of the service it provided.

- The development in the 1990s of the financial instruments known as collateral debt obligations (CDOs) and credit default swaps (CDSs) were touted by their creators as ways to essentially eliminate all investment-related risk. These instruments ran completely contrary to one of the basic tenets of the free market system, namely, the concept of "risk and reward." What is all the more ironic is that the risk "experts" on Wall Street are the ones who concocted these schemes and drove the market into the ground, with many of them collecting huge bonuses for our pains. This proves the point that you cannot sweep uncertainty under the rug or hide it in the closet. It will most surely destroy value if it is not addressed in a rational, responsible manner.

- The proliferation of CDOs and CDSs in turn led banks to lower their lending requirements based on the false belief that the financial risks had been diluted to such an extent that they couldn't possibly lose money on a bad loan. The availability of cheap adjustable-rate loans and the demand for housing led to the boom in house construction during this same period. Between 1997 and 2006, the price of the typical American house increased by 124 percent.[4] During this same period, average U.S. incomes remained virtually flat. Inevitably, borrowers on the riskier loans began to default, which began increasing the supply of homes available and eventually burst the housing bubble. I can remember watching the value of homes in my neighborhood going up and up during this period while my income remained pretty constant. Chatting with my neighbors, we all agreed it couldn't go on forever—and sure enough, it didn't. Between 2006 and 2008, home prices fell an average of 20 percent nationwide and were still falling at the time of this writing.[5] Despite the fact that many of us, at a gut level, felt that something was terribly wrong, we all just went along with it, thinking that the market must be right. Many of us even further leveraged our overvalued homes with home equity loans to buy other things we couldn't afford. When we do not have a clear yardstick for measuring value, we lack the information needed to make critical decisions.

While these examples apply to the general economy at a macro level, they are a reflection of the inability of both individuals and organizations to understand and measure value.

Dan Ariely, in his brilliant book on behavioral economics, *Predictably Irrational*, discusses at length his thoughts on the subprime mortgage crisis. He argues that individuals, organizations, and indeed the global market behave in a manner that is completely irrational with respect to economic decision making. If even only a few of the compelling points he makes are true, then it only further reinforces the importance of developing a rational framework that allows us to assess value.[6]

Lacking the compass of value, an organization is in danger of losing its way. Further, if it can find its compass, it must become fluent in its use in order to interpret its meaning. All of this first requires an acknowledgment that the organization lacks the tools, training, and necessary attitude by its leaders. Developing this insight is the first step, and the greatest hurdle, to overcome.

Managing the change that is necessary for an organization to stay competitive is a difficult challenge. However, the more successful it can become at managing change, the better it can become in meeting its customer's needs, reducing inefficiencies, improving the performance of functions, and managing costs and risks. These changes not only result in improved profits and better efficiency in the present, but continue to pay dividends for years to come. In today's economic environment, maintaining a focus on performance while controlling costs and managing risk are essential for long-term survival and sustainable growth.

In presenting the concept of value optimization, the author challenges the reader to look beyond the traditional indicators of value: price and customer satisfaction, and instead consider value from the perspective of functions and how they are performed relative to cost, time, and risk. This book presents a practical and proven approach, known as Value Methodology, which provides organizations with a cohesive theory, structured framework, and diverse toolset to identify, quantify, and optimize the real value they deliver by transforming the way it is perceived.

Value Methodology

This book is aimed at those new to the discipline with emphasis placed on the practical application of Value Methodology techniques to optimize the value of facilities, products, services, and processes. Value Methodology (VM) has existed under several different names over the years, such as Value Engineering (VE), Value Analysis (VA), and Value Management. There are no essential differences between these designations and they are, for all practical purposes, interchangeable. The term *value engineering* has been traditionally used whenever the Value Methodology is applied to industrial design or to the construction industry; the term *value analysis* for concept planning or process applications; and the term *value management* for administration or management applications. Value *Methodology* is the term most commonly used today and refers to the comprehensive body of knowledge related to improving value regardless of the area of application. Value Methodology is formally defined as:

> *A systematic process used by a multidisciplinary team to improve the value of projects through the analysis of functions.*[7]

Value Methodology is an organized process that has been effectively used within a wide range of private enterprises and public entities to achieve their continuous improvement goals, and in government agencies to better manage their limited budgets. The success of the VM is due to its capacity to identify opportunities to remove unnecessary costs from projects, products, and services while assuring that performance, and other critical factors, meet or exceed the customer's expectations.

The improvements are the result of recommendations made by multidiscipline teams under the guidance of a skilled facilitator, commonly referred to as a value specialist. The multidisciplined teams can comprise those that were involved in the design and development of the project, technical experts that were not involved with the project, or a combination of the two. There are two essential elements that set the Value Methodology apart from other techniques, methodologies, and processes:

1. The application of the unique method of function analysis and its relation to cost and performance
2. The organization of the concepts and techniques into a specific job plan

These factors differentiate Value Methodology from other analytical or problem-solving methodologies.

Value Methodology can be applied to products, manufacturing processes, administrative procedures, and the design and construction of facilities. The VM process is applied in basically the same way for each type of study; however, there are some differences in how preparations are made for the different types of studies and how some of the VM techniques are applied.

VM is often confused with cost reduction; however, cost reduction and VM are distinctly different. Cost reduction activities are component-oriented. This often involves the act of "cheapening" the item. In other words, reducing cost at the expense of performance. Examples of typical cost reduction measures include eliminating components or elements, substituting less expensive systems, relaxing tolerances, and/or the thinning or changing of material. At best, such an approach creates a stripped-down, less expensive version of the original item. At worst, it results in the wholesale degradation of value by forsaking performance in the zeal to reduce cost.

Value Methodology, conversely, is concerned with how things function rather than what they are. This function-driven mind-set demands a radical transformation in our perception, in the way we approach challenges, both old and new. This functional way of thinking is, by its nature, predisposed to lead us to innovative solutions by opening our eyes and deepening our understanding of how things work. This concept of function is the very essence of Value Methodology.

Why Use Value Methodology?

The economic health of an organization relates to the efficient use that is made of available resources. As our society evolves we are confronted with increasing awareness that resources appear to be shrinking. We do not have unlimited choices in materials, types of energy, or sources of labor. The availability of capital is also limited, especially when we consider that the cost of borrowing capital is ever fluctuating and the purchasing power of the dollar seems to be steadily diminishing. Further, the quickening pace of technological advances may find us using designs or methods that are far behind the leading edge of progress. The owner, whether an individual, a corporation, or a tax-supported public body, cannot afford the luxury of paying for design or performance features that contribute nothing to the basic function of the object being acquired. Such unneeded features are often introduced into designs either because there is inadequate communication between the owner, who controls the budget, the user, who identifies the requirements, and the project team, who transform these requirements into plans and specifications.

To achieve maximum benefits from our limited resources we must make full use of our only unlimited resource—our ability to think creatively. By taking advantage of technological advances in materials and methods of production, and by applying our creative ability to each project, we can in some measure offset the rapid rise in the cost of acquiring goods and services. These costs have risen sharply in the past decade, and in almost any year the rise in costs exceeds that of the preceding year. For example, within the construction industry, the cost of building materials has spiked sharply over the last decade for essentials such as steel, concrete, and lumber, as shown in Figure 1.1.[8]

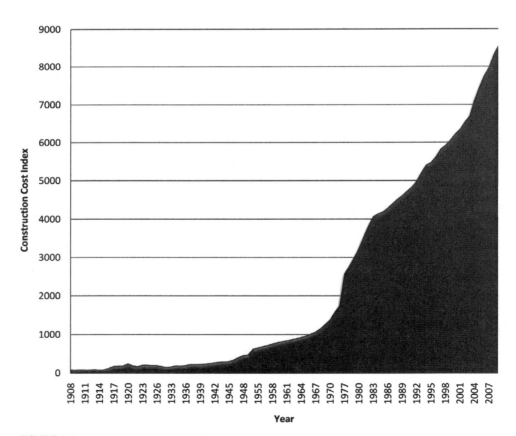

FIGURE 1.1   Construction Cost Index History

In order to acquire the desired projects, products, and processes with the limited funds available, we must use every possible means to attain the required functions at minimum cost. This is precisely what Value Methodology attempts to accomplish through a systematic, organized approach. It is also worth noting that Value Methodology is currently mandated in the United States by federal law. These laws generally apply to the design and construction of facilities, but are also applied for the procurement of some types of equipment and supplies. These laws and regulations include:

- The Defense Authorization Act (Public Law 104-106) states that each executive agency must establish and maintain cost-effective VM procedures and processes.
- The 1995 National Highway System Designation Act requires states to carry out a value study for all federal-aid highway projects with an estimated total cost of $25 million or more.
- The 1986 Water Resources Development Act (Public Law 99-662) requires a review of costs (i.e., value study) on all federally funded water and wastewater treatment projects with a total cost in excess of $10 million.
- The Office of Management and Budget's Circular A131 requires federal agencies to use Value Methodology as a management tool to reduce program and acquisition costs.

As a result, not only is VM required at a federal level, but also at the state and local levels due to the fact that federal funding is an integral part of most major capital improvement projects. In addition, many state and local governments have enacted legislative policy of their own that mandates the application of VM for a wide variety of projects at various budget thresholds.

Project Management and Value Methodology

Value Methodology, as a body of knowledge, is concerned with improving the value of things, whether it is a new facility, a manufactured item, or a management procedure. The application of Value Methodology typically occurs within the context of a program at an organizational level and within a value study, at a project level.

Experienced project managers, especially those with a thorough understanding of the Project Management Institute's *Project Management Body of Knowledge* (PMBOK), will appreciate the similarities between the management of a value study and the management of a project. In fact, a value study, in and of itself, is a project. It meets all of the criteria[9] of a project:

- *Is it unique?* Yes, a value study is a unique endeavor having the goal of improving the value of a product, regardless of whether it is a new product or an existing one.
- *Is it temporary in nature and have a definite beginning and end?* Yes, a value study typically involves an intense expenditure of resources within a very short time, usually occurring over a few weeks or months.

- *Is there a way to determine when it is completed?* Yes, the value study is completed when the formal study process has been completed and oral and written reports have been submitted detailing the specific value improvements developed by the value team.
- *Is there a way to determine stakeholder satisfaction?* Yes, stakeholder satisfaction is determined by holding a formal implementation meeting. This allows the project team and vested stakeholders to determine the acceptability of the value improvements recommended by the value team.

Value studies can be conducted as a part of an ongoing project, or they may be completely free-standing projects in and of themselves. Project managers have a special role to play in the application of Value Methodology.

Project managers are generally positioned within an organization where they may take either a direct or indirect role in the performance of value studies. In projectized and matrix-based organizations, there may be a VM department where value specialists are assigned to facilitate value studies for specific projects. This involvement of a project manager in a value study may take on a variety of forms:

- The project manager may act as a value specialist in facilitating a value study for some projects and organizations. This approach may be preferable if the project is still in the initiation phase.
- The project manager may request and/or sponsor a value study to be performed for a project he or she is actively managing. In this case, the value study may be led by a value specialist from a different department within the organization, by a consultant value specialist, or by a value specialist from an external project stakeholder.
- The project manager may be the recipient of a value study on a project he or she is actively managing. Another entity within the organization, or perhaps an external stakeholder, will have requested that a value study be conducted for the project. In this case, the project manager may be an "unwilling" participant and will be required by the organization to cooperate with the value specialist in participating on the value team directly or in a supporting role.
- The project manager may be a primary decision maker with respect to the acceptance of value alternatives developed as part of a value study.

It is not uncommon for some project managers to take on more than one of the roles identified above. Regardless of which role they will play, it will be an important one in determining the success of the value study. Project managers in all organizations should have a fundamental understanding of VM and be aware of how it can improve the cost, performance, risk, and value of their projects.

It is important to understand that Value Methodology, unlike many management fads, is more than just a concept. VM provides an actual means of achieving improved value. The universality of its application to any project makes it an ideal project management tool. No project manager should be without it.

Value Methodology and Teamwork

The successful application of Value Methodology, as originally conceived by Larry Miles, has always focused on the importance of multidiscipline teams. In fact, VM was one of the first disciplines to recognize the value of drawing upon the group synergism of individuals representing different technical backgrounds. VM is therefore a team process and, as such, requires that members of the value team work together harmoniously and in unison if its output is to exceed the sum of the individual efforts.

Genuine teamwork should always be value-based. In other words, it should be behaviorally rooted in mutually shared values. The value specialist will exert considerable influence over the values that will fundamentally affect teamwork. It must be further emphasized that the value specialist's sphere of influence must extend beyond the boundaries of the value team. The value specialist should think of the value team as an extension of the project team. Further expanding on this idea, the value specialist must seek to include the customer or user, the project team, and the project stakeholders as part of the total team effort, as illustrated in Figure 1.2.

A number of values and principles must be followed in creating successful teams. These include:

- Innovation requires an open discussion about things that are "wrong" about the current project. This is achieved by validating assumptions, strengthening the understanding of the problems that are trying to be solved, and improving communication among team members. Therefore, it is important to establish a basic level of trust among the team members that is based upon the understanding that the goal of the value effort is the overall improvement of the project. It is not about criticizing team members for perceived shortcomings.
- No one individual must ever intentionally be praised or rewarded for looking good at the expense of another. When team members sense that such behavior is rewarded, they will use information about the project in ways that will subvert the value effort and prevent teamwork. Team players are committed to the success of the project, which in turn will make everyone a success.
- Large organizations and bureaucracies tend to shield individuals from conflict through policies and procedures. Discomfort with conflict runs higher in these

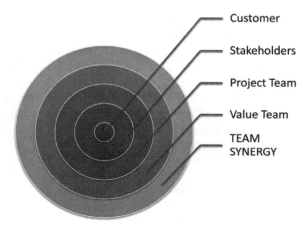

FIGURE 1.2 Teamwork and Value Methodology

environments for this reason. Therefore, the value specialist needs to develop strong facilitation skills in order to make people more comfortable with resolving conflicts in a team or group setting. The value effort by nature should be a process of consensus rather than an autocratic one.

- Managers within a bureaucracy generally understand that clarifying responsibility is necessary in order to prevent the paralysis that can develop when there is uncertainty within a team about who is responsible. Within the context of the value effort, teams, rather than individuals, must be empowered to solve problems.

- Individuals must have respect for data and objective analysis in order to foster teamwork. Members of a team are more willing to create interdependencies involving trust and vulnerability when they feel that facts and neutral data are valued.

- All members of the team that are part of the value effort must be valued equally, no matter how far down within an organization's hierarchy they are. The value specialist should seek to solicit information and ideas from everyone. Often, those within the lower echelons of an organization hold important information that is usually overlooked.

- It is not at all unusual for there to be both superiors and subordinates from the same organization participating simultaneously within the context of the value effort. The value specialist must emphasize the importance that team members demonstrate tolerance in the acceptance of constructive criticism of their own ideas. Teamwork improves when people feel that they have the freedom to constructively criticize and evaluate the group's efforts without fear of reprisal, and when superiors become more "hands on" and less authoritarian.

A "teamwork culture" must acknowledge interdependencies that exist in a complex organization. Values about fairness and equality must support the interdependencies within the total team comprising the value effort; otherwise, teamwork is undermined and the outcome will be compromised. Teambuilding is further discussed in Chapter 4, "Preparation."

History of Value Methodology

The genesis of the Value Engineering methodology was during the period of World War II, from 1938 to 1945. Lawrence Delos Miles, regarded as the father of Value Analysis/Engineering, was an engineer for General Electric Company.[10] During this time, every facility was scheduled to the hilt and prioritized to AAA and higher. Steel of all types was totally scheduled. All vital products and materials were heavily controlled including copper, bronze, tin, nickel, ball bearings, roller bearings, electrical resistors, and capacitors. Miles was assigned the task of "finding, negotiating for and getting" a number of these vital materials, such as materials to expand production of turbo-superchargers from 50/week to 1,000/week for B-24s, capacitors and resistors for skyrocketing military electronic needs, armament parts for expanding production of B-29s, and so forth. In this environment, it was not possible to stop short of achieving the essential results.

Frequently, suppliers, already overextended, said no to increased schedules or new necessary products. In this desperate situation Miles was forced to basics. "If I can't get the product, I've got to get the function. How can you provide the function by using some machine or labor or material that you can get?" Time and again there was a way to do it. Engineering tests and approvals were rushed and schedules met. Thus "function" grew in vitality and was to later mature into the development of the VA techniques.

To assure materials for these and other vital programs, Miles usually worked two days in the vendors' plants, one to two days in GE plants, one day in the Pentagon keeping priorities suitable, and Saturdays and Sundays in his own office. One particular incident will illustrate the function emphasis that pressed itself upon him.

A production manager gave Miles a schedule calling for thousands of a few dozen types of resistors and capacitors to be delivered weekly starting in one week. Manufacturing schedules at the time were nine months out, with six months firm. He was told it was an absolute requirement. Miles asked, "Who agrees with you that this must be secured regardless?" The manager said, "Tom Garahan, overall production manager of GE." Miles asked, "Does Harry Erlicher [vice president of purchasing] agree?" The manager said yes.

The resistors and capacitors were secured. They were for Oak Ridge, Tennessee. Much later it was learned they were for atomic bomb research and development. Their priority overrode everything; still the others were vital too. Miles went to vendors and made schedule changes, but told each he would find some way to provide the essential functions of resistance and capacitance through a different shape or type or material or equipment, which would keep other vital electronic equipment on schedule for the military. The function approach proved to be so effective that he would never abandon it.

Critical years passed. In 1944, Erlicher asked Miles to become Purchasing Agent of a GE plant. Miles experienced more benefits from the functional approach in buying.

In March 1944, he was transferred to Locke Insulator in Baltimore, Maryland, a subsidiary of GE, as manager of purchasing. He took line responsibility for delivery and cost of millions of dollars worth of materials and products per year. During nearly the next four years, he developed patterns of engineering, laboratory, and purchasing teamwork that limited costs and improved products. He learned firsthand both the productive and the destructive force of human attitudes and practices, and their effect on appropriate designs and appropriate costs. His thinking was becoming more and more "What *function* am I buying?" rather than "What material am I buying?"

In 1947, Miles wrote a letter to Erlicher saying that he believed that much good could come to GE if he were relieved of line operation responsibilities and assigned full-time to cost reduction work in the central purchasing office. Mr. Erlicher bought the idea and moved him back to Schenectady in late 1947, where his activity was named the Purchasing Department Cost Reduction Section, PDCRS.

In late 1947, back in Purchasing on Mr. Erlicher's staff, his schedule was cleared so that he could research and develop workable techniques, which would secure more cost effective achievement by the decision-making employees in a plant or business.

Larry Miles described the early technique:

To an exceptional degree it focuses on what is important, develops knowledge about it, and then causes great creativity in that area. You select from the creative approaches, answers that may not have come in years with other thinking methods. When the system was put to work the first time, it resulted in replacing a bronze clip holding a cover on a refrigerator control (that could flex millions of times without breaking) with a lower cost brass clip (that would flex thousands of times). Quality was not sacrificed because the clip would be flexed only about six times in the lifetime of the refrigerator. The $7,000 per year savings may seem like nothing, but when the same technique was applied to everything in the control box, the yearly savings jumped to $1.25 million.

The new functional approach was introduced to Mr. Winne, vice president of engineering. Mr. Winne listened, understood, and said, "This is the best method I have seen to get competitive costs and retain quality. What are you going to call it? Proper quality at proper costs equals *value*. Why not call it *value analysis?*" Thus the new methodology was named. Then he said, "The vice president of manufacturing, Mr. DuChemin, will be most interested in this." Mr. DuChemin set up a 20-minute appointment with Miles. After two hours of listening and learning, he said, "Train 1,000 people per year." With the support of these people, Miles set up training programs that were available to GE's plants. He accepted people and products from different plants, applied the techniques, and showed them how they could increase earnings and maintain competitive positions. He learned that great benefits were derived when technical people used the VA system and geared training to them.

For the next three years, Larry continued training personnel and doing work for the plants. He did this using a revolving team of six to eight people. Training was moved into plant locations with a goal of 1,000 per year to be trained. Later, GE often exceeded that number. Larry and his training team learned that greatest benefits come when customers and vendors also know and use the VA functional and methodical thinking approaches. On his advice, GE agreed to provide VA training to other industries as well. During the four years from 1948 to 1952, $10 million in benefits were reported.

In 1950, GE gave Larry Miles its highest award: the Coffin Award. This is given in honor of their first president, for benefits to the company resulting from the creation and use of the VA System.

This highest GE award, at that time, went to fewer than one in each 10,000 employees. Larry Miles was the first and only purchasing man to ever receive it. The citation was:

In recognition of his outstanding accomplishment through the establishment, organization, and development of a Value Analysis Program, which has resulted in substantial cost reductions.

In 1954, the U.S. Navy Bureau of Ships implemented the first federal government program with the assistance of Miles and his staff. There followed a period of gradual growth in federal agencies until 1963, when the Department of Defense established specific requirements for a formal program within the three military services. This involved their design and construction activities as well as suppliers, and mandated incentive-sharing clauses in construction contracts. Contractors were permitted to propose Value Engineering changes and share in net savings. It also introduced full-time value engineers within agency staffs to promote and administer the program. The high level of success achieved by the Department of Defense led to further recognition in civil agencies. Great expansion followed in the next fifteen years. Today, every federal agency with a significant construction or purchasing program employs VE in some form. In addition to the Department of Defense, such agencies include the General Services Administration, the Environmental Protection Agency, the U.S. Forest Service, the U.S. State Department's Overseas Building Operations, Veteran's Administration, the Federal Highway Administration, and the Department of the Interior. This was further expanded during the 1980s by the executive branch, with the support of congress, to include requirements for the application of Value Engineering to all agencies within the federal government. In addition, many states and city governments have directed, through legislative action, that value methodology be applied to all capital expenditures. Thus the value technique, born of necessity in a single company, has become a widely used technical methodology for effective utilization of resources throughout the public and private sectors.

SAVE International

SAVE International, originally founded in 1959 as the Society of American Value Engineers, is the premier international society devoted to the advancement and promotion of the Value Methodology. Value Methodology benefits include decreasing costs, increasing profits, and improving performance.[11]

Society members practice the Value Methodology in the public and private sectors for organizations in more than 35 countries. VM applications span a variety of fields, including management, construction, manufacturing, transportation, health care, government, and environmental engineering.

SAVE International offers member services such as education and training, publications, tools for promoting Value Methodology, certification, networking, and recognition within the value field. The SAVE International certification program is linked to a number of value societies in other countries. Additional information concerning professional certification is provided in Chapter 12, "Value Leadership."

Mission

SAVE International will promote, support, and advance the practice of value enhancing methods through global exchange, networking, certification, member services, professional growth, and recognition. Its strategic goals include:

- Promote the value methodology worldwide
- Collaborate with societies and organizations with common interests
- Identify new opportunities for application of the value methodology
- Embrace new tools and techniques

- Create more flexible and comprehensive value education
- Expand and diversify membership
- Enhance the image of the profession

Core Values and Beliefs

The following core values and beliefs give SAVE International boundaries in the pursuit of its vision:

- Foster an environment for personal and professional growth
- Embrace honesty and integrity
- Celebrate the accomplishments of members
- Advance the profession worldwide
- Concentrate on strengthening the knowledge of members

Projected Role for the Future

SAVE International has identified the role it will play in the future with regard to Value Methodology as summarized in the following points:

- SAVE International will continue to influence the development and dissemination of Value Methodology to chief executive financial officers of corporations and government agencies worldwide.
- SAVE International is known as the premier value organization, with highly skilled members providing value-based leadership in every facet of VM application.
- Opportunities abound for SAVE International members to enjoy top career advancement and business success. This is mainly due to the variety of educational and value-based research offered by the society at universities, symposia, on the Internet, and in collaboration with societies of similar interests.
- SAVE International is the repository of all methodologies related to value improvement, as well as information knowledge databases, for people everywhere.

Current VM Applications

Today, Value Methodology is widely used within the public and private sectors to improve the value of their outputs. Value programs have been instituted in order to ensure that value improvement occurs as a matter of choice. Profiles of three of the most prolific users of VM at the federal, state, and local levels are provided below. Each of these entities has found unique ways in which to apply the Value Methodology to improve the value of their facilities and services to the public.

U.S. Army Corps of Engineers

The U.S. Army Corps of Engineers has one of the longest-running programs within the construction industry and has been a leader in applying the Value Engineering to construction projects since 1964, solidly demonstrating the Corps' cost effective-

TABLE 1.1   USACE VE Program Results

Fiscal Year	Military	Civil	Total
2004	$59,771,000	$84,630,000	$144,400,000
2005	$102,020,000	$100,672,000	$202,692,000
2006	$386,124,000	$111,285,000	$497,409,000
2007	$222,815,000	$102,733,000	$325,548,000
2008	$186,684,000	$114,764,000	$301,448,000

ness. The program has resulted in construction of over $5.5 billion in additional facilities, without additional funds requests.

The basic focus of the program is to increase project value by proactively searching for and resolving issues through very open, short-term workshops, and to maximize precious taxpayer resources to provide the required function(s), amenities, and the highest quality project(s), at the lowest life cycle cost.

The Corps has recently used Value Management/Value Engineering:

- Programmatically to create and implement transformation in how the Corps executes all Military Programs workload
- Shorten schedules significantly, and provide quality projects with reduced budgets
- Ensure full project coordination with all stakeholders
- Assist in preparing project scopes, negotiating environmental contracts, planning optimization, and project review
- Provide planning assistance to states and communities
- Assist in program review

The Corps regularly helps others initiate VM/VE programs by advising headquarter offices, exporting or established training workshops, and by furnishing appropriate Certified Value Specialist leadership and/or teams (consultants and in-house) to perform Value Management Workshops.

In 2008, the Corps invested $8.3 million in the program, performed 287 workshops, and had a return on investment of over 36:1. Table 1.1 summarizes the *net* USACE VM/VE savings and cost avoidance for the last five fiscal years as reported to the Departments of Army, Defense, and OMB.[12]

Over the past decade, there has been an increasing use of charrettes (intense design workshops focused on developing the conceptual design of a project) by U.S. Army Corps of Engineers (USACE) Districts to initiate the design process for military construction. Many districts within the Corps are now utilizing the Value Methodology in the form of a "Value-Based Design Charrette" to ensure that a project meets its scope, schedule, and cost targets at the earliest stage in the design concept.

California Department of Transportation

The California Department of Transportation (also know as Caltrans) uses Value Methodology, where it is referred to as Value Analysis. Caltrans uses VA for a variety of reasons, including:

- *Maintain federal funding.* Value analysis studies are now required on all projects greater than $25 million (construction, right of way, and capital outlay costs) on the National Highway Systems (NHS). The project is defined by the environmental document and may include multiple contracts over many phases. The NHS Act of 1995, the subsequent Federal Rule (February 1997—Subpart 627), and the Federal Aid Policy Guide, which added a new Chapter 6—Value Engineering to define the application of this regulation.
- *Building consensus with its transportation partners.* Federal and state legislation over the last several years has given the local authorities a greater role in deciding local transportation issues. Value Analysis is an effective tool to break down the conflicts and build consensus with project stakeholders and partners.
- *Solving difficult transportation projects.* The steps and tools of Value Analysis provide an excellent tool to focus on and solve our most difficult transportation problems. The more complex a project in terms of geometry, staging, environmental impacts, and so on, the more opportunity it provides a skilled, well-led VA team to provide an in-depth analysis and subsequent innovative solutions for the project.
- *Cost reduction while maintaining or improving product quality.* The public is demanding more performance for less cost. Project costs should consider the total cost of ownership, which includes both the original (construction) cost and subsequent operation and maintenance costs. VA recommendations should not include cost reduction at the expense of project functions.
- *Elimination of detrimental design influences.* Many influences can negatively affect a project's design, ranging from a lack of information to the unwavering adherence to design standards. The VA review process can overcome the above influences by use of an objective, multidisciplined team of individuals applying the VA methodology in a controlled environment.

Caltrans regularly conducts three types of value studies:

1. *Highway construction projects.* Performing value studies on highway projects is the primary focus of the Caltrans VA Program. Caltrans typically conducts more than 50 value studies per year on the design of highways, bridges, and other supporting facilities, resulting in implemented cost savings averaging over $100 million per year.
2. *Product studies.* The VA process can be used to improve the quality of highway products. Typically, engineering products are items and systems as described in Caltrans' standard plans and specifications. Value Analysis can help identify products that need to be updated due to changing technology, outdated application, or any other changes that affect our standard engineering products.
3. *Process studies.* The VA process can be used to improve the quality of Caltrans' processes, such as policy and procedures and business practices.

Caltrans experienced a major boost to their Value Analysis program in 1995, when the FHWA began mandating that value studies be conducted on all projects involving the National Highway System. Between 1996 and 2008, the implemented savings have been considerable, over $2.2 billion. Figure 1.3 summarizes the results of the Caltrans VA Program over the past two decades.[13]

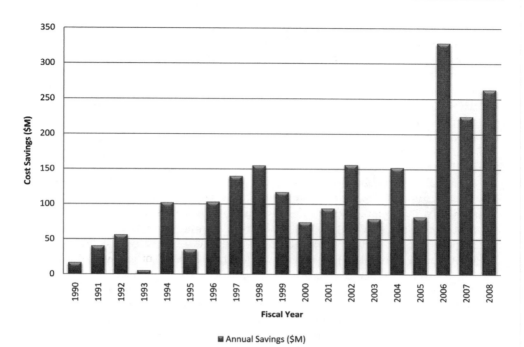

FIGURE 1.3   Caltrans VA Program Results

City of New York, Office of Management and Budget

The New York City Value Engineering/Value Analysis (VA/VE) Program began in 1983 as a response to a series of capital projects that had become very public embarrassments for the mayor. He asked the budget director for a capital project cost management tool to ensure that agencies would catch problems at an early stage, before costs escalated and construction schedules and public perception were affected.

The program has evolved and expanded over the past twenty years to focus on more than just cost management. OMB's objectives include getting a full reality check on a capital project's cost, program, and schedule, and on offering alternative proposals to improve the project's cost effectiveness, functionality, and schedule. The routine use of VM has become linked to OMB funding approval for large capital projects. Agencies use these reviews as an opportunity to get a second opinion from relevant experts to confirm or modify the technology choices and functional arrangements for their projects, and to identify ways to make them more cost effective, especially in times of fiscal constraints.

Additionally, Value Methodology has been used successfully to streamline or redesign agency operations or processes. Agency staff becomes the team of experts who suggest improvements and changes to upper management, using the structured VM job plan and professional VM facilitation. This tool is much in demand, as agencies must do more with less and deal with changes in technology. Often, "business as usual" is no longer an option.

OMB has reviewed hundreds of capital projects of great complexity and diversity using VM. Subjects have included schools, hospitals, jails, water pollution control plants, bridges (movable and fixed, roadway and waterway), computer systems, parks, museums, zoos, garages, courts, health and social services facilities, police and fire facilities, vehicle maintenance facilities, corrections food services, combined sewer overflow facilities, water treatment plants, sludge and ferry boats and ferry terminals, landfill closures, lab buildings, data centers, and environmental projects.

The scale and variety of projects reviewed in the NYC program is unique, as almost all city agencies are administered by OMB. The wide range of projects demands that OMB undertake extensive outreach for appropriate and credible team expertise. In addition, OMB has used VM to recommend improvements to operational processes or delivery of services. Examples of subjects reviewed include the city's procurement process for professional design services or human services contracts, leasing and space acquisition, daycare contracting, mail handling, the construction change order process, the emergency housing intake process, information technology services, social services payment and case documentation, and hospital revenue enhancement processes.

The VE/VA program reviews the largest, most complex or important capital projects from within the city's capital. From 2001 to 2007, OMB reviewed 101 major projects resulting in cost savings of just under $1.2 billion, with an average reduction of 4.7 percent per project and a return on investment of $71 for every $1 spent on value studies. The NYC VE/VA program has been a model for other government agencies, and it continues to evolve in response to the needs of its demanding stakeholders.[14]

Major Corporations

Numerous major corporations throughout the world representing all spheres of manufacturing, construction, and professional services maintain active VM programs. A representative list of these includes:

- Bechtel
- Bristol-Meyers Squibb Inc.
- Ford Motor Co.
- General Dynamics
- Ingersoll-Rand Company
- Kellogg Brown & Root
- Kraft Foods Inc.
- Navistar
- Pratt & Whitney
- Raytheon Systems
- Samsung Electro-Mechanics Co., Ltd.
- Teco-Westinghouse Motor
- URS Corporation
- Whirlpool

While the scope and focus of the application of Value Methodology within these organizations varies widely, all maintain formal VM programs.

Summary

In today's global economy, Value Methodology is being used to improve the value of construction projects, consumer and industrial products, manufacturing processes, and business practices around the world. Value Methodology achieves this by:

- Identifying areas of poor project value
- Developing innovative ways to better perform key project functions at less cost
- Maximizing the use of the most valuable resource—people!

CHAPTER 2

Value

© Magixl 2009, www.magixl.com

Consumption is the sole end and purpose of all production; and the interest of the producer ought to be attended to, only so far as it may be necessary for promoting that of the consumer.

—Adam Smith, Economist

Adam Smith is perhaps the most well-known advocate of capitalism in history. He was born in Kirkcaldy, Scotland, in 1723. Smith was educated at Glasgow University and at Balliol College in Oxford, England. He later lectured at Edinburgh and became a professor at Glasgow University. After a time, Smith went to France to tutor the duke of Buccleuch. While in France, he began work on his famous economic treatise *The Wealth of Nations* and continued writing it upon his return to Scotland. This influential work was published in 1776. In 1778, he followed in the footsteps of his father as a customs official. He died in Edinburgh.

The light of higher learning has shone brightly on Adam Smith's contribution to the field of economics. As a result, his views of religion and morality have been eclipsed. In the *Theory of Moral Sentiments*, he discussed the role of sympathy in connecting self-interest with virtue. One of the primary themes of this work was his view that if the free market is allowed to function and people become affluent, they will then have time to worry about the plight of the indigent. In contrast, he argued that in a primitive society, people primarily focus upon survival. Smith also postulated that a free market promoted virtues such as responsibility, honesty, frugality, ability, and self-control. In the quest for acquisition of wealth and power, he believed these virtues were needed to succeed. In the past, there was no such channeling mechanism or incentive within the market to harness virtue. Smith wrote that the rich and powerful had depended upon privilege and deception in the precommercial era.

Besides the market, other institutions such as the church and public society would reinforce virtue. Smith asserted that religion was the manifestation of humanity's need for justice and benevolence in the material world and would "enforce a natural sense of duty." Despite this, Smith wrote that the funding of religion through taxation would remove its proclivity for evangelism in spreading the faith. He also argued that in society, association with like-minded people would foster like effects. If one chose to affiliate with good people, good results would tend to occur.

Adam Smith spent much of his life's work dedicated to the research and analysis of the concept of value on both an individualistic and societal level. Smith made direct correlations between the properties of value as it relates to morality and the economy, which was seen as a radical approach for its time. The writings of Adam Smith provide the foundation for our contemporary understanding of value, which introduces us to the primary focus of this chapter.

The Concept of Value

The objective of Value Methodology is to improve the *value* of whatever is being studied. Unfortunately, we all have our own opinions regarding what affects the value of a product, project, or service, and this may vary greatly depending on our own perspective. Too often decisions are based on just one criterion, such as cost, performance, or schedule, which can lead to less than optimum decisions. A decision that improves performance but increases the cost to a point where the product is no longer marketable is just as unacceptable as one that reduces cost at the expense of performance. It is also important to avoid confusing cost with value. Added material, labor, or overhead will increase cost—but will not necessarily increase value. Value is lessened if added cost does not improve the ability to perform the necessary functions.

Key to understanding the value concept is an awareness of several other critical terms and their definitions as used in Value Methodology:

- *Function.* Function is the natural or characteristic actions performed by a product or service—that which a product, facility, or service does as it is currently designed or conceived.
- *Project.* The Project Management Institute defines a project as a temporary endeavor undertaken to create a unique product or service.[1] The word "temporary" implies a finite beginning and end. For the purposes of this book, a project refers to any endeavor whereby a product is brought into being. A project begins at the inception of a concept, moves into its design and/or development, and continues through its production, construction, or implemen-

tation. This book uses the term "project" in referring to the subject of a value study whether it is a product, service, process, or facility.

- *Customer.* The word "customer" refers to anyone who receives a product "downstream." A customer is also sometimes referred to as a "user," depending on the application.

There are four basic elements that provide a measure of value to the user. To use project management terms, these are *performance, time, cost,* and *risk.* These four elements provide the basic building blocks on which all projects are managed:

1. *Performance.* In project management terms, performance is defined through a project's scope. There are two aspects of scope that must be considered: product scope and project scope. Every successful project produces a unique product: a tangible item or a service. This could be a new highway, a better mousetrap, or a new management process. Customers or users typically have expectations about the features of products they seek to acquire. *Product scope* describes the intended performance and features of the product. *Project scope* describes the work required to deliver a product or a service within the intended product scope. Although product scope focuses on the customer or user of the product, project scope is mainly the concern of the people who will execute the project. In discussing scope, we will use the concept of *performance* as the means of defining it.

2. *Time.* The customer requires acceptable delivery, usually at a specific place within a given time. The best products or services are of no value if they cannot be provided to the customer in a timely fashion. Time is also commonly referred to as "schedule."

3. *Cost.* Similar to the previous definition, costs include all the resources required to deliver the project. Cost includes the people and equipment that do the work, the materials they use, and all the other circumstances that require an expenditure of *resources.*

4. *Risk.* We can never be certain that a project will be delivered in a manner that goes exactly according to plan. Therefore, we must consider the impact that uncertainty can have on the project. Risks may be classified as either threats (negative risks) or as opportunities (positive risks). There can be many risks to a project, both known and unknown, that can affect one or all of the aforementioned elements.

Project managers should be able to relate to these four elements, as it is their job to strike a balance among them in order to achieve the best possible value to the customer or user. Maximizing the relationship of these elements is important to satisfying the customer (see Figure 2.1) and optimizing value. From this relationship it is easy to see that value can be enhanced by improving either scope or schedule or by reducing cost. While most value studies have specific objectives, such as performance improvement, cost reduction, improved delivery, or the management of risk, the value relationships identified here require a balanced approach. A properly facilitated value study should seek to adjust the contributions of these four elements in an effort to optimize value.

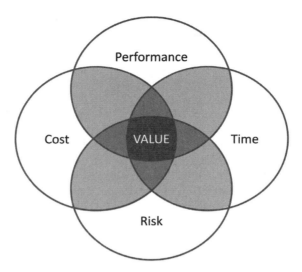

FIGURE 2.1   Value Optimization

Value Theory

The evolution of the concept of value has been a long process. The philosophical groundwork for the concept of value was first established in ancient Greece in Plato's dialogue *Protagoras*. Closely following this philosophical work, in 350 B.C., Aristotle identified seven classes of value that are still used today: ethical, judicial, religious, political, social, aesthetic, and economic.

Our present understanding of the concept did not begin to fully take shape until the eighteenth century. During this period, Adam Smith published *An Inquiry into the Nature and Causes of the Wealth of Nations*, his landmark economic treatise, and perhaps of equal if not greater importance, *The Theory of Moral Sentiments*, which discusses the influence of moral values on economic values. Meanwhile, Immanuel Kant's writings on moral philosophy, including *Groundwork of the Metaphysic of Morals, Critique of Pure Reason*, and *Metaphysics of Morals*, considered the humanistic basis for value. Kant, who was a contemporary of Smith, differentiated between preferences and values and argued that considerations of individual rights tempered the calculations of aggregate utility.

Value Methodology is primarily concerned with economic value on a more fundamental level. There are four types of economic value:

1. *Use.* The properties or qualities of an item that permit the required work or service to be performed. The concept of *utility* is integral to the understanding of use value.
2. *Esteem.* The properties, features, or attractiveness of a given thing that makes its ownership desirable.
3. *Exchange.* The price for which a good or service will trade in a given market.
4. *Market.* A rational and unbiased estimate of the potential price of a good, service, or asset, considering factors such as:

- Acquisition/production/distribution costs
- Supply versus demand
- Uncertainty (risk)
- Actual utility
- Subjective utility—which includes individual appraisals of worth as well as the effects of cognitive bias. (It is worth noting that subjective utility is neither rational nor biased and actually conflicts with the root definition of "market value.")

All four of these types of economic value are important; however, it should be noted that market value incorporates the concepts of use, esteem, and exchange value and adds a host of other macro and microeconomic considerations. Therefore, if we can improve market value, we can improve total value.

Theories of Utility

The concept of *utility* is an important one in considering "use value," which is an essential concept in Value Methodology. Utility is essentially a measure of the degree of satisfaction one derives from the use of goods or services. It is closely related to *performance*, which provides a means of measuring utility and is one of the key components of value presented earlier in this chapter. Several theories have evolved over the centuries to help describe how people incorporate the concept of utility in making decisions: Expected Utility Theory, Marginal Utility Theory, and Prospect Theory.

EXPECTED UTILITY THEORY Expected Utility Theory was first suggested by Daniel Bernoulli in 1738. Bernoulli was a skilled mathematician, and his interests were wide ranging. Bernoulli's work formed the groundwork for the future development of Expected Utility Theory and the idea of risk aversion.

One of his key contributions to Expected Utility Theory is his solution of a hypothetical problem referred to as the St. Petersburg Paradox. Incidentally, his cousin Nicolas Bernoulli is credited with originating the Paradox. The Paradox challenges the idea that people value games of chance according to expected return. The Paradox posed the following situation:

You are invited to play a game of chance. The game consists of flipping a coin. On the first flip, a tail ends the game and you win nothing, but a head earns you $2 and the opportunity to flip again. Every time you flip another head, your cash prize for the rounds doubles the one from the previous round. The game ends when the first coin comes up tails. How much would you be willing to wager to play this game?

From a purely mathematical standpoint, the answer is that you should be willing to pay any amount up to the expected prize, the value of which is obtained by multiplying all the possible prizes by the probability that they are obtained and adding the resulting numbers. The chance of winning $2 is 1/2 (heads on the first toss); the chance of winning $4 is 1/4 (tails followed by heads); the chance of winning $8 is 1/8 (tails followed by heads followed by heads); and so on. Since

TABLE 2.1 Expected Prizes in the St. Petersburg Paradox

n (Flips)	Probability (n)	Prize	Expected Prize
1	1/2	$2	$1
2	1/4	$4	$1
3	1/8	$8	$1
4	1/16	$16	$1
5	1/32	$32	$1
6	1/64	$64	$1
7	1/128	$128	$1
8	1/256	$256	$1
9	1/512	$512	$1
10	1/1024	$1024	$1

the expected payoff of each possible consequence is $1 ($2 × 1/2, $4 × 1/4, etc.) and there are an infinite number of them, the total expected prize is an infinite sum of money (see Table 2.1).

A rational gambler would enter the game if and only if the price of the wager was less than the expected prize, or sum of expected prizes. In the St. Petersburg Paradox, any finite price of entry is smaller than the expected prize of the game, which is infinite. Thus, the rational gambler would play no matter how large the entry price was! But there's clearly something wrong with this. Studies have shown that most people would offer between $5 and $20 on the grounds that the chance of winning more than $4 is only 25 percent and the odds of winning a fortune are very small.[2] This is the paradox upon which Bernoulli opined:

> *The determination of the value of an item must not be based on the price, but rather on the utility it yields. ... There is no doubt that a gain of one thousand ducats is more significant to the pauper than to a rich man though both gain the same amount.*

Bernoulli's solution to this mystery touches upon the realm of behavioral economics and psychology. He pointed out that a given amount of money isn't always of the same use to its owner. It is, in fact, relative. For example, to a billionaire accustomed to thinking in terms of tens of millions of dollars, $1 is insignificant. However, to a penniless beggar, it may represent the difference between starvation and survival.

In a similar way, the utility of $2 million is not simply twice the utility of $1 million. Thus, the important quantity in the St. Petersburg Paradox is the *expected utility* of the game. In this context, expected utility refers to the utility of the prize multiplied by its probability, which is far less than the *expected prize*.

The insurance industry operates on this principle. The existence of a *utility function* means that most people would prefer, for example, having $98 in cash to gambling in a lottery where they could win $75 or $125 each with a chance of 50 percent, even though the lottery has the higher expected prize of $100. The difference of $2 is the premium most of us would be willing to pay for insurance. It is interesting to note that while most of us pay hefty premiums for insurance to avoid risk, we are also willing to seek a certain amount of risk by purchasing lottery tickets whose price far exceeds the expected utility.

Expected Utility Theory was subsequently refined by Oskar Morgenstern and John von Neumann in 1944. This theory states that people will always choose the outcome they expect will give them the greatest degree of utility.[3]

Subjective Expected Utility Theory was first suggested by Leonard Savage in 1954. This permutation of Expected Utility Theory adds the variables of personal utility and personal probability, which suggests that people evaluate these elements through their own unique perspective. This theory is closely related to the concept of worth, which is discussed later in this chapter.

MARGINAL UTILITY THEORY   Marginal Utility Theory was developed at the same time in the 1870s by several economists, including William Stanley Jevons, Carl Menger, and Marie-Esprit-Leon Walras. Marginal Utility Theory, also known as Marginalism, is the theory that economic value results from marginal utility and marginal cost. Marginalism is the notion that what is most important for decision making is the marginal or last unit of consumption or production.

For example, one automobile is very useful for getting around. An additional automobile might be useful in case the first is being repaired or for spare parts, but it is not as useful as the first. A third automobile has even less utility than the first two. Given the price of cars, one would not expect many people to own three cars, as the benefit derived from the third car would not likely equal or exceed its price.

PROSPECT THEORY   Prospect Theory was first presented in 1979 by Daniel Kahneman and Amos Tversky, two psychologists who were subsequently awarded the Nobel Prize for their research. It suggests that most people do not evaluate prospects from the "*maximum* utility" perspective suggested by the Expected Utility Theory. Consider the following situation.

Imagine that the United States is preparing for the outbreak of a deadly strain of influenza that is expected to kill 60,000 people. Two alternative programs to combat the disease have been proposed. Assume that the exact scientific estimates of the consequences of the programs are as follows:

- If program A is adopted, 20,000 people will be saved.
- If program B is adopted, there is a one-third probability that 60,000 people will be saved and a two-thirds probability that no people will be saved.

Which of the two programs would you choose?

Assume that two alternative programs to combat the disease have been proposed. Assume that the exact scientific estimates of the consequences of the programs are as follows:

- If program C is adopted, 40,000 people will die.
- If program D is adopted, there is a 33 percent probability that nobody will die and a 66 percent probability that all 60,000 people will die.

Which of these two programs would you choose?

A scientific study was conducted by Kahneman and Tversky posing similar questions to people. The results were quite remarkable:

- If program A is adopted, 20,000 people will be saved (72 percent).
- If program B is adopted, there is a one-third probability that 60,000 people will be saved and a two-thirds probability that no people will be saved (28 percent).
- If program C is adopted, 40,000 people will die (22 percent).
- If program D is adopted, there is a one-third probability that nobody will die and a two-thirds probability that 60,000 people will die (78 percent).

The results of Kahneman's and Tversky's study were fascinating. Mathematically speaking, programs A and C are identical while programs B and D are identical.[4] However, the majority of people selected programs A and D, which is completely illogical from a mathematical standpoint. What could have caused this breakdown in logic?

The explanation has to do with the manner in which the prospective outcomes are framed. The implicit reference point of the question is that if no program is adopted, then 60,000 people will die. The outcomes of programs A and B are stated in terms of gains, and people tend to be risk averse when encountering opportunities for gain—respondents typically prefer to take the known outcome rather than the gamble.

The outcomes of programs C and D are stated in terms of losses, and people tend to become risk seeking when confronted by the likelihood of loss—respondents will typically prefer the gamble over the certainty of losses.

Prospect Theory postulates that people evaluate from the perspective of the status quo suggested by the way a prospect is stated, and think of each prospect as involving a gain, a neutral outcome, or a loss. The influence on decision making by the way in which the problem is asked or stated is called a *framing* effect, and can lead to irrational decision making and, consequently, poor value.

Figure 2.2 illustrates how the framing of a prospect impacts the value that is placed on the utility of expected outcomes.

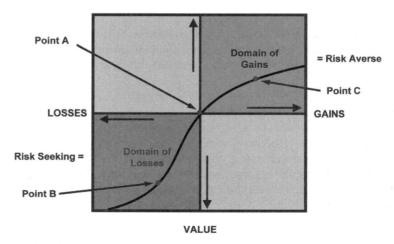

FIGURE 2.2   The Effect of Prospect Framing on Value

The "status quo" serves as the reference point, which is indicated on the graph as Point A. Many choices involve decisions between retaining the status quo and accepting an alternative to it. Because prospects are evaluated in relation to the status quo, gains will be evaluated cautiously from a risk-averse point of view, and losses will be evaluated in a risk seeking manner.

At Point B, further losses do not lead to a large decrease in value; however, comparable gains lead to a large increase in value. The person at Point B will risk small losses in order to obtain potentially large gains. This predisposition is referred to as the Sunk Cost Effect. The Sunk Cost Effect has two key aspects to it. First, people tend to have an overly optimistic probability bias, whereby after making an initial investment, the perception of that investment paying dividends is increased. Second, sunk costs appear to operate chiefly in those who feel personal responsibility for the investments that are to be viewed as sunk.

The Sunk Cost Effect is often witnessed in the domain of public projects. Projects whose costs spiral wildly out of control are effective examples of this, where public officials refuse to cancel a project due to the large financial and political investments made, even though doing so would offer much better value to the public welfare.

Conversely, a person at Point C will be reluctant to risk even small losses for large gains. This is because losses tend to loom larger than gains, and therefore a decision maker will be biased in favor of retaining the status quo. This is termed the Endowment Effect—it explains the reluctance of people to part with assets that belong to their "endowment."

The study of utility and value is a fascinating area of scholarship. The field of behavioral economics continues to develop new theories to explain how people make value judgments in seemingly irrational ways. It is clear to see from this brief overview that understanding value is challenging and can be often perplexing.

Functional Value

In 1947, Lawrence Miles established the concept of value as a technical field of study. In 1961, Miles published *Techniques of Value Analysis and Engineering*, which laid forth the concept of function as an integral part of value.

Miles's codification of function as a component of value has had far-reaching implications within the sphere of human industry. It spurred a new wave of thinking with respect to the value of goods and services. Miles defined value in terms of the relationship of function and cost. This was eloquently stated in his now famous axiom "All cost is for function."[5] Of equal importance, he stressed that value is established by the user's—or the customer's—needs and wants. This basic understanding of value is essential if we are going to set about improving it.

Building upon Miles's theory of value, Carlos Fallon further refined these concepts. Fallon recognized that while function lay at the heart of value, it was the manner in which the function performed that allowed it to be quantified. Through his work with RCA, Fallon developed a methodology for quantifying performance, which he described using the concept of utility. In his book *Value Analysis*, Fallon discusses at length the concept of utility and its relationship to value. He describes the elements of utility as consisting of "performance, quality (including appearance), reliability, service, and opportune delivery."[6] These elements describe the term *performance* used in this book. So, for all intents and purposes, utility and performance are synonymous.

In a monograph published for RCA in 1965, Fallon outlined a process, also known as *Combinex*, for measuring the utility of manufactured goods.[7] This process consisted of (1) defining the product's objective; (2) defining key utility factors and related measurement scales; (3) identifying the relative importance of the utility factors; and (4) quantifying net value. Fallon's method for weighing the relative importance of utility factors is simple yet direct—the customer or user directly assigns them.

David De Marle provides several simple equations to define value.[8] The first is based upon Miles's understanding of value, where F = function and C = cost.

$$V_{max} = \frac{F}{C_{min}}$$

The next equation is an expression of Fallon's theory of value where the term *utility* is defined as the product of a need (n) and the ability to satisfy that need (a).

$$V = \frac{na}{c}$$

Finally, he proposes a simple equation for value that also captures the idea that the customer or user determines value.

$$Customer\ Value = \frac{performance}{price}$$

This equation addresses several observations made by Miles on value. Miles stated that a product or service is considered to have good value if that product or service has appropriate performance and cost. He also made the following observations:

- Value is always increased by decreasing costs (while, of course, maintaining performance).
- Value is increased by increasing performance *if the customer needs, wants, and is willing to pay for more performance.*[9]

There are indeed other ways, however, to improve value. One way is to increase performance while increasing costs such that the improvement in performance is greater than increase in cost. Another way is to decrease *performance* while decreasing costs such that the decrease in cost is greater than the decrease in performance. The two methods of improving value described here are less obvious and require specific techniques to measure performance in order to evaluate the relationship of cost and performance.

Where does the concept of function fit into these notions of value? The equation suggested by Miles states that maximum value is achieved by providing the function for the lowest possible cost. The term "function," as it is commonly understood within the context of Value Methodology, is defined as the means by which an expressed need or want is fulfilled. When we discuss the concept of value, what we are really expressing is a measure of how well that need or want is being fulfilled relative to the cost to do so. The "how well" question refers to the performance of the function rather than to the function itself. Function is tied directly to value such that it provides us a framework for establishing value. It could thus be said that Value Methodology is a body of knowledge focused on improving *functional value*. Functional value forms the basis for *Value Metrics*, a process for measuring value improvement, which is introduced in Chapter 3, "Value Methodology Job Plan."

$$V_f = \frac{P}{C}$$

In other words, the value of a function is equal to its performance (P) relative to its cost (C). To be more precise, we are talking about the value of a specific manifestation of the function. For example, if we were considering a carpentry hammer, whose function is to "transfer force," then the value would be considered as the relationship of the hammer's performance (i.e., how well it "transfers force") relative to the resources used to produce and acquire it (i.e., cost, time, etc.). From this discussion the following definition for value emerges:

> *Value is an expression of the relationship between the performance of a function, and the resources required to obtain it. Hence the term "best value" refers to the most efficient means to reliably accomplish a function that will meet the performance expectations of the customer.*

Some will recognize the similarities between this algorithm and cost benefit analysis. A key difference, however, is that instead of trying to convert benefits to costs, we are seeking to measure total performance (not just benefits) using non-monetary means.

The integration of time into this equation requires further dissucsion. On the one hand, we could choose to consider time as an input similar to cost. On the other, we could choose to consider it as an output like performance. There are arguments for both expressions. In one sense, time is directly related to cost—one need only consider the effect of price escalation over time on costs. In another sense, time could also be viewed as an output as it has importance outside of its effect on cost.

$$Value = \frac{Performance}{Cost + Time}$$

$$Value = \frac{Performance + Time}{Cost}$$

The last element to be incorporated is risk—the impact of uncertainty to a project. The application of risk analysis can shed light on how uncertainty can affect schedule and cost as it relates to project value.

$$Value = \frac{Performance \times Risk}{(Cost + Time) \times Risk} \quad \text{or} \quad Value = \frac{(Performance + Time) \times Risk}{Cost \times Risk}$$

Incorporating these concepts back into our equation for functional value,[10] we can summarize (where T = time and R = risk):

$$V_f = \frac{PR}{CR + TR} \quad \text{or} \quad V_f = \frac{PR + TR}{CR}$$

This definition of value incorporates use, esteem, exchange, and market value and links them with the powerful concept of function.

Finally, it has been postulated that value can be interpreted as a form of energy with properties similar in nature to other convertible forms of energy. This "value force," though subjective in nature, can be measured and modeled. De Marle argues that it is, in fact, the driving force behind the evolution of products, services, and societies to meet human needs.[11] Ultimately, Value Methodology must focus on functional value, that is, the value of the function the customer or user is seeking to acquire. At this level of understanding, Value Methodology provides a framework in which we can measure the components of value, identify where there are value deficiencies, and direct our efforts at improving it.

Worth

There is usually some confusion in discussing the concepts of worth and value. The two words are often used interchangeably, although they have two distinctly separate meanings.

Carlos Fallon presents the following definition for worth:

An appraisal of the properties rendering a product useful or esteemed in the eyes of a person; a measure of such usefulness or esteem; the monetary equivalent of utility. From the West Germanic wert through the Anglo-Saxon worth, this very English word reflects the direct approach to economic goods of Anglo-Saxon warriors, hunters, and farmers. By extension it has come to mean an appraisal of the effectiveness with which a product performs its function or a system accomplishes its mission. Either appraisal can yield a monetary figure that represents the customer's regard for the capability of a product to satisfy his wants. Closely related terms are merit and system effectiveness. The monetary connotation of the term worth makes it possible to quantify utility in the same units as cost.[12]

Fallon's definition of worth sounds very similar to the one proposed by this author, referred to as *functional value*. The primary difference between the two is in who the subject is making the value judgment. In Fallon's definition, worth is value from the "eyes of a person." In other words, value is determined by the individual.

Fallon presented this concept of worth within the context of a book that was focused on the application of Value Methodology on manufactured goods that are purchased by individuals. For this application, there is indeed a distinction between worth and value.

As such, it tends to reflect subjective perceptions of esteem that a person holds for things. Value, on the other hand, describes an average worth that a group of people attribute to something. For example, a particular customer might purchase a very expensive suit for $5,000 because he feels the image he is able to convey while wearing the suit is well worth the price. On the other hand, another less style-conscious customer may feel that paying $5,000 for the same suit is ridiculous. The manufacturer of the suit, on the other hand, is less interested in these individual perceptions of worth and more interested in what the broader market's perception of value is. Good market research should provide data on exactly what that price point is. The following equation illustrates the relationship between individual worth and total customer value.[13]

$$Customer\ Value = \frac{\sum(worth\ 1 + worth\ 2 + worth\ n)}{n}$$

Another use for the term *worth* within the context of Value Methodology is that worth is the least cost method for performing the function without respect to criteria or codes.[14] This definition falls far short of Fallon's and is not particularly sophisticated.

Worth can be used as a simple means of quickly assessing the potential of a concept for improving value. Suppose that we were studying a ceramic teacup. The basic function might be "contain liquid." The cost of the teacup might be $5.00. The worth of the teacup would be the lowest cost method the value team could identify to "contain liquid." Let's assume that the value team decides that the cheapest way to "contain liquid" is using a paper cup, which costs only $0.02. Therefore, the "worth" of the function is stated as $0.02 while the cost of the function is still $5.00. Cost and worth can be used to develop a "value index" by dividing the function cost by the function worth. In this case, $5.00 ÷ $0.02 = 250. Ideally, the "value index" would be 1, which would mean the cost equals the worth. The cost/worth value index approach would normally be used during idea evaluation to determine the "value" potential of the ideas.

Please note that this is the "traditional" way to determine function value using this approach to a value index. It is markedly different from the concept of functional value previously discussed, which is stated as $V_f = P/C$. Cost/worth approach to value really tells us little about value because nowhere is performance considered, which of course is all important. In the previously stated example, there is a huge difference between a ceramic teacup and a paper cup, despite the fact that they both contain liquid. A possible solution to this would be in recognizing that the teacup potentially has more than one basic function, perhaps another being "convey style." If this were the case, we could identify the least cost way to perform this function, which requires us to consider alternative materials and methods of manufacture. Nevertheless, this approach is crude at best and lacks the sophistication to thoroughly consider such complexities.

Customer Value

The concept of customer value is built on the idea that people make their buying decisions based upon the relationship between price and performance. The primary principle in this decision is overall value; or, simply said, is the customer getting the most for his or her money? The two variables are what have been determined to be the primary components of value: overall price and overall performance. The impact of price versus performance is very different depending on the industry or products being measured. Customer value is clearly illustrated using a Customer Value Map (see Figure 2.3).

Once again, it is important to remember that customer value relates directly to the function or functions that the customer is trying to acquire. The fair value line represents the points at which price and performance are "in balance." A service,

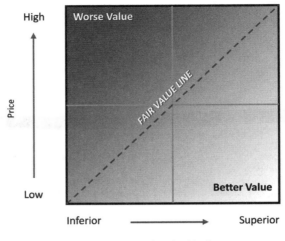

FIGURE 2.3   Customer Value Map

product, or facility that falls to the right of the line (superior performance, lower price) would be perceived as offering "better value" to its customer or user. Conversely, a service, product, or facility that falls to the left of the line (inferior performance, higher price) would be considered as offering "worse value" and would stand to lose the confidence and/or a portion of its customer base.

The study of customer value is important because it can help us better understand how people choose among competing suppliers of goods and services. This approach, which ties into the traditional marketing disciplines, can help lead companies to search for the answers to a number of important customer value questions such as:

- What are the key buying factors that customers value when they choose among a business and its most closely related competitors?
- How do functions support customer "wants and needs"?
- How do customers rate a business' performance versus its competitors on each key buying factor?
- What is the relative importance of each of these components of customer value?

By highlighting the best performer on each key buying factor, marketers can obtain important data regarding a given customer's value position for the organization and that of its competitors. Often the view from the marketplace differs from the organization's internally developed perception of customer values. Although it is not the intent of this text to review the way in which organizations choose to market their products, it is important that those seeking to apply Value Methodology develop an appreciation of the importance of understanding the wants and needs of its customers in improving value.

Ultimately, the success of an organization will depend on how well it satisfies the needs of its customers. The key criterion in measuring this is value. The Value Methodology, as described in the chapters that follow, will provide the reader with a means of creating and improving value for the products, services, or facilities

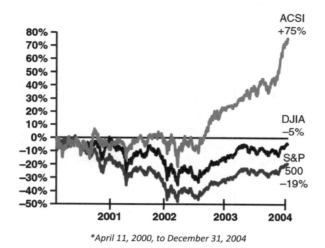

April 11, 2000, to December 31, 2004

FIGURE 2.4   ACSI Portfolio versus DJIA and S&P 500*

your organization provides. An organization must strive to see value through the eyes of its intended customers or end users. Once the organization has accomplished this first step, it will be in a better position to achieve the following:

- Understanding what customers value from your facilities, products, and services
- Measuring value and communicating it to the customer
- Prioritizing what a customer wants as value and delivering it
- Retaining existing customers (the cost of finding a new one is typically five to ten times that of servicing an existing customer)
- Converting unknown customers to known ones
- Creating a competitive advantage through the development of a customer-focused organization

A good indicator of an organization's understanding of customer value is captured in the American Customer Satisfaction Index, which was developed by the National Quality Research Center at the Stephen M. Ross Business School at the University of Michigan. The American Customer Satisfaction Index (ACSI) is an economic indicator based on modeling of customer evaluations of the quality of goods and services purchased in the United States and produced by both domestic and foreign firms with substantial U.S. market shares.[15]

A recent paper published in the *Journal of Marketing* illustrates the importance of understanding customer value. The paper asked, "Do investments in customer satisfaction lead to excess returns? If so, are these returns associated with higher stock market risk?" The evidence presented in the article suggested that the answer to the first question was yes, and that the answer to the second question was no, suggesting that satisfied customers are economic assets with high returns and low risks. The portfolios studied were compared against the stock market performance of the S&P 500 for the same period of time. The results are presented in Figure 2.4.[16]

Reasons for Poor Value

Value seems to be something most organizations would want to strive for in delivering their products and services to the customer; however, seldom is optimum value achieved. Why is this so? There are many reasons why an organization's efforts result in less than optimal value. Some of the more common ones are as follows:

- Focus on internal value rather than customer value
- Poor communication or lack of consensus in developing project scope
- Changes in the customer's needs or wants
- Outdated design standards or changing technology
- Incorrect assumptions based on poor information
- Fixation with previous design concepts
- Temporary circumstances
- Honest wrong beliefs
- Habits and attitudes

The first three bullet points are the primary contributors to poor value. The first is universal in nature and relates to virtually every organization, regardless of whether they are involved with products, services, or facilities. The second and third apply primarily to businesses and organizations involved in the development of facilities and services.

Focus on Internal Value Rather Than Customer Value

Consider this statement: "Organizations should focus first on the products and services they provide." Would you be inclined to agree or disagree? While this may seem like a reasonable statement, too many companies and organizations place internal value measurements in considering the value of their products and service ahead of their customers. Sometimes this can lead to negative consequences.

Basing important decisions related to product development on internally derived values can produce disastrous results for an individual company or, as in the case of the U.S. automotive industry, an entire business sector. Over the past few decades, automakers focused on just such internal value measurements. In order to minimize up-front design costs and produce a greater variety of models in a shorter time period, they extended "platforms" by modifying body styles but leaving the basic structure unchanged by basing new models on existing ones. The problem was that customers didn't want more cars in a shorter time period; they wanted models with unique characteristics that captured their imaginations and made it easy to differentiate between models. While companies met their internal goals, they lost the differentiation of their products, resulting in customer confusion, which ultimately damaged sales.

A recent article cited eight reasons for the decline and bankruptcy of General Motors (GM) by a noted professor at the Harvard School of Business. The first, and most important reason, was GM's focus on products, not customers.

> *For years, Detroit wrongly viewed product types as market segments. Cars were classified as subcompacts, compacts, intermediates etc. But no consumer ever left home passionate to buy an "intermediate car." Segments are groups of customers, not products. Later, Detroit discovered lifestyle marketing but GM was trumped by Chrysler on minivans, was late to market with SUVs, then missed the mood swing of consumers towards crossovers. There must be pockets of consumer insight at GM, but they do not readily translate into market-shaping product initiatives.*[17]

Too few companies use customer value as a parameter in managing their portfolios. In his book *Product Leadership*, Robert Cooper found that nearly 90 percent of the thirty-five companies he studied did not include customer value in their portfolio management process. The few that did, still seemed to come up short as they typically took an internal view, looking at how attractive the market was to their own company, rather than how attractive the products they offered were to their customers.[18]

The application of VM techniques and processes, such as Value Metrics, brings together users and key project stakeholders to develop a broad understanding of the project's performance to develop the best value solutions.

Poor Communication or Lack of Consensus in Developing Project Scope

Most projects, especially those dealing with facilities and management processes, involve multiple stakeholders. Nowhere is this more evident than within public organizations where there are typically a number of regional and local government entities, regulatory agencies, special interests, and citizen groups involved in the project development process. Many times, these stakeholders will hold radically different views with respect to the importance of a project's objectives. Typically, the dominant stakeholder (usually the project's "owner") will place its objectives ahead of all others, which are often not aligned with the customer's or user's. This bias often leads to the development of a project scope that does not optimize value to all stakeholders.

Related to this phenomenon is the type of communication structure that is still pervasive in most organizations, which is essentially one-way.[19] In a one-way communication structure, information essentially flows from the top down. This is especially true of most public and many corporate structures that are functional or departmental in nature. Figure 2.5 illustrates a functional organizational structure and the associated communication model.

Under this structure, most communication passes one way, from the upper echelons of management down through the hierarchy. Just like an army, which also uses this model, it is easier to maintain control over the organization in meeting objectives, especially in very large ones. However, there are only limited opportunities for communication back up the chain, and as a result, the probability is that the information received by the lower tiers will be misunderstood or misinterpreted. Further, this model tends to stifle constructive criticism and feedback, which are essential to innovation and improvement.

VM utilizes a cross-functional, team organizational structure. One of the primary strengths of this structure is that it utilizes a completely different communication

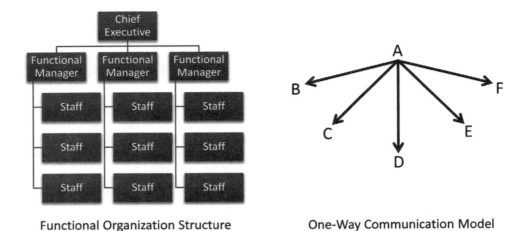

Functional Organization Structure   One-Way Communication Model

FIGURE 2.5 Functional Organization Structure and One-Way Communication Model

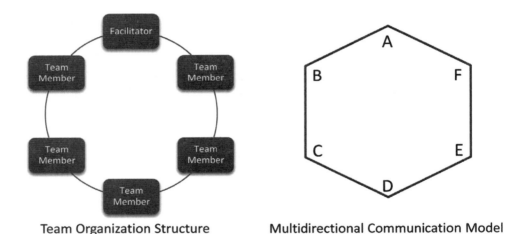

Team Organization Structure   Multidirectional Communication Model

FIGURE 2.6 Team Organization Structure and Multidirectional Communication Model

model, which is multidirectional. In a multidirectional communication model, information flows freely between all participants. This is much more conducive to innovation and improvement. Figure 2.6 illustrates the organizational structure and communication model.

In order for this structure to be effective, a skilled, objective VM facilitator needs to provide direction and structure while allowing for the free flow of information.

The application of VM within the context of a value study is an intense, focused effort where members of the value team, project team, owner, and user representatives come together in the same room as a single team possessing a single goal—that of improving project value. In addition, the VM techniques applied at each step of the Job Plan gather, organize, and develop information regarding the project;

draw meaningful conclusions from it through the application of Function Analysis and Value Metrics; and fosters direct communication between the team members through a consensus-driven process.

Changes in the Customer's Needs or Wants

Changes in customer needs or wants can occur within a relatively short time frame, often right under the noses of a project team. Examples of this phenomenon abound in virtually every type of project. Even in the design and development of facilities, user requirements can change quickly. With respect to public facilities, which can take many years to deliver, population growth can make the original design criteria obsolete by the time the design is ready for construction.

Many local departments of transportation struggle with the issue of highway improvements not keeping pace with the demands of growing traffic patterns. The project scope cannot keep pace with the changing scope of the problem and is therefore unable to satisfy the users' needs at the time of project delivery.

Similarly, military construction projects in the United States must pass through a multiyear funding process. Typically, several years pass from the time the user's needs are assessed, a program document is prepared, and the request is approved by congress. By the time that funding is finally available, the user's needs have changed and the approved budget may no longer match the requirements of the program.

Value Methodology can be used to accelerate the project delivery process by bringing together the project stakeholders, who often hold differing wants and needs with respect to the project's outcome, and helping them see the broader picture. The key to doing this is to distill complex organizational and technical issues into simple, easy-to-understand elements and to identify their relationships within the context of the larger framework of the total project. Furthermore, the application of the processes of Function Analysis and Value Metrics will provide a means for identifying and defining incomplete or overlooked project issues, risks, and objectives. With a well-defined project at the onset, the project effort can be better focused and the project delivery accelerated, thereby providing better value by addressing stakeholder needs as quickly as possible.

Outdated Design Standards or Changing Technology

In today's world, technological change is an accepted part of life. Despite this, organizations still fall prone to maintaining outdated standards or relying upon aging technology. Much of this resistance is rooted in a belief that new technologies are unproven and inherently flawed. With this line of thinking, individuals and organizations can quickly fall behind the competitors. Some relevant examples are:

- *Highway design standards*. The author was once leading a value study on a project by a state department of transportation. During function analysis, the function "Improve Sight-Distance" was identified as describing one of the major project elements involved regarding the current design concept. To achieve this function, the grade of an existing highway was going to be lowered in order to allow motorists to see over the crest of a gentle hill. The cost to do this was estimated to be in the tens of millions of dollars while creating significant disruptions to existing traffic and requiring extended detours. During the Speculation Phase of the VM Job Plan, one of the ideas that the value team came up with was to adopt a different design standard. In fact, such a standard had been recently adopted by the American Association of Highway and Transportation Officials (AASHTO), which resulted in the elimination of this work. The state had not yet adopted this standard, but was in the process of doing so. The change in question was the manner in how driver sight lines were calculated. With the higher volumes of SUVs and light trucks on the roads today, the average driver was sitting significantly higher above the roadway than was a counterpart from previous decades. This lag in the adoption of new standards nearly cost taxpayers millions of dollars and thousands of hours in traffic delays.

- *Computer processing power.* Bill Gates is often quoted as having said, "640kB ought to be enough for anybody." This is incorrect. What he really said was, "I laid out memory so the bottom 640K was general purpose RAM and the upper 384 I reserved for video and ROM, and things like that. That is why they talk about the 640K limit. It is actually a limit, not of the software, in any way, shape, or form, it is the limit of the microprocessor. That thing generates addresses, 20-bit addresses that only can address a megabyte of memory. And, therefore, all the applications are tied to that limit. It was ten times what we had before. But to my surprise, we ran out of that address base for applications within—oh five or six years people were complaining."[20] Regardless, the fact is that even an industry innovator like Bill Gates can be misguided in predictions regarding technological development. He had thought that 640kB would be sufficient for about 10 years, when in fact it lasted only five.

Value studies that are initiated by an organization are conducted under the premise that innovation is necessary in order to improve value. In light of this, VM provides an excellent vehicle for presenting the ideas and technologies of tomorrow, and challenging yesterday's standards, within an environment that is conducive to introspection and thoughtful consideration.

Incorrect Assumptions Based on Poor Information

A basic lack of information can lead to some amazingly bad decisions. History books are filled with countless examples of the world's greatest leaders and thinkers making faulty assumptions based on poor or outdated data. An excellent example of this concerns a value study the author recently facilitated.

In a project for a new highway facility, four potential alignment options were initially developed. Three of these bisected a wetlands area according to project documentation that was less than a year old. Based on this information, the project team selected the alignment option that avoided this area due to concerns related to obtaining environmental clearances from regulatory agencies. During the course of the value study for this project, the value team noted that three alignment options that had been eliminated from consideration because they all impacted the same wetland area. Furthermore, all three of these alignment options offered numerous significant advantages over the "preferred alignment." In light of this, the value team decided to further investigate the nature of the affected wetlands to see if there might be ways to mitigate the impacts.

After contacting a number of individuals who had firsthand knowledge of the area, a rather surprising discovery was made—the wetlands no longer existed! Apparently, the "wetlands" were a series of man-made ponds, which were fed by the outflow of a nearby wastewater treatment plant and used by local sportsmen to hunt ducks. These ponds had not been formally designated as emergent wetlands at the time of the initial environmental studies and, in the meantime, a local developer had purchased the land and filled them in. In addition, the same developer had even constructed new ponds in the direct path of the "preferred alignment." In light of these findings, the three alignment options that had been previously eliminated instantly became viable options.

What is today's good information often becomes tomorrow's bad information. Conditions can change quickly and without our knowledge, as was the case in the preceding example. In this respect, an accurate assessment of value is only as accurate as the information upon which it is based.

All projects generally begin with a number of basic assumptions. Too often as projects progress, these assumptions become "criteria" or "requirements" if they are not challenged and either verified or changed. Value studies provide a structured way to question original assumptions, identify their cost and performance impacts, and replace or challenge them with facts.

Fixation with Previous Design Concepts

There is a natural tendency for humans to resist change, especially in relation to longtime solutions that appear to be working just fine. We are all familiar with the mantra "If it's not broken, don't fix it!" While there is an undeniable common sense to this phrase, we should not let it dull our creativity and the desire to find a solution that works better.

The noted American geologist Thomas C. Chamberlin (1843–1928) addressed this concept as it applies to the application of the scientific method. He had observed that there was a strong tendency among scientists and researchers, in their desire to reach an interpretation or explanation, that commonly led them to a tentative interpretation based on an initial examination of a single example or case. He realized that this tentative explanation, as such, was not a threat to objectivity, but if it began to be trusted without further testing, it could blind us to other possibilities that were ignored at first glance. This premature explanation can become a tentative theory and then a *ruling theory*, and subsequently our research becomes focused on proving that ruling theory. The result is a blindness to evidence that disproves the ruling theory or supports an alternate explanation. Only if the original tentative hypothesis was by chance correct does our research lead to any meaningful contribution to knowledge.

Through these observations, Chamberlin developed the Method of Multiple Working Hypotheses,[20] which involves the development, prior to research, of several hypotheses that might explain the phenomenon to be studied. Many of these hypotheses will be contradictory, so that some, if not all, will prove to be false. However, the development of multiple hypotheses prior to the research lets us avoid the trap of the ruling hypothesis and thus makes it more likely that our research will lead to meaningful results. Through this approach, all the possible explanations of the phenomenon to be studied can be open-mindedly envisioned, including the possibility that none of the explanations or solutions is viable and the possibility that anew explanation may emerge.

As in the case of the first example, "If it's not broken, don't fix it!" Chamberlin's observations are quite relevant. Generally, there is a fixation with the existing solution or standard way of doing things. This can inhibit the potential for value improvement.

The VM process helps to address this issue, as alternatives are free to be developed that challenge the status quo. The benefits and risks associated with the change are quantified for the decision-makers. Often it is the risk associated with not changing that becomes the compelling rationale for action.

Temporary Circumstances

Temporary circumstances arise in response to a disruption in the usual flow of work and could manifest in a variety of ways, such as a shortage of a particular material or an unexpected production problem. When these circumstances arise, invariably a solution will be developed as a stop-gap measure. Generally, the work-around is more expensive or time-consuming, and the intent is to return to the old method as soon as the disruption is over. However, in many circumstances, and especially within larger organizations, there is a tendency to overlook these quick fixes as temporary, and the shift back to normal operations never happens. Value can be diminished in this manner, although rather insidiously.

The communication that occurs during a value study within the multidisciplined team as they apply the Value Methodology helps to bring to the surface these issues and provides a means of correcting the situation.

Honest Wrong Beliefs

These may result from mental conditioning as well as the ready acceptance of opinion, rumor, and speculation without justification or verification. They are often a result of the longtime propagation of many of the other poor reasons for value cited here. There is a certain mythology that has arisen in modern society to which we all have a tendency to subscribe. In his bestselling book *Freakonomics*,[22] author Steven Levitt identifies a number of underlying economic principles, which he discusses at length. Two of them dovetail nicely with the notion of "honest wrong beliefs." These are:

1. *Conventional wisdom is often wrong.* It is a commonly held belief in the United States that money wins elections. One need only look at the 2008 presidential election to confirm this, right? The Obama campaign significantly outspent the McCain Campaign and guess who won? We often see correlations where we want to see them; however, it doesn't mean they are correct. Based on an analysis of data presented in *Freakonomics*, a winning candidate can cut his spending by 50 percent and lose only 1 percent of the vote, while a losing candidate who doubles his spending can similarly expect to pick up 1 percent more votes.

2. *Experts use their informational advantage to serve their own agenda.* Here, Levitt shows how experts can easily exploit our trust and lead us to believe they are working for us rather than themselves. Real estate agents typically work for a commission of the total sale of a property. It stands to reason that their interests are in line with their clients—the higher an agent can sell a client's property, the more money they will both make. However, as Levitt shows, the data paints a very different picture. The average realtor makes 3 percent more on the sale of their own homes than they do for everyone else. That's $9,000 more on the sale of a $300,000 house! Why don't the rest of us get the same value from their services?

The application of the Value Methodology facilitates challenging such beliefs with current facts and helps to dispel them by developing alternatives that would otherwise be dismissed without analysis and quantification of the benefits in the current environment. Through VM's focus on the user, misconceptions, such as those identified above, can be revealed and strategies developed to address them.

Habits and Attitudes

Habits and attitudes are developed by individuals over a lifetime. This ingrained form of behavior can lead to an appalling degree of ignorance with respect to making decisions that will lead to good value. There are a number of layers of habits and attitudes that all of us possess related to our culture, religion, profession, and lifestyle. While many of our habits and attitudes are quite positive, they can also create blind spots with respect to our ability to make value decisions in the workplace. Companies often get into trouble when the motivation profit, which is ingrained in corporate culture, takes control.

Habits and attitudes represent the greatest obstacle in achieving good value. Habitual thinking can be extremely difficult to overcome. If you repeatedly ask somebody "Why do you do it that way?" usually by the third time, they will respond, "Because that's the way I've always done it!" This type of response is apt to come up even sooner if asked in the workplace. People perform tasks all the time without really thinking about them or knowing why they are doing them. If they stopped to ask things like "Why are we filing these reports?" or "Why do accounting and purchasing both need to approve this requisition?" they might find that the answer is "You don't need to!" What follows are all good examples of habits and attitudes influencing behavior in the workplace:

- We did it that way on our last job.
- It deviates from standard procedures.
- We've never done that before.
- It will set a precedent.
- It's too risky.
- Management won't like it.
- It hasn't been tested.
- It doesn't agree with company policy.
- Headquarters will never approve it.

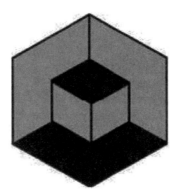

FIGURE 2.7   Ambiguous Cube

The responses identified above represent obstacles to change based upon habitual ways of doing things. It is important to recognize these for what they are and not to let them get in the way of innovation. Remember, habits are a necessary part of our life; however, their very nature is thoughtless. The best way to overcome habitual thinking is to make people aware of what they are saying and then get them to think about it. People are usually not even aware that their habitual responses are rooted so deeply and, once the roots are exposed for what they are, people are more apt to accept changes.

Another aspect of habitual behavior is related to those that are formed by our perceptions. It is important to remember that, to a large degree, the brain functions by interpreting the world around us through the senses. Perhaps the most important of these is vision. Most people depend greatly upon their eyes every single day. Because of this, we are prone to take what we see for granted, and the habits and attitudes that arise from our visual interpretations can inhibit our ability to make good decisions. The following exercises are intended to demonstrate the limitations of our visual senses.

Figure 2.7 appears to be a normal cube with a piece missing from one corner; however, this cube is ambiguous, and may suddenly turn into any of three different aspects. You can empower these transformations by concentrating a little.

Look at the cube, and in your mind's eye, turn the missing corner piece into a solid cube. The small cube will appear to float in space, tilted slightly forward, with a dark top. When this aspect is realized, the cube will take on a completely new three-dimensional appearance. Now try to make the larger cube appear as a *room* with two vertical walls and a darker floor. In this new aspect, the missing corner piece fits snugly into the far corner of the *room*. Remember—*all this is happening inside your head!*

Try turning the cube inside out so that you are instead looking at a small cube floating in space into a room with two walls and a darker floor. It may take some effort on your part to achieve this transformation. This exercise is useful in demonstrating that it is the brain, and not the eyes, that interpret what we see. Although our eyes see the same image, we can perceive the image in different ways depending on how we choose to think about the visual information.

Our eyes possess millions of specialized light receptors, but only a few of them are active when we look at something. Next to the active receptors are receptors

FIGURE 2.8 Hermann's Grid

at rest that are recovering from just being used. The image shown in Figure 2.8 takes advantage of these "sleeping" light receptors.

This figure is known as Hermann's Grid, and it is used to demonstrate a visual phenomenon known as lateral inhibition. The fuzzy little black dots in the intersections of the grid are not really there. The rule: White tends to look darker when it is surrounded by black, therefore the intersections appear darker. An active light receptor is an honest light receptor, so the fuzzy dots fade when you look right at them. The fuzzy dots are proof that you can see with nearby, "sleeping" receptors, but you shouldn't always believe them. These are just two of the many physiological and cognitive illusions that can fool our visual perception.

To summarize, the old adage "Seeing is believing" is simply not true. Our brains and our senses can betray us if we choose to let them by falling into habitual patterns—and habitual thinking can inhibit our ability to make good value decisions.

Attitudes, emotions, and beliefs tend to become habitual. People tend to think, feel, and act the same way whenever they encounter what is interpreted as the same sort of situation that has been previously experienced. As creatures of habit, attitudes support the habits we have acquired. Attitudes can rob us of value. Attitudes support the continuation of existing habits and the acceptance of roadblocks to progress. Attitudes and habits go hand-in-hand. Change one, and you will automatically influence the other.

If we approach our projects with a negative attitude and say, "We have been doing it this way for a long time, and it works, so why change it?," chances are as we examine it we will not find many ways to improve it. However, if we say, "This is a good design, but we might be able to make it better," chances are that we will find ways to improve it. A quote by the ancient Chinese philosopher Confucius summarizes this discussion rather well:

> *It is our habits that take us where we were yesterday, and our attitudes that keep us there.*

While there are many reasons poor value exists in the products and services provided today, the systematic approach of the Value Methodology is a proven, effective way to overcome these factors and improve the products and services provided.

Summary

Developing a basic understanding of value is not only essential for the value specialist but for all individuals and organizations involved in the creation and delivery of products, facilities, or services. It is really quite astonishing that so little is understood about the nature of value when so much depends upon ensuring that good value is achieved. Ultimately, it is the customer or end user who will decide value, and not the organization.

CHAPTER 3

Value Methodology Job Plan

© Magixl 2009, www.magixl.com

I was taught that the way of progress is neither swift nor easy.

—Marie Curie

Marie Curie was born Maria Sklodowska in Warsaw, Poland, in 1867. She was the fifth and last child of piano player and teacher Bronsilawa Boguska and mathematics and physics professor Wladyslaw Sklodowski.

In 1891, at the age of 24, Sklodowska went to Paris to study mathematics, physics, and chemistry at the Sorbonne. She was consumed by her studies and subsisted almost entirely on bread, butter, and tea. During her years there, she changed the spelling of her name to the French version, Marie. She met Pierre Curie in Paris while she studied there and they soon married in a civil ceremony.

Marie and Pierre Curie devoted themselves to the study of radioactivity and were among the first to work with radium and polonium. It was Marie Curie who coined the term *radioactivity,* and she named polonium after her home country of Poland. Pierre was chiefly concerned with the physical properties of radium and polonium, while Marie worked to isolate radium in its pure state. She and one of Pierre's students, Mr. Debierne, accomplished this, and Marie received her doctorate in 1903 based on her findings. Also in 1903, the Curies won the Nobel Prize for their work along with French physicist Antoine Henri Bacquerel, who had first discovered natural radioactivity.

She also had to fight the prejudices of her day: hatred of foreigners and sexism, which, in 1911, prevented her from entering the Academy of Science. Despite the challenges she faced, soon after, she was honored with a Nobel Prize for Chemistry for determining the atomic weight of radium. But her real joy was "easing human suffering." The founding of the Radium Institute by the University of Paris and the Pasteur Institute in 1914 would enable her to fulfill her humanitarian wish.

During the First World War, Marie felt that the use of X-rays would help to locate shrapnel and bullets and would therefore better facilitate surgery. With this need in mind and realizing that it was important to avoid moving the wounded if possible, she created mobile X-ray vans. She would later provide X-ray equipment to hospitals and ultimately train 150 female X-ray operators.

Madame Curie died of leukemia in 1934, exhausted and almost blinded, her fingers burnt and disfigured through her work with radium. In her dedication and tireless pursuit of science through her methodical approach to problem solving, Marie Curie demonstrates the value of following a proven process. The scientific method, as will be discussed later in the chapter, shares some parallels with the Value Methodology Job Plan.

The Value Methodology Job Plan

Within the Value Methodology, there is a specific approach that must be followed if significant results are to be obtained. This organized, multiphase approach is called the Job Plan. Key to the success of the Value Methodology approach is following these steps in sequence and avoiding the temptation to jump ahead—to try to solve a problem before it has been thoroughly understood and analyzed.

Before introducing the Value Methodology Job Plan, it is useful to first discuss the *scientific method*, which is perhaps the most widely understood and applied approach to problem solving. The original development of the scientific method is largely attributed to Francis Bacon, a persuasive seventeenth-century English statesman and philosopher (1561–1626), who argued that knowledge was gained only through the gathering of empirical data rigorously and logically refined to a single, essential conclusion. The scientific method (see Figure 3.1) consists of four distinct steps:

1. *Observation.* State the problem and research it. Observe a phenomenon or a group of phenomena and gather data.
2. *Hypothesis.* Formulate a hypothesis (or multiple working hypotheses) to explain the phenomena. In many fields of study, the hypothesis can often take the

FIGURE 3.1   Scientific Method

form of a causal mechanism or a mathematical relation, while in general problem-solving instances, a potential solution to the problem or a prediction of the expected outcome, is identified.

3. *Experimentation*. Perform experiments to test the predictions. In science, the use of numerous independently reproduced experiments to verify and validate the original findings is generally required.

4. *Conclusion*. Draw conclusions from the experiments. Summarize the results of the experiments into meaningful conclusions relative to the original hypothesis.

The original Job Plan, as presented by Miles,[1] consisted of five steps, as shown in Figure 3.2:

1. *Information*. Develop an understanding of the project. The key to this step is the process of asking questions of the project team.

2. *Analysis*. Develop an understanding of the project functions. This step represents the main point of departure of Value Methodology from other problem-solving approaches, including the scientific method. Miles created an entirely different way of thinking about problems and systems based on what an object *does* rather than what it *is*.

3. *Creativity*. Identify alternative concepts of achieving the project functions. Although creativity is a fairly routine component of just about every type of problem solving methodology, the creative process in VM focuses on functions rather than objects. This may at first appear to be a rather subtle difference; however, the implications are profound.

4. *Judgment*. Evaluate the alternative concepts based upon their merits. Miles regarded this as a rather straightforward step, and the assumption was that basic common sense would be used to select the best ideas for additional development.

5. *Development Planning*. Develop the alternative concepts into detailed recommendations. Also originally included within this step was the implementation of the alternative concepts into the project.

How does the VM approach to problem solving differ from that of the scientific method? There are several important differences that merit further discussion. These differences are best introduced by two quotes attributed to Albert Einstein (1879–1955), one of history's greatest thinkers and scientists.

The significant problems we have cannot be solved at the same level of thinking with which we created them.

FIGURE 3.2 Miles's Original Job Plan

The scientific method first states the problem and then gathers pertinent data. The Job Plan states the problem, gathers data, and then defines the underlying *functions*. This is an essential difference in understanding the problem. The process of breaking problems down into functions broadens the level of abstraction involved in order to understand and to solve the problem at the most appropriate level.

"Imagination is more important than knowledge."

The scientific method develops a hypothesis (solution), or in some cases multiple working hypotheses. The Job Plan dedicates an entire step to the creation of ideas that will address the *functions*. There is a deliberate separation of creativity (imagination) and judgment (knowledge and experience). This separation is essential if our imagination is to be fully realized and applied to the problem.

Since the creation of the original Job Plan, a multitude of variations have been developed to address the specific needs and requirements of individuals and organizations applying VM. This proliferation notwithstanding, the five basic steps as conceived by Miles continue to serve as the foundation for these variations. Any Job Plan that does not include these steps, and in the same relative order, is not properly applying the Value Methodology.

The Job Plan that is being presented in this book consists of eight phases. The phases include the five original steps identified by Miles in the same relative order, but some of these have been divided into subphases and most have been renamed to add clarity to the Job Plan. The eight phases of the Job Plan are:

1. Preparation
2. Information
3. Function
4. Speculation / Creativity
5. Evaluation
6. Development
7. Presentation
8. Implementation

The modern VM Job Plan is illustrated in Figure 3.3. Typically, the Preparation Phase is performed before the value study, and the Implementation Phase is performed after the value study. A detailed discussion of each of the phases in the

FIGURE 3.3 Value Methodology Job Plan

Job Plan is provided in the chapters that follow. Provided below is a brief introduction of each phase that includes a description of the objectives sought and considerations relevant to each phase.

Preparation

Thorough preparation is critical to the success of any value study. The first part of this preparation is identifying what project is to be studied and when it is to be studied. A variety of techniques may be employed to select the best projects for study and identify the proper timing for the value study with respect to the project's life cycle.

A basic level of understanding is provided by gathering and reviewing the appropriate information before starting a study. Depending upon the type of study, the information required will vary slightly. However, in all studies the project's need and purpose, performance attributes and requirements must be understood; specific goals must be defined; and current costs must be gathered and organized.

One of the key steps in meeting these requirements is conducting a prestudy meeting to organize and plan for the value study. This meeting typically includes the value specialist, the project manager, the project team, stakeholders, and in some cases the rest of the value team. This meeting will result in a well-defined value study and will identify goals, objectives, assumptions, and constraints.

Information

The primary objective of the Information Phase is to obtain a thorough understanding of the project under study. The information gathered prior to and during the study is reviewed and discussed by the team. Typically, the project team and/or the project manager will present the current project status to the value team and answer their questions. Key considerations in this phase include:

- Human relations are very important to the success of any value study. "People problems" are oftentimes more difficult to resolve than technical problems. The effectiveness of a value specialist's efforts depends upon the amount of cooperation he or she is able to obtain from the project development team, customers, stakeholders, and value study team members.
- All pertinent facts concerning the project must be uncovered and drawn together, including customer and owner objectives, the history of the project and its development, cost, and performance requirements. All aspects of the project must be questioned and examined: How is it produced, constructed, shipped, installed, repaired, maintained, replaced, operated, and what materials are used in its manufacture? It is often helpful if the item can be observed in actual operation. The main considerations are getting all the facts, and getting them from the best sources.
- All relevant information is important, regardless of how disorganized or unrelated it may seem when gathered. After gathering all available information, the facts should then be organized and copies of all important documents obtained. The more information brought to bear on the problem, the more likely the possibility of a successful and productive value study. A lack of information

should not preclude the performance of the VM effort, as more information will likely become available as the study progresses. Indeed, the availability of information should play a significant role in defining the scope and objectives of the value study effort.

Function

Function Analysis is the heart of the Value Methodology. The ultimate objective of the Function Phase is to identify functions that are not providing good value and those that are unnecessary. There are three steps in the Function Analysis phase:

1. Identify the project functions. The basic function(s) should also be identified at this time.
2. Classify the functions by type, preferably using the Function Analysis System Technique (FAST). FAST diagrams show how the functions relate to each other and provide the team with a visual image of these functional relationships.
3. Evaluate the functions by developing relationships between cost, performance, time, risk, and function by assigning component or process costs, risk levels, time or schedule durations, and performance attributes to the various functions. Through this process, referred to as *dimensioning*, the team can analyze how the functions provide value to the customer. Select functions are then focused on during the Speculation Phase for improvement.

In a typical project, several functions usually stand out as requiring improvement, either from the cost/performance/functional relationships that were developed or through the identification of a function(s) as a root cause of a performance problem.

Speculation

In the Speculation Phase of the Job Plan, a creativity session is conducted for each function targeted for improvement during the Function Phase. During these creative sessions, any idea that can be associated with that function is recorded so that it may be evaluated later. Brainstorming techniques are typically used to identify numerous ideas on each function requiring improvement. Generating a large *quantity* of ideas is the goal, rather than the *quality* of the ideas. A large quantity of ideas will lead to a greater number of quality ideas. A key element of creativity is to avoid evaluating the ideas during the creative process.

Speculation should not begin until the problem is thoroughly understood and the specific time for speculation has arrived. Only when the required function has been defined and evaluated should speculation begin. A variety of creative techniques can be employed to stimulate the value team's imagination. Team brainstorming is typically used to initiate the creative process. It is the role of the value specialist to act as coach during the Speculation Phase. All members of the value study team must be encouraged to participate. A high level of participation will serve to motivate and energize the creative process. Every attempt should be made during this phase to depart from the "usual" or conventional way of doing things.

Experience has shown that it is often the new, fresh, and radically different approach that uncovers the best value solution. The focus should first be on the development of ways of performing the function, and secondly on ways to improve the performance of the function.

Evaluation

The objective of the Evaluation Phase is to reduce the large quantity of ideas generated in the Speculation Phase to a few high-quality ideas through the evaluation process. The value team will discuss and evaluate each idea relative to the project's performance attributes and cost. This process identifies the major advantages and disadvantages of each idea and how it would impact project performance. Once this is done, the team agrees on a rating for the idea. This serves as a filter, and the better ideas are generally taken to the next step and developed further.

Frequently, several ideas or a combination of ideas that compete with one another remain. When this occurs, an evaluation matrix is used that better quantifies the impact of the competing ideas to identify which will best meet the project's need and purpose, performance, and cost objectives. Key considerations include:

- Spend project money as you would your own. This is an important rule when considering the cost of implementing an idea.
- Evaluate the ideas relative to project performance attributes. How will the idea affect project performance relative to need and purpose?
- Similar to performance, consider how the ideas will impact time and risk. Will the idea take more or less time than the current approach? Will it reduce uncertainty by maximizing opportunities or minimizing threats?
- Compare the advantages and disadvantages of each idea relative to the baseline project concept or design.
- Once the three previous considerations have been taken in evaluating each idea, rank the ideas based upon their overall merits.
- Refine ideas that may be otherwise rejected. Often additional team brainstorming can develop a "fix" to a problem that arises during idea evaluation. It is useful to think of the Speculation and Evaluation Phases as cyclical in nature. The surviving ideas are then refined and more cost information is obtained. Detailed estimates are prepared only for the more promising alternates.
- Select ideas for further development. Ideas with the greatest value improvement potential are normally chosen to be developed with further study, testing, refinement, and information gathering. If there is more than one idea addressing a specific function that is outstanding, or the differences between two or more ideas are not clear enough to eliminate any of them, then all should be retained and carried over into the next phase.

Development

Depending on the type of study, the Development Phase may be completed as part of the study or in a follow-up to the study. The objective of this phase is to develop the "best ideas" that were identified during the Evaluation Phase into specific value alternatives that have been technically validated. The impact of each value alternative should also be quantified as much as possible. Before presenting the recommendations, it is necessary to establish an action plan to organize the team's efforts. Some of the work is performed by individual team members and some by the team as a whole. The action plan should identify the work that needs to be done on each concept to resolve any unanswered questions and confirm that the concept should be formulated into a recommendation. With a good action plan in hand, the team can then finalize and develop each recommendation. Key questions and considerations include:

- Are the costs accurate and representative for the project?
- Do the cost estimates include all costs of implementation and testing, and are all costs accurate?
- Have schedules for implementation and testing been included?
- How will the concept affect uncertainty? If it is an "untested" concept, will it pose a risk to the project? Conversely, will it reduce uncertainty by better managing risk?
- The best ideas in the world will not be accepted unless reasons are provided for accepting them.
- Prepare all pertinent technical and cost information and list all of the advantages and the disadvantages for each alternative concept.
- Provide graphical information relevant to the value alternative if possible.
- Prepare value alternatives for testing and implementation.
- Determine what changes will be required in existing schedules, drawings, specifications, or contracts.
- Make sure all the pertinent information is reviewed that may change the value alternative.
- If multiple value alternatives have been developed that address the same issues, the value team should select the one alternative they feel is best for implementation. Others may be prepared in the event the first choice is not accepted by the approval authority.
- Ensure that each value alternative has been fully documented and is presented in a format that will enable decision makers to clearly understand all relevant information. This information should include:
  - A brief summary of the project and/or project element, including a narrative description of the baseline and alternative concepts
  - Graphic information such as design drawings, diagrams, sketches, or process flowcharts
  - The estimated cost of the baseline and alternative concepts, including the life cycle and implementation costs
  - A description of the anticipated impact the value alternative will have on project performance
  - A thoughtful analysis of risk, whether it be qualitative or quantitative. Remember, uncertainty can affect performance as well as cost and time.
  - An estimate of the time or schedule impacts.
  - Technical data supporting the value alternative
  - Actions necessary for implementation of the value alternative
  - A suggested implementation schedule

Presentation

A final report containing the value team's alternatives and a presentation to the project team concludes the value study. The objective is to inform the owner, project team, stakeholders, and the customer or user of the value team's findings. This initial presentation should not be advertised as a decision meeting—the decision making process should occur in the final phase: implementation. The value team typically provides the written report after the presentation. Key considerations in presenting results include:

- The presentation of the value alternatives, both written and oral, must gain the cooperation of the decision makers and their advisors. It is therefore important that the value alternatives be made in as clear and concise a manner as possible. This will help separate technical objections from emotional ones when it later comes time to make decisions regarding the acceptability of the value alternatives.
- Use specifics and avoid generalities where possible. If one exception can be found to a generality, this exception can be used to defeat the entire value alternative, even if the exception does not bear directly on the problem. Present facts and be prepared to support them.
- Both the written and oral presentations will draw the attention of people who do not have time to waste. Make sure all the required facts are presented in a concise manner, and then stop.
- Conducting an oral presentation is most helpful when presenting the value alternatives to the project team. The value team can elaborate on those points that are not clear to the listeners, and questions regarding the value alternatives can be answered on the spot.
- The value team must be diplomatic in the presentation of its alternatives. Often, members of the project team may feel threatened by the value team's findings. Care must be given to respect the work that has gone before and the constraints under which the project team may have been working. Change is not always easy to accept.

Implementation

The implementation activities are critical to the ultimate success of the Job Plan. During this phase, the project team and the decision makers will review and assimilate the data given to them in the Presentation Phase. An implementation meeting should be conducted once sufficient time has passed to review the value team's findings. The purpose of this meeting is to make a determination regarding the disposition of each of the alternative concepts. Ideally, the value team will be present to provide clarifications and assistance to the decision makers. Alternatives that are accepted will require the development of an implementation plan and schedule for integration into the project. Those alternatives that are rejected should have the reasons for their rejection documented.

Tracking the implementation of value alternatives and auditing the results helps to measure the effectiveness of the VM effort. The project should have some kind of mechanism put in place that will allow the changes to the project's scope, schedule, and cost to be managed.

Value Metrics

Value Metrics was originally developed as a means to measure the effect of value studies on project performance for the State of California's Department of Transportation, where it was first called the *Performance Measures Process.* This process was later expanded and refined as a means of measuring value.

Value Metrics is composed of a group of techniques that establish a means for the measurement of a project's inputs (cost and time) and outputs (performance) as they relate to value. *Value Metrics* uses the algorithms for *functional value*, as discussed in Chapter 2, "Value," as the basis for measuring value improvement.

As discussed earlier in this chapter, the quantification of cost is relatively straightforward. The quantification of performance is not. There are several reasons for this:

- Performance varies for each product, process, and facility.
- Performance is often subjective in nature.
- Performance standards often do not exist for the project.

Value Metrics provides a standardized means of identifying, defining, evaluating, and measuring performance. Once this has been achieved, and the costs for all value alternatives have been developed, it is a relatively simple matter of measuring value.

Value Metrics is a complementary system of concepts and techniques developed to augment the traditional Value Methodology Job Plan. It is not absolutely essential that *Value Metrics* be utilized in order to perform a value study; however, it is well worth the additional effort, as there are a number of significant benefits that it can convey. *Value Metrics* can improve value studies by:

- Building consensus among project stakeholders (especially those holding conflicting views)
- Developing a better understanding of a project's goals and objectives as they relate to purpose and need
- Developing a baseline understanding of how the project is meeting performance goals and objectives
- Identifying areas where project performance can be improved through the VM process
- Developing a better understanding of an alternative concept's impact on project performance
- Developing a deeper understanding of the relationship between performance and cost in determining value
- Using value as the basis for selecting the best project or design concept

The concepts and techniques used in *Value Metrics* will be introduced in conjunction with each of the subsequent chapters that deal with each specific phase of the Job Plan. A summary of each of these complementary steps is provided in Figure 3.4, which shows the relation of *Value Metrics* to the traditional Value Methodology Job Plan.

Value Methodology Job Plan

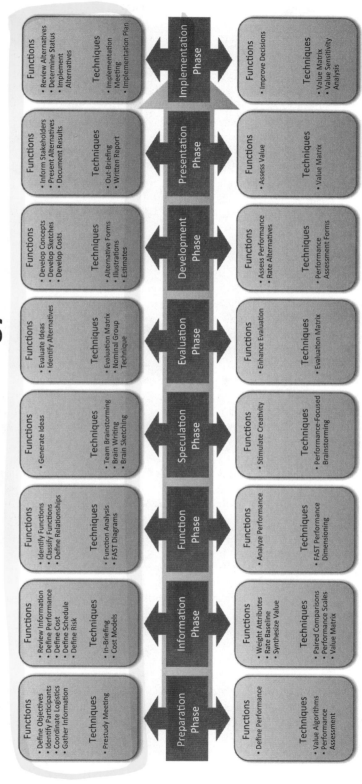

Value Metrics

FIGURE 3.4 Value Methodology Job Plan: Value Metrics

Summary

The VM Job Plan provides a vehicle to carry a value study from inception to conclusion. It assures that proper consideration has been given to all necessary facets of the study. The Job Plan divides the study into sets of work elements. The Job Plan requires those performing the value study to clearly define the functions of the project or project element to be studied and provides the value team with a plan for obtaining all the information needed for the study. The Job Plan affords the value team time for creative work and analysis of alternates. This leads the team to the selection of the best value alternatives. The Job Plan concludes with a presentation of specific recommendations to project stakeholders, a proposed implementation schedule, and a summary of benefits.

CHAPTER 4

Preparation

© Magixl 2009, www.magixl.com

They call it coaching but it is teaching. You do not just tell them . . . you show them the reasons.

—Vince Lombardi

Vincent Thomas Lombardi was born on June 11, 1913, in Brooklyn, New York. He was the first of Henry and Matilda Lombardi's five children. Vince was raised in the Catholic faith and studied for the priesthood for two years before transferring to St. Francis Preparatory High School, where he was a star fullback on the football team. After playing college football at Fordham University, Lombardi took a job as a high school teacher and coach. Later, he returned to his alma mater, where he coached the football team. A few years later, he was hired as the defensive line coach at West Point Military Academy. In 1954, he was hired by the New York Giants as an assistant coach. In three years, he helped bring the Giants from a losing record to become the champions of the National Football League.

In 1958, Lombardi received his first head coach position with the Green Bay Packers. Prior to this time, the Packers had established a reputation as perpetual losers. In 1967, after nine phenomenal winning seasons with the Packers, Lombardi chose to retire as head coach, deciding to continue only in the front office as the general manager of the team. During his tenure as head coach, the Packers had dominated professional football, collecting six division titles, five NFL championships, two Super Bowls (I and II), and posting a record of 98–30–4. They had become the yardstick against which all other teams were measured.

Compared to offenses in the twenty-first century, Lombardi's offensive playbook was basic and methodical. Its most famous play is often referred to as the "Lombardi sweep" or the "Packer sweep," and consists of the tailback following pulling guards to either side of the field. Lombardi was famous for his pursuit of perfection, often dedicating long hours of film or practice to study just one element of a play.

Lombardi was also known as an innovator. In 1967, at a cost of $80,000, Lombardi had heating coils installed under the "frozen tundra" of Green Bay's Lambeau Field in order to keep it from freezing in the winter months. During the 1967 NFL Championship, better known as the "Ice Bowl," due to the subzero temperatures under which the game was played, the system failed. However, some suggest that Lombardi actually turned it off intentionally to gain even more of a home field advantage. Regardless, Lombardi's heating grid lasted until 1997, when the Packers replaced it with the current system, which contains more than 30 miles of radiant heating pipe, to maintain a root-zone temperature of 70-plus degrees.

In less than a year after retiring, however, Lombardi realized that he still wanted to coach. He accepted the head coaching position for the Washington Redskins in 1969. During that season, he kept what had become the Lombardi tradition and led the Redskins to their first winning record in 14 years. In January 1970, his professional coaching record stood at a remarkable 105–35–6, unmarred by a losing season. The NFL named him their acclaimed "1960s Man of the Decade."

The hallmark of Vince Lombardi's success was his discipline and slavish attention to preparation. The time spent off the field, mentally and physically preparing his team, was where he won the game. Vince Lombardi's story is instructive in introducing the first phase of the Value Methodology (VM) Job Plan—the Preparation Phase.

Preparation Phase

Regardless of whether we are looking at a large, multistory building or a small manufactured item composed of various parts, the general impression is one of complexity. Humanity has succeeded in creating increasingly complicated structures and products that are intended to improve the quality of life. Thus, when starting a value study, the value specialist is immediately confronted with the task of separating a distressingly complicated entity into subsystems, selecting certain items for study, and ignoring others. Time and labor limitations do not permit everything to be studied; he or she must become skilled in rapidly identifying items that have a high potential for value improvement to the project at hand. This chapter provides guidelines on how to select, schedule, and prepare for a value study.

The Preparation Phase features the following steps:

- Identify the projects for the value study
- Identify the timing of the value study
- Conduct a prestudy meeting

Each of these steps is detailed further in this chapter and addresses the questions of what project, or parts of a project, will be studied; when in the project's life cycle it will be studied; and how the value study will be organized and executed.

Identify Projects for Value Study

Identifying the right project or parts of a project (if it is of substantial size, cost, or complexity) is the first challenge in preparing for a value study. In most cases, the need for a value study on a specific project will be obvious.

In large organizations where there are either limited funds to conduct value studies or simply too many potential projects to choose from, it may be necessary to give careful consideration in selecting those projects that will offer the greatest return on investment.

In the situations described above, a program to stimulate the generation of items for value studies is essential, particularly during the early stages of a value management program. As personnel become more familiar with VM and its benefits it will be found that generation of good study areas becomes automatic, making formal methods of generation less essential. The following techniques may be used:

- *Cost models.* Cost data is an excellent source of information available to most organizations. This can take the form of historical or parametric cost data on past construction projects; bills of materials for product lines; or resource reports for businesses processes. Summaries of such cost data are frequently available and often continuously updated, based on information obtained on an organization-wide reporting system. Cost information gleaned from this information can be organized in the form of cost models. When applied to a meaningful population of comparative costs, a cost model can enable management to identify the high cost areas within a project. These areas may be earmarked for value study. Cost modeling is discussed in greater detail in Chapter 5, "Information."
- *Publicizing the need.* The value manager should explain to the organization what types of studies are wanted and the criteria used for selection. An invitation to all personnel to submit suggested projects and items to the value manager usually gives good results.
- *Quotas and project generation teams.* Periodically issuing instructions to internal departments or divisions within the organization to submit a given number of projects for study by a specific date can result in a healthy number of items. The appointment of a team of about four persons to brainstorm an assigned design for high value study potential usually results in numerous worthwhile projects for study.
- *Standing VM committee.* A committee of top personnel that meets periodically for selection of items or areas will produce a good list of candidate studies. Studies originating from these sources have a better-than-average chance of implementation because they will have been selected by persons who are also the decision makers.
- *Design-to-cost targeting.* A cost model that establishes cost targets for each element of a project will readily show which ones exceed a given budget. This information can be determined at any stage of design and can serve as a warning to the value specialist to concentrate effort on these items.

- *Pareto analysis.* The Italian economist Vilfredo Pareto (1848–1923), developed the curve known as Pareto's law of distribution. This curve applies to any project where a significant number of elements are involved. It points out that, in any area, a small number of elements (20 percent) contain the greater percentage of costs (80 percent). Similarly, a small number of elements will contain the greater percentage of unnecessary costs. Thus, if costs of each element are arrayed, with the most costly items at the head of the list and the less costly following in order, it will enable the value specialist to concentrate on the relatively few components that contribute the most to the total cost (see Figure 4.1). It should be emphasized that Pareto analysis can be applied to other elements as well, such as time, performance, and risk—whatever is important to the customer or user.

- *Spatial cost analysis.* This method assumes that area or volumetric costs (e.g., square feet, cubic meters) is a direct index of design efficiency. This method is particularly useful to construction applications. A design having a high cost per square foot would be considered less efficient than one with a lower unit cost. This is not necessarily true and must be applied with caution. For example, a poorly designed building with an excessive amount of wasted space may spread the cost of expensive areas such as plumbing fixtures, kitchens, mechanical, and electrical spaces over a larger area, thereby lowering the per-square-foot cost. On the other hand, in an efficiently planned building with a minimum of wasted space, the cost per square foot will be higher, although the overall cost of the building will be less. Similarly, the enclosure method of estimating

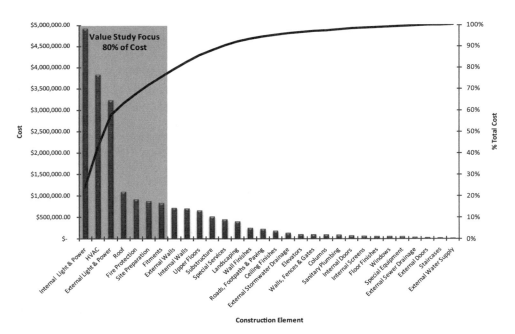

FIGURE 4.1 Pareto Cost Model—Data Center

compares the cost per square foot of the original design with unit costs of alternatives on a basis of total surfaces enclosed. "Enclosure," as used here, means any surface such as floors, walls, partitions, roof systems, columns, piers, stairs, railings, and similar items. Thus the cost of the alternative design, which has, let us say, 25 percent less surface area in the form of fewer partitions and so on, would be assumed to cost 25 percent less. This method can be used to quickly determine the probable cost of alternatives early in the value process.

- *FAST diagrams.* Functional Analysis Systems Technique (FAST) diagrams give a graphic portrayal of the interrelationship of the functions of any project. On projects that are massive in scale, such as a mass transit project or a complex manufactured item such as a vehicle, FAST diagrams are useful for revealing key functional areas on which value studies can focus. They permit the analyst to see where simplifications can be achieved. The process for using FAST diagrams to aid in identifying candidates for value analysis is covered in detail in Chapter 6, "Function."

Each system and subsystem must be examined to identify high-cost elements, which then become prime candidates for study. For each such item, the following questions will provide further guidance:

- Is the item expensive? Remember that Pareto's Law states that 80 percent of the cost of an item is contained in 20 percent of its components.
- Is it complex?
- Is it a high-volume item? Can a simple change in one item produce large savings within the total project?
- Does it use critical materials?
- Is it difficult to construct or require specialized skills to create?
- Does it have high maintenance and/or operations costs?
- Does it use obsolete materials and methods?
- Are costs simply "out of line"?
- Was the design rushed?
- Is there a high degree of uncertainty related to performance, cost, or time?
- Would the consequences of failure be catastrophic?
- Does it suffer from performance problems?
- Is it a state-of-the-art component with a low level of proven acceptance?
- Are life cycle costs unacceptable?
- Does it contain redundant features?
- Does it create an unwanted function of high future cost?
- Does it use traditional design?
- Is the competition producing the item at a lower cost?
- Does top management want improvement?

Identify Timing of Value Study

It is the responsibility of the project manager or, ideally, the value program manager to ensure that the studies of each project are scheduled at the right time. This requires awareness by all management and project development personnel of the benefits that can be achieved through the VM process and the necessity to incorporate them into all phases of project development. Too often, projects are well advanced before value studies are made. This must not be allowed to happen, and it is the value program manager's responsibility to ensure that all projects are considered for a share of the available VM effort.

When should VM be applied to a project? Theoretically, VM can be applied at any time during a project's life cycle, from conception to completion and eventual replacement. More practically, VM should be applied at specific phases of a project's development in order to achieve maximum results.

PROJECT PLANNING PHASE   The first application of the VM effort should be made during the project planning stage. This is the point in the project life cycle where maximum flexibility exists to make changes without incurring undue expenses for redesign. As the project development progresses, the cost to make changes increases until a point-of-no-return is reached, where the potential benefits are swallowed up in the cost of redesigning, reordering, and rescheduling. This is shown in Figure 4.2. Early in the concept phase, a budgetary estimate is produced, which defines goals, requirements, and applicable criteria. The owner establishes most of this input and makes it available to the project development team. The project team, in turn, establishes broad objectives and a cost framework, which become the budgetary estimate.

Studies have shown that it is the project team that has by far the largest impact on the total life cycle cost of a project. The owner, too, has a significant impact on costs by establishing requirements, which become the basis for the project development team's efforts. Between them, the owner and the project team will establish roughly 70 percent of the total life cycle cost of the project by the

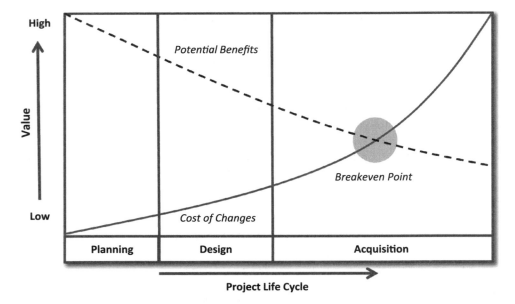

FIGURE 4.2   Potential for Value Improvement

end of the project planning stage. Thus it is apparent that a VM analysis made during the planning stage has a tremendous potential for improving performance and reducing costs. At this stage of project, the VM effort can assist the owner to establish his or her true requirements. This requires a complete understanding of the basic function to be performed by the project. Dialogue between the value specialist, the owner, and the project team must be searching and in depth, for VM takes nothing for granted, questions everything, and insists on justification of all requirements. The project team should welcome this process, as it assists it in understanding the owner's and/or user's true requirements and eliminates ambiguities.

PROJECT DESIGN PHASES   As project development advances from the conceptual stages through to the final development stages, the VM effort should keep pace. Preferably, the value specialist should accompany each project milestone in order to provide continuous guidance to the project team and ensure that value judgments are brought to the attention of the owner for decision. At a minimum, VM analysis should be performed early in the design stages and accompany the preliminary milestones. At this point, project development decisions have been made that permit a reasonable degree of exactitude in determining initial costs. Additional VM studies can profitably be performed as late as the final development phase, although the elements that can be changed without inordinate delays and costly redesign expenses are limited.

ACQUISITION PHASE   The VM effort can also be applied during the acquisition phase (production, construction, or implementation) of the product. This arises from two possible situations: when an item has been identified by an earlier VM study, which needs further investigation before a decision is made; and when the contractor, manufacturer, or vendor identifies areas that he or she feels can be improved. The first situation may arise when, for example, an item has been identified by the VM effort during the preliminary project development phase, but that requires testing or research prior to decision. Even after with the delay inherent in such a process, it may be profitable to pursue it when the potential savings and improvement are of significant magnitude. Value Incentive Clauses provide a means for sharing cost savings between the contractors and owners.

The application of VM during the construction of new facilities is standard practice among major public agencies, such as the U.S. Army Corps of Engineers. Contractors are provided incentives to identify and develop proposals to reduce costs and/or improve performance after the construction contract has been awarded. This can also be used in manufacturing applications where components of an assembly are subcontracted to vendors or to other companies for production. In this case, vendors and subcontractors receive a cash incentive to develop innovations that will reduce cost and/or increase performance.

A great many variations of VM contract provisions are in current use, but there are only two basic types. They are commonly known as the Value Incentive Clause and the Value Program Requirements Clause.

Value Incentive Clause   The method normally used for soliciting the contractor or vendor input is the value incentive clause. This general provision to construction and production contracts solicits the contractor's or vendor's proposals for change through an instrument known as a value change proposal (VCP—traditionally referred to as Value Engineering Change Proposals, or VECPs). It calls for the owner and contractor to share the savings resulting from any approved and implemented VCP. The usual savings sharing rate is 50:50; however, this may be varied in the contract provisions as desired. An acceptable VCP must meet two tests: It must require a change in some contract provision, and it must reduce the contract price. A complete VCP should contain information similar to that of a value alternative, as discussed in Chapter 9, "Development."

Program Requirements Clause This type of clause requires the contractor to perform value studies to a specified level, for which it is paid by the owner as a separate item of work under the contract. Clauses with program requirement provisions may also permit incentive sharing for individual proposals, but the contractor's proportion of the savings is considerably smaller than under an incentive provision.

The principle reason for the program requirement approach is to ensure that potential innovations are continuously considered, beginning with the initial project development stages. This type of clause has not been used in construction contracts to any significant degree. It is more appropriate for research and development and supply contracts, and it has been very successful in these applications. In a comparatively recent construction-related innovation, however, agencies such as the U.S. Army Corps of Engineers, the Environmental Protection Agency, and the General Services Administration have established modified value program requirements for architect-engineer and construction manager contracts for major facilities.

Conduct Prestudy Meeting

Getting off on the right foot on a value study is akin to starting a new job. Laying out the responsibilities of each participant will lead to a well-coordinated effort. This can best be handled in an orientation meeting with the owner, the project team, and the value specialist who will be facilitating the study. At this meeting, the value specialist should outline the entire Value Methodology process. It is important to remember that, in many cases, this will be the owner's and the project team's first exposure to Value Methodology. The project team may be perplexed, realizing that the value specialist is evaluating the project. There will be many underlying fears and questions that should be addressed in this session.

The following is a list of steps that contribute to a successful prestudy meeting:

- Collect project information
- Identify project scope, schedule, and cost
- Define performance requirements and attributes—*Value Metrics*
- Establish value study goals and objectives
- Define value study scope
- Identify value study participants
- Define value study schedule
- Organize value study logistics

COLLECT PROJECT INFORMATION It is important to have necessary data available prior to commencement of the value study, in order to conserve time and effort. This data is normally procured by the value specialist and given to the value team members for review prior to the first team meeting. The following are required for a typical value study:

- A clear description of the project's intended purpose and need
- Project work breakdown structure and scheduling information
- Up-to-date project scope information (e.g., project reports, design drawings, flow charts, etc.), as it exists at the time the value study is undertaken
- Specifications such as any applicable codes, regulations, owner guidance, and any technical requirements
- Cost figures, including budgets, unit costs, design-to-cost targets, and the latest cost estimates
- Special information such as historical data, status of design, user requirements, and so on
- Schedule information
- Project risk register and any risk analysis that has been performed
- Persons to be consulted with to provide any specific project information, guidance, or approval
- Anticipated use of the project's output

IDENTIFY PROJECT SCOPE, SCHEDULE, AND COST The information identified above will provide the value specialist with specific details relevant to the project's scope, schedule, and cost. Value Methodology should begin at this fundamental level. Most projects include a "scope statement" or a "need and purpose statement" as a standard element within the project development process. A scope statement should include the following elements:

- *Project Justification or Need.* A narrative describing the need that the project was undertaken to address.
- *Project Purpose.* A narrative describing the project's purpose.
- *Project Deliverables.* A list and description of the project's outputs (e.g., design drawings, specifications, reports, prototypes, etc.)
- *Project Objectives.* A list and description of quantifiable criteria that must be met for the project to be considered successful. This usually includes cost, schedule, and qualitative measures.

A well-written scope statement should serve as the foundation upon which a project is based. Despite their fundamental nature, scope statements are frequently taken for granted and are often poorly prepared. This can lead to serious problems as the project is developed, most of which can be linked to disagreements between stakeholders possessing differing perspectives. The reconciliation of the differences becomes increasingly difficult as the project progresses. The following is an excerpt from a Federal Highway Administration Memorandum concerning this issue:

> *The Project Development Branch (HEV-11) in its review of environmental impact statements has noted a systematic deficiency in the purpose and need*

section. In our view this deficiency is particularly critical because it helps define what alternatives must be evaluated and, in some cases, selected in order to comply with the myriad of Federal environmental laws, Executive Orders, and regulations.[1]

The realization of this problem for projects within the sphere of design and construction has been addressed through refinements to the way in which VM is applied. The U.S. Navy's Naval Facilities Engineering Command developed the Function Analysis Concept Design (FACD) as a way to validate project scope through the application of function analysis at the earliest stages of the design process.

The value specialist should begin preparations for a value study with a similar notion of using Function Analysis to validate a project's scope. Function Analysis provides us with a powerful technique for developing a better understanding of wants and needs through the identification, classification, and organization of functions. Identifying the project's basic and required secondary functions is really all that is needed at the beginning. Refer to Chapter 6, "Function," for a comprehensive discussion of functions.

DEFINE PERFORMANCE REQUIREMENTS AND ATTRIBUTES—*VALUE METRICS*

Once the basic functions and requirements are understood and agreed upon relative to project scope, the next step is to begin the process of defining performance. Performance—or project objectives in project management terminology—can be divided into two categories: requirements and attributes. The term "requirements" is used to describe performance characteristics that are mandatory and absolute in nature, while "attributes" can possess a range of acceptable values. Attributes are flexible, while requirements are rigid. A potential solution that does not satisfy a performance requirement cannot be considered, but a performance attribute can be further defined by establishing a range of acceptable parameters. Both performance attributes and requirements should be identified at this early stage of the VM job plan.

The process should begin by identifying what is important to the customer or user in terms of project performance. A good place to start would be with the project's objectives. For example, if the project concerned the design and construction of a new building, the value team could begin with the building's design objectives. Oftentimes, project objectives can easily be adopted for use as performance attributes. In his book, *Enhancing Value in Design Decisions*, Stephen Kirk identifies a number of typical design objectives that often appear in buildings.[2] These include:

- *Image.* The visual concept of the building.
- *Community.* How the building and site project a "good neighbor" image.
- *Functional efficiency.* The degree to which the building is able to respond to the activities occurring within it.
- *Security.* The degree to which the building can segregate sensitive functions and prevent unwanted entry.
- *Expansion.* The ability of the building to grow to meet projected changes.
- *Flexibility.* The degree to which the building can be rearranged to conform to revised work processes.

Additional examples of building-related performance attributes and requirements are illustrated in the case study section at the end of this chapter.

In thinking about performance attributes and requirements, key questions to ask include:

- What does the customer or user care about?
- What *must* the project do to successfully meet the customer's or user's *needs?*
- What *should* the project do to successfully meet the customer's or user's *wants?*

With respect to performance requirements, there can be any number since these are only considered as binary values: yes/no. The number of performance attributes, however, should range from 4 to 8. The reason for this is that, theoretically, there are a nearly infinite number of details we could attempt to measure in a project but only finite amount of time to do so. The value specialist must help the customer or user focus their thinking in terms of categories of performance. It should be noted, however, if specialized software is used, then the number of attributes that can be considered can be considerably greater. Chapter 5, "Information," provides an example of such software.

A performance requirement should be made as a statement of fact that identifies specific measures. A performance attribute should be stated using a broader definition that identifies significant elements within it. By nature, the language must be a little less specific because an attribute is concerned with defining a range of potential levels of performance as opposed to a requirement that need only satisfy a single, discrete performance level. In all cases, the definition should be descriptive enough to provide enough information to allow measurements, even if they are qualitative measurements. For both attributes and requirements, select a one- or two-word title for the attribute or requirement followed by the definition.

The participants of the value study will need to have a clear understanding of both the performance attributes and requirements before moving into the subsequent phases of the VM job plan. Performance attributes need to be discretely defined and must not overlap in meaning. Parameters defining the lower and upper range of desired performance should be included as well. Performance requirements should be similarly defined, but in a more detailed manner relevant to the actual conditions of the requirement. The value specialist should lead this discussion with the project's stakeholders during the prestudy meeting, preferably in the presence of the value team members. Only those attributes that are identified as the most critical in meeting the project's purpose and need should be included.

Performance optimization requires a balanced approach. In discussing the nature of customer performance, Fallon observes:

> *Once the customer's requirements have been defined, they must be studied systematically in order to generate a number of satisfactory combinations. The key concept here is that of a balanced combination rather than the most of the best of everything. This is the difference between well-allocated effort and maximum effort in all directions.*[3]

In Figure 4.3, a performance requirement and a performance attribute have been identified. The examples provided are for a product study of a 1.5-ton forklift

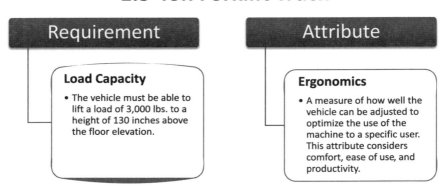

FIGURE 4.3   Performance Requirements versus Attributes

truck. Of course, there would be numerous requirements and attributes defined for such a project, but we will focus on just one of each in this example.

The performance requirement describes a condition that MUST be met by any potential design solution: that the forklift must be able to lift 3,000 pounds to a height of 130 inches off the floor. It is important to emphasize that performance requirements are binary in nature—they are conditions that are either met or not met. If a design solution exceeds the conditions of the requirement, the excess performance offers no additional value. In this example, because the manufacturer markets its forklifts in specific load capacity classes, there is no additional benefit in producing a vehicle that exceeds a load capacity of 3,000 pounds. Customers with needs beyond this level will be directed to the next vehicle class. The project owner and/or users must be made clear on this point and it must be emphasized during the development of the performance requirements and attributes. If the answer is that additional performance in excess of the requirement will add value to the project, then this requirement must also be considered as an attribute. In such a case, the requirement describes the lowest level of acceptable performance for the attribute.

The performance attribute describes an aspect of performance that may have a range of potential acceptable levels of performance. In Figure 4.3, "ergonomics" describes a measure of how well the design of the forklift interfaces with the operator. A large number of designs could be developed offering a variety of ergonomic features in a manner acceptable to the user to a greater or lesser degree. Therefore, it would be useful to consider a wide range of solutions that could satisfy the users' performance needs.

Chapter 5 will discuss the creation of measurement scales that are necessary to adequately compare the differences in the performance of competing design solutions.

ESTABLISH VALUE STUDY GOALS AND OBJECTIVES   Establishing the goals and objectives of a value study is critical. Value studies may have varying objectives, depending upon the types of issues that the project team may face. The VM team participants should have a clear understanding of what the study sponsor's VM goals are prior to the commencement of the value study. They could vary dramatically, depending upon the state of the project or the reason for performing the value study.

For example, a value study's goals and objectives could be:

- Goal: Identify a means to reduce processing time.
  - Objective: Reduce it by two weeks.
- Goal: Build consensus among stakeholders as to what the project scope should be.
  - Objective: Identify a project scope that can be delivered within the annual budget
- Goal: Improve product market share.
  - Objective: Improve it by 5 percent.
- Goal: Reduce project costs.
  - Objective: Get the project back within budget.
- Goal: Reduce production costs.
  - Objective: Reduce them by 10 percent.
- Goal: Reduce project risk.
  - Objective: Identify specific methods to reduce litigation risks.

As these goals and objectives indicate, the Value Methodology can be used in a number of different ways, all of which aim at improving value. They should always relate back to the project's scope, schedule, risks, and cost and can be general or specific in nature. Having a clear statement of the value study's goals and objectives will help the value team stay focused on the study sponsor's expectations for the VM effort.

DEFINE VALUE STUDY SCOPE   The scope of the value study should be determined during the Preparation Phase. The value specialist will need to be given guidance from the study sponsor and/or the project team. Will the value study consider the entire project or just certain elements? Related to the issue of value study scope is the need to identify the parameters in which the value team can recommend changes to the original project scope. For example, can the value team challenge project objectives, such as design criteria or project delivery milestones? Correctly setting the scope of the value study will help ensure that the value team does not overstep its boundaries or expend valuable time on issues with which they have no ability to influence change.

Projects of all types are generally growing more complex, and time available for development is always limited. Personnel and time available for value studies are also in short supply. In order to maximize benefits of the value study, identified tasks must be matched with available resources (talents, skills, knowledge, and time).

The correlation of resources is often overlooked, yet it is as important as selection of the proper project if maximum return is to be gained. Furthermore, it is not desirable to select items for VM study where it can be anticipated that the net savings will be drastically reduced by the cost of the study itself and the cost of implementation. A yardstick often used is that net cost savings should be at least $10 for every dollar spent on the VM effort.

IDENTIFY VALUE STUDY PARTICIPANTS Once the value specialist has developed a basic understanding of the project, he or she will be in a position to begin identifying the participants for the value study team. Depending upon the value study's budget and the study sponsor's desires, the value team participants may be drawn from a variety of sources:

- Members of the project team
- Project owner or study sponsor's representative
- Customers or users
- External project stakeholders
- Expert technical consultants

Most value study teams include a mix of individuals from these sources. This is desirable because it provides the best cross-section of perspectives on the current project. Members of the project team will be able to contribute their intimate knowledge of the project and its history. Customers or users will be able to provide invaluable information pertaining to how the project's output will be utilized. External project stakeholders can provide important guidance regarding regulatory issues, approval processes, and other indirect project impacts that may not otherwise be considered. Expert technical consultants will provide specialized knowledge and will also be able to provide a fresh perspective to the project and its challenges. Although training in Value Methodology is always preferable for value study participants, it is not essential. It will be the job of the value specialist to educate and lead the study team through the VM process.

Another key consideration in selecting value study team members is the technical composition of the team. Ideally, a multidiscipline team will be arrayed, representing expertise from each specialized field of knowledge required to fully develop a project. Selecting a well-balanced technical team will greatly multiply its effectiveness. As the value study team develops alternative concepts, IT will need to be able to address technical issues that may arise. Frequently, a new alternative will have unanticipated impacts on other technical areas or even other related projects. Having the right expertise on the team will ensure that these issues can be adequately addressed as they arise. A few examples of value study teams organized for different types of projects are provided in Figure 4.4 to illustrate the diversity recommended in achieving a good balance for value studies.

Once the participants of the value study team have been identified, the project documents should be given to them for review and study prior to the start of the value study. Each member of the VM team should spend a sufficient period of time in going through the background information of the project. Usually, 8 to 16 hours per person is allowed for this task, depending on the size and magnitude of the project. Familiarization can be done independently.

DEFINE VALUE STUDY SCHEDULE One of the most important concerns for the project team will be the schedule for the value study. The value study schedule must fit very closely with the project schedule. Ideally, the value study can be scheduled during a milestone, when the project will be undergoing an interim review or approval period.

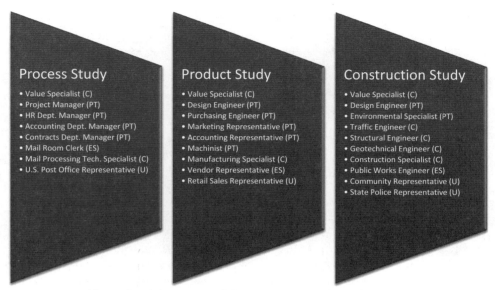

Process Study

- Value Specialist (C)
- Project Manager (PT)
- HR Dept. Manager (PT)
- Accounting Dept. Manager (PT)
- Contracts Dept. Manager (PT)
- Mail Room Clerk (ES)
- Mail Processing Tech. Specialist (C)
- U.S. Post Office Representative (U)

Product Study

- Value Specialist (C)
- Design Engineer (PT)
- Purchasing Engineer (PT)
- Marketing Representative (PT)
- Accounting Representative (PT)
- Machinist (PT)
- Manufacturing Specialist (C)
- Vendor Representative (ES)
- Retail Sales Representative (U)

Construction Study

- Value Specialist (C)
- Design Engineer (PT)
- Environmental Specialist (PT)
- Traffic Engineer (C)
- Structural Engineer (C)
- Geotechnical Engineer (C)
- Construction Specialist (C)
- Public Works Engineer (ES)
- Community Representative (U)
- State Police Representative (U)

(C) – Consultant, (PT) – Project Team, (ES) – External Stakeholder, (U) – User/Customer

FIGURE 4.4 Examples of Value Study Participants

Determining the appropriate length for the team portion of the value study should be the first priority in determining the overall value study schedule.[4] For many years, there has been a widely perceived notion that a value study should be five days long, or 40 hours. In fact, the duration of a value study should be based on a number of different factors, which include the following:

- Size and complexity of the project
- Value study goals and objectives
- Value study scope
- Size and expertise of the value team
- Resources available to conduct the study

For a typical five-day value study, the baseline includes time allotments as shown in Table 4.1. The shaded area represents those phases of the Job Plan that occur as a "team" effort.

Some value practitioners will require that a longer period of time be devoted to the value study. Reasons for why a study may need to be longer include solving problems, creating new concepts or designs, planning strategies, or streamlining processes or procedures. This may vary from six or eight days to as long as twelve days or more. Longer studies typically require a split schedule and, depending upon the study target, may necessitate a variation in the time allotted to specific VM Job Plan activities.

In some cases, value study sponsors may attempt to limit value studies to three days, or sometimes even shorter periods, without regard for the scope of the study

TABLE 4.1   Five-Day Value Study Model

Job Plan Phase	Number Hours per Study Value Type			
	Construction	Product	Process	Procedure
Preparation	8–24	8–16	20–30	40–60
Information	4–6	2	2	2
Function	4	8–16	8	6
Speculation	4	6	4	4
Evaluation	6–8	16–20	12	8
Development	16	4–8	12	8
Presentation—Oral	4	4	4	4
Presentation—Report	48	80	40	20
Implementation	Times will vary and depend on value study sponsor.			

target or the integrity of the Value Methodology Job Plan. Time limitations may result in more enthusiastic participation by the study sponsor's personnel, because they are "losing" less time away from their normal work effort. At the same time, these time constraints require that some portion of the Job Plan be compromised. The Value Methodology Job Plan is often construed to apply only to the formal phases included in the team study: Information, Function, Speculation, Evaluation, Development, and Presentation. The Preparation and Implementation Phases, while not always considered formal steps of the VM Job Plan, are integral to the success of any value improvement effort, and are addressed as such in this discussion.

Regardless of the study type, the study target, or the length of the value study, certain prestudy activities must always occur. In addition to project identification, definition of the value study schedule, and team selection, extensive preparation work is required in the form of data collection, cost analysis and models, team information packages, and logistics arrangement. Once the team study is concluded, additional documentation may be required to complete or further refine the developed value alternatives. A complete report is prepared to document the study efforts and its results and to determine what implementation actions must occur.

None of the phases and activities associated with the Value Methodology Job Plan (as described in Chapter 3) can be eliminated by reducing the length of a team study; all must occur for every value study, regardless of how long the team sessions last.

Using a construction project as an example, assume the study sponsor has requested a three-day value study. The compressed time is required to maintain the design schedule, the budget to conduct the value study is limited, and the key team members are unable to commit more than three days of time away from their regular responsibilities. Table 4.2 shows how the hours per phase would differ for a three-day study compared to the 40-Hour Model previously illustrated. The shaded area represents those phases of the Job Plan that occur as a "team" effort.

There are both advantages and disadvantages associated with the three-day value study approach. While it reduces the value study sponsor's cost for the study, the value team and value specialist are put under tremendous pressure to accomplish a great deal in a short period of time. In order to maintain the integrity of the Job Plan and, at the same time, prevent the activity from being simply a cost

TABLE 4.2 Three-Day Value Study Model (Construction Project)

Job Plan Phase	Number of Hours	Effect of Reduced Time
Preparation	24–32	More prestudy time required by the value specialist to prepare for the abbreviated value study
Information	4	Site visit eliminated
Function	2–3	Less time for team interaction; increased value specialist influence; reduced time for cost/performance/function analysis
Speculation	2–3	Fewer ideas generated; potential loss of significant ideas
Evaluation	4	Reduced depth of team discussion and analysis of ideas
Development	8–10	Less detail and potentially less credibility related to value alternatives
Presentation—Oral	2	Fewer value alternatives to present
Presentation—Report	64	More time required in report writing to complete development of value alternatives
Implementation	Times will vary and depend on value study sponsor.	

reduction exercise, the value specialist's job of keeping the value team focused and on track becomes even more critical than usual. As noted earlier, every phase of the Job Plan is impacted in some way. Of additional consideration is that the prestudy and poststudy time will need to be increased as a result of the compressed team study schedule.

Results of a three-day value study may be limited to mere validation of a project's functional concepts rather than significant project improvements. Alternatives that are developed during a shortened study are likely to be more conceptual, and less detailed, than value alternatives produced in a longer study and, as a result, may prove more difficult to implement. Most important, the results may not be optimized due to the limited time the value team has had to exploit the techniques of the Value Methodology and gain the benefits of team communications and project understanding that these techniques offer.

Even when constrained by a three-day study, it is possible to have impressive results that will dramatically demonstrate the power of the VM process. However, this scenario represents a double-edged sword because impressive results only encourage more use of the abbreviated value study approach. Note that a successful value study in a three-day period is highly dependent upon an experienced value specialist and value team.

There are many reasons why a value study might require more than the typical five days. A high-profile, controversial project or multiple funding entities may create specific issues that require more attention by the value team. A more involved study may be required if the project is over budget, has problems associated with its completion, or is a very complex project, having more elements on which to focus and requiring a larger team to perform the study.

There is much to be gained by increasing the time available for a value study. First and foremost, the value team can be more intimately involved in the prestudy planning (Preparation Phase), resulting in increased and improved information gathering. Of equal importance, the value team may meet with project stakeholders and decision makers at the midpoint of the study to validate the direction the team is taking with their value alternative development. Additionally, when complex problems are considered, multiple FAST diagrams may be developed.

Obviously a study spanning more than five days requires a split schedule of some sort. There is a significant advantage to having a break of several days between team sessions, as it offers the opportunity for team members to do research and gather additional information needed for development of value alternatives. Too much time between team meetings should be avoided, to reduce the potential for loss of the value team's momentum.

Assuming an eight-day VM Team Study, the breakdown of time spent on each phase of the Job Plan might be as shown in Table 4.3.

Table 4.4 provides an example of a value study agenda that is five days in length.

The true issue is not whether a value study is conducted over three days or three months. The key is maintaining the integrity of the Value Methodology Job Plan and making the necessary adjustments in time allotted for all elements of the process to maximize the results generated. The key is achieving that "fair return" for something exchanged—in this case, time.

ORGANIZE VALUE STUDY LOGISTICS   The value specialist should prepare a contact list identifying the roles the various participants will play. This list should include everyone that will be involved in the value effort, including all meeting participants. Names, addresses, phone numbers, and e-mail addresses should be included. This list should be distributed to all participants in addition to the value study's objectives, scope, and schedule.

TABLE 4.3 Eight-Day Value Study Model (Construction Project)

Job Plan Phase	Number of Hours	Effect of Increased Time
Preparation	32	Includes prestudy meeting
Information	8	Enhanced site visit and discussions with stakeholders
Function	8	Increased function analysis possible; multiple FAST diagrams can be constructed
Speculation	4–8	Additional time for creativity; different techniques may be employed
Evaluation	12–16	Increased evaluation time allows more thoughtful consideration of ideas
Development	24–28	More credible, well-developed value alternatives
Presentation—Oral	4	Increased number of value alternatives to present
Presentation—Report	72	More time required in report writing due to greater number of value alternatives developed
Implementation	Times will vary and depend on value study sponsor.	

TABLE 4.4 Example of a Five-Day Value Study Agenda

Value Study Agenda	
Day 1	
	Kick-Off Meeting
8:00	Introductions (All) and agenda review (Value Team Leader)
8:15	Project overview (Project Manager and Engineers)
9:15	Stakeholder issues and concerns
10:00	Break
10:15	Development of performance requirements and attributes
11:15	Assessment of project performance
12:00	Lunch
1:00	Site visit
3:00	Break
3:15	Function analysis/FAST diagram
5:00	Adjourn
Day 2	
8:00	Team brainstorming
10:00	Break
10:15	Team brainstorming (cont.)
12:00	Lunch
1:00	Evaluation of ideas
3:00	Break
3:15	Evaluation of ideas (cont.)
4:45	Team assignments for development
5:00	Adjourn
Day 3	
8:00	Review alternative development process, research, and refine ideas
10:15	Break
10:30	Research and refine ideas (cont.)
12:00	Lunch
1:00	Alternative development
3:00	Break
3:15	Alternative development (cont.)
5:00	Adjourn
Day 4	
8:00	Alternative development (cont.)
10:15	Break
10:30	Alternative development (cont.)
12:00	Lunch
1:00	Complete alternative development
5:00	Adjourn
Day 5	
8:00	Group review and ranking of value alternatives and strategies; presentation preparation
11:00	Finalize alternatives and prepare presentation
12:00	Lunch
1:00	Finalize alternatives and prepare presentation
2:00	Presentation of alternatives meeting
3:30	Adjourn

If a site visit will be included as part of the value study, it will be necessary to coordinate transportation arrangements with the project manager. The value specialist should have the project manager identify key areas on which to focus at the site, in order to maximize the time spent out in the field. Ensure that the schedule includes enough time to travel from the location of the value study to the project site and back.

The logistics of a value study should be made with consideration to the overall project. Keep in mind that value studies involve intense effort employing a group of people. Therefore, it is helpful to have the study in a place where interruptions are limited and the arrangements are comfortable. Ideally, studies are conducted in locations removed from the daily work flow, such as hotel meeting rooms or other similar conference areas. Outside calls coming into the team should be restricted.

Other disturbances should be kept to a minimum when possible. It is also helpful to have facilities with windows that open to the outside. This helps to provide a good working environment. Printers, scanners, photocopiers, and office supplies required for the study should also be available. The location of the study may be in the city where the owner or the project team is located or in the offices of the value specialist. If an existing facility is involved, or where unusual site conditions warrant, the study should take place near the site. This gives the team a chance to visually observe the location and surrounding area of the project. In any event, a site visit by the value specialist and one or more of the other team participants is recommended during the VM effort.

The Value Team

Once the participants of the value team have been identified, the next step will be to begin the process of teambuilding. Most of the time, the members of the value team will not be familiar with one another. The value team may consist of people from different departments within an organization or they may be consultants. In any case, it is likely that this will be the first time that many of them will have worked together. The value specialist may want to consider utilizing teambuilding exercises to help develop a strong working relationship and to instill the values identified in Chapter 1, "Introduction."

Teambuilding Exercises

Successful teams must hold common values as described in the preceding paragraphs. However, before these values can be shared, it is recommended that the team members share something about themselves. A popular way to accomplish this is by employing simple team-building exercises that will help break the ice and introduce the team members to one another. It is always quite surprising how much people have in common with one another, regardless of what walk of life they come from.

In some cases, the value specialist may want to also consider including individuals outside of the value team, such as members of the project team, project stakeholders, and even the customers or users as participants in these teambuilding exercises. The use of teambuilding exercises will vary greatly, depending upon the size of the group and the amount of time available in the value study. Two effective teambuilding exercises are described below:

- *Acronym builder*. The business world is full of acronyms. There are GANTT charts, PERT diagrams, and SMART goals. The objective of this exercise is to have everyone develop an acronym that relates to their first name or their initials. This exercise includes the following steps:
  1. Each team member is asked to write the initials of their names vertically on a flip chart, white board, or chalkboard. Optionally, first names could be used; however, this may not be appropriate for larger groups or where time is short.
  2. A word that somehow describes them should be selected for each initial of their name and written horizontally. It may be a bit of a challenge for some, especially those with long first names!
  3. Each participant should do this in front of the group as they write their acronyms.
- *To tell the truth*. This exercise is loosely based upon the old game show of the same name. The participants each present three interesting facts to the rest of the team about themselves. The rub is that only two of the facts are true: One is a lie. The other team members must determine whether each is true or false. This exercise includes the following steps:
  1. This works best in groups of four to six people. Larger groups should be divided into ones of this size.
  2. Each person should write down two truths and a lie about themselves. The others in the group will then try to guess each other's lie. The objective is to convince others that your lie is the truth and to correctly guess other people's lies.
  3. Allow about five minutes for everyone to write their truths and lies.
  4. Once completed, each person in the group should read off their truths and lies without revealing which is which. Once a person has read all three statements, he or she should read them again and have the rest of the group vote on which is a lie and which is a truth.
  5. The exercise can be run competitively by counting up how many correct guesses of other people's lies and take away the number of people who correctly guessed your own lie. The highest score wins.

These exercises can be completed in a relatively short time, usually between 15 to 30 minutes. It is easy to dismiss these activities as frivolous; however, the very positive effect they can have in developing a better level of familiarity for the participants should not be underestimated. If team members do not feel comfortable about their environment, they will be less likely to trust others. This can act as a significant impediment in getting everyone to freely contribute to the value effort. Take full advantage of any opportunity to foster teambuilding—it will yield excellent dividends.

Summary

Proper preparation is essential to the success of any undertaking. The value specialist must remember that the results of the value study for a project will be closely scrutinized by the very people who originally developed the project. Establishing a strong, early relationship with the project team, customers, and other stakeholders will also help inform and mentally prepare these participants, as well as the value study team members, for the Value Methodology process, and help pave the way for managed change.

Appendix 4A: Case Study

Chapters 4 through 11 include an example of a value study that was led by the author in 2008. The purpose of this case study is to demonstrate the application of principles and techniques of Value Methodology on a complex, real-world project. This particular case study focuses on the design and construction of a technical high school, which is a facility that everyone should have some familiarity with. The names of the project, location, and participants have been changed for obvious reasons.

Project Background

The author was retained to organize and lead a value study for a new technical high school (i.e., trade school) by a state budget agency. The "customer" agency was a regional school district that was required by state policy to undergo a value study as part of the budget approval process. The school district, which had hired the design team, was concerned about the potential impact that the value study could have on their project. The perception was that Value Methodology was a "cost cutting" process rather than a value improvement process and, as such, the district was a little apprehensive that the funding could be reduced and result in a reduction in the project scope. Similarly, the design team was concerned that they could potentially lose control of the design process. Sadly, these reactions are typical in the sphere of design and construction and primarily stem from an ignorance of VM.

As part of the contract with the state budget agency, the author's firm would also select and manage a large portion of the value team. Other responsibilities included the preparation of reports and presentations.

Project Description

The state's technical high school program came into existence as a response to the need for Career and Technical Education (CTE) programs that were too expensive for individual school districts to pursue. The development of the CTE program has been driven by the region's population growth and its diverse employment base. These factors have caused a greater demand for a wider array of career education opportunities. The technical high school envisioned in this project was designed to expand on the courses already offered in the local high schools and also to provide a dedicated pipeline for individuals to attend post-secondary and other training options in the region. The purpose of the project is to provide high-skill, high-wage training as part of students' high school experience.

The new technical high school was programmed to offer twelve educational programs to high-school-aged students in ten school districts. The site that was selected, and subsequently acquired by the regional school district, was formerly a supermarket. The Supermarket Building was about 35,000 square feet in area. The current Predesign Concept was to renovate this building to serve as a new Technology Building and construct two new facilities, a 25,000-square-foot Administration Building and a 25,000-square-foot Classroom Building.

The project will be delivered in two construction phases. Phase 1 will include the following programs: Emergency Services/Homeland Security, AP Environmental Science, Construction, Culinary Arts, Auto Technology, Marine Technology, Food Science (organics), Metal Fabrication, Welding, Allied Health, VCR Repair, Web Design, Network Security, Aerospace Maintenance, and Pilot Training. Phase 2 programs at the core campus offerings will include Engine Technology, Creative Digital Design, and Criminal Justice. Phase 2 offerings at satellite/branch campuses will be developed and planned as needed.

Phase 1 will construct all of the Administration and Classroom Buildings and renovate about 25 percent of the Supermarket Building. Phase 2 will complete the renovations to the Supermarket Building. The current predesign cost estimate antici-pates Phase 1 will cost approximately $36 million, while Phase 2 will cost $11.8 million for a total project cost of $47.8 million.

Prestudy Meeting

A prestudy meeting was held at the offices of the regional school district to discuss the project about three weeks before the value study. Those in attendance included:

- Value Specialist (Team Leader)
- Value Specialist (Assistant)
- VM Program Manager, State Budget Agency
- Budget Analyst, State Budget Agency
- Superintendent, School District
- Technical High School Principal, School District
- Facilities Manager, School District
- Project Manager, Design Team
- Architect, Design Team

The prestudy meeting was approximately two hours long and included the following activities:

- Overview of the Value Study process
- Overview of the project, including a review of the project documents
- Discussion of the Value Study goals and objectives
- Identification of the project's performance requirements and attributes
- Identification of Value Study schedule and participants

The project had just completed the predesign concept phase, and a large amount of information had been developed. A list of project documents available for the value study included:

- Predesign Concept Report
- Predesign Concept Drawings
- Predesign Concept Cost Estimate
- Site Phasing and Master Plans
- Preliminary Project Schedules, Phases 1 and 2
- Existing Supermarket Site Plan

The State Budget Agency identified the following goals and objectives for the Value Study:

- *Value improvement.* Review the program requirements and identify alternative methods of performing key project functions that will enhance project value by reducing cost and/or improving performance. The project was about $8 million over budget at the Predesign phase.
- *Cost estimate validation.* Review the predesign cost estimate and prepare an independent cost estimate to assist the State Budget Agency in assessing the project budget.

The State Budget Agency utilizes Value Methodology as a means of both enhancing project value as well as a means of cost control. The cost estimate validation objective is not a "typical" component of value studies; however, it is easily conducted as a parallel activity and utilizes the skills of the value team in a complementary capacity.

Following the design team's presentation of the predesign concept and the discussion of the value study's goals and objectives, the participants focused on discussing project performance. The value specialist facilitated the discussion and elicited the performance requirements and attributes from the group (see Tables 4.5 and 4.6, respectively).

It was decided that project schedule would be considered as an input, similar to cost. Due to the early stage of design development, risk analysis had not yet been initiated by the project team and was therefore not formally considered; however, the Value Team would consider the potential impact of risk informally. Therefore, the following equation for functional value was agreed upon:

$$V_f = \frac{P}{(C + T)}$$

The last item on the meeting agenda, determining the value study participants and schedule, was then discussed. Despite the early stage of design development, it was agreed that the size and scope of the project warranted a five-day team effort. The dates and times were discussed and agreed upon and an agenda was developed (see Table 4.7).

It was also decided that the out-briefing and presentation would be held two weeks after the end of the value study, on August 14, 2008, in order to allow additional time for the value team to finalize the results. The participants in the out-briefing would include additional staff from both the School District and the State Budget Agency.

The study would take place at the offices of the School District, while the out-briefing and presentation would be held at the State Budget Agency's offices.

TABLE 4.5 Performance Requirements for New Technical High School

Performance Requirement	Definition
Accessibility	All facilities must meet ADA requirements.
Safety/Security	The campus is intended to be segregated (by schedule) between high school students and adult students during evenings and weekends and must be an open campus. Security cameras and key card locks will be standard. Minimum site lighting of 1 foot-candle must be maintained for security.
Sustainability	Must meet standards for the State's Sustainable Schools Program (LEED Silver).
Environmental Approvals	No special approvals are required; typical permitting required per county and state policies.
Critical Milestones	Goal is to have the Skills Center operational within three years (however, this is not a "hard" requirement). Must release funds for construction by Summer 2009, so construction must begin by July 1, 2009.
Code Requirements	All building(s) must meet current building and zoning codes.
Compatibility with Land-Use	The project must comply with the Fredrickson Development Plan.

TABLE 4.6 Performance Attributes for New Technical High School

Performance Attribute	Definition
Program Compatibility	A measure of how well the building(s') interior spaces meet their intended function and the objectives of the overall educational program. This attribute considers the size and shape of spaces; sound attenuation; lighting characteristics; and special amenities (e.g., data, audio/visual, storage, etc.)
Building Organization	A measure of how well the interior spaces within the building(s) are organized. This attribute considers elements such as the adjacencies of interior spaces; the efficiency of interior circulation, and ease of way finding.
Site Organization	A measure of how well the campus is organized. This attribute considers elements such as the efficiency of site circulation; orientation of the building(s); adjacencies of site elements (i.e., buildings, parking lots, walkways, and other features).
Aesthetics	A measure of the building(s) aesthetic appeal. This attribute considers how well it responds to the site, the surrounding structures, the locale, and the building's function.
Phaseability	A measure of the ease with which the project can be incrementally constructed over 4+ years. This attribute considers the construction impacts of new buildings to existing operations; the effects of "throw-away" work, and so on.
Maintainability	A measure of how easily the building(s) and site can be maintained over its expected useful life. This attribute considers energy consumption; the frequency of equipment replacement; the durability and longevity of building finishes. Assumes a 30-year life cycle before a major remodel.

TABLE 4.7 Value Study Agenda, New Technical High School

July 28, 2008	Monday	
8:00 to 8:30	Opening comments *Welcome *Introductions *Value study overview and schedule	Value Specialist
8:30 to 10:30	Presentation of predesign concept *Project history and objectives *Designer's presentation	School District Representatives Design Team
10:30 to 12:00	Project issues and performance *Construction issues *Discussion *Project performance *Stakeholder issues	Value Specialist
12:00	Lunch	
1:00 to 3:00	Site visit	School District Representatives Design Team Value Team
3:00 to 5:00	Function analysis	Value Team
July 29, 2008	**Tuesday**	
8:00 to 12:00	Speculation phase: Team brainstorming	Value Team
12:00	Lunch	
1:00 to 5:00	Evaluation phase: Idea evaluation	Value Team
July 30, 2008	**Wednesday**	
8:00 to 12:00	Evaluation phase (cont.)	Value Team
12:00	Lunch	
1:00 to 5:00	Development phase *Assign ideas for development *Discuss write-up requirements *Develop alternatives	Value Team
July 31, 2008	**Thursday**	
8:00 to 12:00	Development phase (cont.)	Value Team
12:00	Lunch	
1:00 to 5:00	Development phase (cont.)	Value Team
August 1, 2008	**Friday**	
8:00 to 12:00	Development phase (cont.)	Value Team
12:00	Lunch	
1:00 to 5:00	Development phase (cont.)	Value Team

(The rows for July 28 Monday 8:00–12:00 are bracketed as "Kick-Off Meeting.")

Finally, the group discussed what the role of the participants would be and what additional technical disciplines were needed to round out the value team. It was decided that the following participants would comprise the core of the value team:

- Value Specialist (Facilitator)
- Assistant Facilitator
- Architect
- Educational Planner
- Executive Director (from another technical high school)
- Civil Engineer
- Cost Estimator

These participants would be selected and retained by the value specialist. Due to the conceptual nature of the design, it was decided that it was not necessary to include a mechanical and electrical engineer on the value team. Further, the State Budget Agency had identified the executive director of another technical high school that was recently constructed to participate on the value study. This "core" group would be supported by two representatives from the School District: the principal of the new school and the district's facilities manager.

Information

© Magixl 2009, www.magixl.com

Sometimes when you innovate, you make mistakes. It is best to admit them quickly, and get on with improving your other innovations.

—Steve Jobs

Steven Paul was an orphan adopted by Paul and Clara Jobs of Mountain View, California, in 1955. Jobs was not happy at school in Mountain View so the family moved to Los Altos, California, where Steven attended Homestead High School. His electronics teacher at Homestead High, John McCollum, recalled he was "something of a loner" and "always had a different way of looking at things."[1]

In 1972, Jobs graduated from high school and registered at Reed College in Portland, Oregon. He dropped out of Reed after one semester but continued to hang around the campus for a year, taking classes in philosophy and immersing himself in the counterculture of the day. Early in 1974, Jobs took a job as a video game designer at Atari, Inc., a pioneer in electronic video games. After meeting Stephen Wozniak, a fellow electronics whiz, the two decided to create a computer of their own.

Jobs and Wozniak managed to scrape together enough money to start a garage-based computer company that was later to be named Apple. Together, they developed the first personal computer. The Apple I, as it was called, began to change people's view of the types of operations a computer could perform and the fledgling company grew rapidly as a result.

The subsequent development of the Macintosh reintroduced Xerox's innovative idea of a user-friendly interface system that used a pointing device called a mouse. The Macintosh also utilized revolutionary software that represented specific computer functions or programs with picture-like icons on-screen that the user clicked on with the mouse-operated pointer or curser to run. This feature would later be imitated by software giant Microsoft in the form of a program known as Windows.

In 1985, Jobs left Apple to concentrate on the software side of the industry. After founding a new company called NextStep, Jobs developed a revolutionary programming language called object-oriented programming (OOP), which allowed programmers to write complex software programs in a fraction of the usual time. NeXT Software was sold to Apple Computer in February 1997.

Steve Jobs later became chairman and CEO of Pixar, the Academy Award–winning computer animation studios, which he cofounded in 1986. Pixar's first feature film, *Toy Story,* was released by Walt Disney Pictures in November 1995 and became the highest-domestic-grossing film released that year and the third-highest-grossing animated film of all time. Pixar has since created many more blockbusters and award-winning animated feature films, including *Toy Story 2, Monsters Inc., Finding Nemo, Cars, The Incredibles, Ratatouille, Wall-E,* and, most recently, *Up.*

Steve Jobs, along with pioneers like Bill Gates, ushered in the Information Age. He understood the importance of making information accessible and has played a monumental role in the development of hardware and software designed to manage information on a scale unprecedented in history. Jobs is a fitting front piece for this chapter, which will focus on the Information Phase of the Value Methodology Job Plan.

Information Phase

It is said that we live in the Information Age, which, like all stages of societal evolution, carries with it the inevitable dualities of growth and decay. During the Industrial Age, the world saw unprecedented growth in the efficiency of human effort, especially within the realm of construction, manufacturing, and transportation. At the same time, it also witnessed the widespread, and sometimes catastrophic, decay of the environment in terms of pollution, deforestation, and the wholesale extinction of species.

As we have moved from one era to the next, the tendency has been for these unbalanced forces to move back toward equilibrium. The growth we have seen in the past decade in terms of our ability to create information has far exceeded our ability to organize, analyze, and draw meaningful conclusions from it. We are bombarded by words and images watching television, listening to the radio, reading the newspaper, or merely walking down the street. Much of the information that is developed in the workplace is equally overwhelming. We need only open our e-mail accounts after a few days away from the office to appreciate this phenomenon. The challenge of the day then, it seems, is to focus on ways to direct our efforts toward the development and organization of data into meaningful forms.

If the success of a project is directly related to the quality and timeliness of the information on which it is based, then this is doubly true for value studies. Most projects, especially during the latter phases of their development, will have generated volumes of information. The project team, which has been responsible for generating, collecting, and organizing the data, possesses a level of familiarity with it that the value team will be unable to match. Furthermore, few, if any, members of the project team will have a full appreciation and understanding of all aspects of the information used to develop the project.

With respect to project information, the value team will be in an unusual position. While the members begin the study from a relatively uninformed standpoint, this lack of knowledge also frees them from the assumptions and conclusions that have been made by the project team. The goal of the value specialist, as well as the other value team members, in this phase of the job plan will be first to develop a thorough understanding of the project relevant to its scope statement (i.e., the need and purpose), which, if properly written, is predicated on the customer's or user's requirements. Once this has been accomplished, each member of the value team can then focus on his or her respective areas of expertise in preparation for the development of alternative concepts.

The Information Phase features the following steps:

- Gather and analyze project scope information
- Gather and analyze project schedule information
- Gather and analyze project cost information
  - Initial costs
  - Life cycle costs
- Gather and analyze project risk information
- Conduct value study kick-off meeting
- Identify and measure project performance—*Value Metrics*
- Conduct site visit (if applicable)

In the Preparation Phase, consideration was given to collecting the project information. The focus of the Information Phase is on the review and analysis of this information by the value study team. It is important to remember that the Information Phase is not a one-way street. In other words, developing a thorough understanding of the project is best achieved through the establishment of an active dialogue between the project team, customers, owners, stakeholders, and the value team.

Gather and Analyze Project Scope Information

It is critical that the value team have ample opportunity to review all relevant project information prior to the commencement of the value study. It is recommended that at least a week be allotted for value study team members to review the information. Additional time may be warranted for particularly large and complicated projects.

In a perfect world, the different types of project information identified in the previous chapter would exist and be distributed to the value team members in a timely fashion. However, as we all know, we do not live in a perfect world. Invariably, there will be pieces of information that will either not have yet been developed or that are not organized into a format that is immediately useable by the value team. Hopefully, these "information gaps" will have been identified during the Preparation Phase and the project team will be working to develop this information so that it can be made available during the value study. Often, however, the information will simply not be available in time. This is a rather common phenomenon for value studies, especially those that are performed early in the project life cycle (i.e., at the project initiation or planning stages). When, for whatever reason, this situation occurs, it will be necessary to identify the assumptions that will be used in place of the information. The value specialist should work with the project team to identify these assumptions and document them for inclusion in the report that will summarize the value team's findings.

Value studies conducted for projects that have been developed and managed by a conscientious project team will have a significant advantage, in terms of the completeness and quality of project information, over those that have not. The standards for project management developed over the years by organizations such as the Project Management Institute provide the basis for the sound development and management of projects.[2] Projects that have not taken advantage of these guidelines are generally not as well organized, tend to suffer from poor internal communication, and are more likely to produce information gaps. While value studies conducted for projects that are less well managed tend to be more challenging to conduct, they are also more likely to reap greater benefits. However, this is not to say that well-managed projects will not benefit from the application of the Value Methodology—there is always room for improvement.

As mentioned previously, many times project information will exist; however, it will be in a form that is not readily useable by the value team. This situation is typical for projects that are farther along in the project life cycle where large quantities of information have been developed with respect to detailed design aspects. In these instances, it may be beneficial to prepare summaries of this data, using tables, charts, or matrices to illustrate trends and/or the relationship of this detailed information to the project as a whole. The value specialist should request that the team members prepare such summaries where appropriate as they review the project information for distribution to the rest of the team.

It is recommended that the value specialist request that the team members prepare a memo detailing questions, issues, and concerns they might identify during the course of their review of the project documents. These should be submitted to the value specialist to augment his or her own review of the project. This will help the value specialist in identifying trends within the project (e.g., lack of information, incorrect assumptions, inconsistencies between technical disciplines, etc.) and provide him or her with a better understanding of the project and potential issues.

Those questions that arise regarding project information that the team feels are critical to address prior to the value study should be directed to the value specialist. It is recommended that a single point of contact be established between the project development and value study teams. Generally, this should be between the value specialist and the project manager. Allowing value team members to make direct contact with the project team can lead to communication problems or misunderstandings that may be otherwise avoided. Some of the potential issues include:

- Interrupting or distracting project team members from their work
- Creating the perception that the value team members are criticizing the work of the project team
- Developing lines of communication that may contravene internal project communication protocols
- Accidentally or unintentionally sharing sensitive project information with parties that should not be privy to it

The project manager will probably have the best overall understanding of the dynamics of the people and issues related to the project. They will logically be in the best position to efficiently collect the additional information needed by the value team, while minimizing disruptions to the ongoing project development process.

Gather and Analyze Project Schedule Information

A thorough review of a project's schedule information is an important step in the Information Phase. Hopefully, the project will have a well-developed work breakdown structure. For those unfamiliar with this concept, a work breakdown structure (WBS) is a deliverable-oriented grouping of project elements that organizes and defines the total scope of the project. A WBS identifies all activities that occur in delivering the project's output, whether a product, process, or facility. The value specialist should be aware that a WBS may exist at several different levels within the project. For instance, one WBS may define the delivery of the design of a facility, while another WBS may define its construction. Depending on the timing and scope of the value study, one or both WBS may be relevant.

A project schedule is generally derived from the WBS. There exist today numerous project scheduling tools and techniques for project managers. Some of the more prevalent software programs on the market today include *Microsoft Project* and *Primavera P3*. Programs such as these allow detailed schedules to be developed from a WBS. In addition, these programs allow project resources to be linked to activities occurring within the WBS.

There are a number of different ways in which a project schedule can be graphically represented, all of which can be accomplished through the use of project management software. These include:

- Bar charts (also known as Gantt charts)
- Project network diagrams (also known as PERT—Program Evaluation and Review Technique—charts)
- Workflow diagrams
- Process flowcharts

Bar charts are useful for showing the relationship of activity start and end dates. These are easy to read and are the standard project schedule representation used for construction and manufacturing projects (see Figure 5.1).

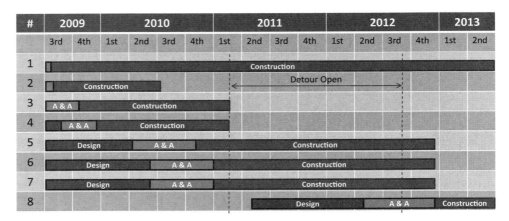

FIGURE 5.1   Project Schedule (Gantt Chart)

Workflow diagrams and process flowcharts are excellent for modeling the relationship between activities and time for all manner of procedures and services (see Figure 5.2). Often an organization will not have developed such a graphic tool for many of their processes and may lack a clear understanding of them. Developing a process flowchart or workflow diagram as part of the Information Phase can clarify the various activities, resources, and time involved. Chapter 6, "Function," will further demonstrate the use of these types of charts and diagrams in developing an understanding of project functions.

While the use of project scheduling software has become commonplace, the value specialist may encounter projects where it is not being used. It is suggested that the value specialist consider utilizing such software to develop a project schedule, as doing so can be an invaluable aid in identifying potential areas for improvement in project delivery, as well as understanding how the alternatives the value study team will develop later will impact the project schedule. Surprisingly, some project teams do not develop schedules, although this is more common for public entities with respect to construction schedules. Some public agencies may be responsible only for developing a design, while construction will be taken care of by a contractor. Therefore, a detailed project schedule for delivery of the design may exist but a construction schedule may not. The argument for the project team not preparing a schedule is usually "We aren't responsible for how it will be built or manufactured" or "We don't know how the contractor will bid the work or how manufacturing will assemble it." The value specialist should regard such an attitude as a major opportunity for value improvement.

If this is the case, it is strongly advised that the value specialist work with the project team to create a "straw man" construction schedule. If they are unable or unwilling to do so, then the value team should create one. Similar circumstances may also occur for product and process studies where one entity develops a concept and/or design and another is responsible for its production, implementation, or acquisition. Value studies performed on a design should consider the impacts on acquisition.

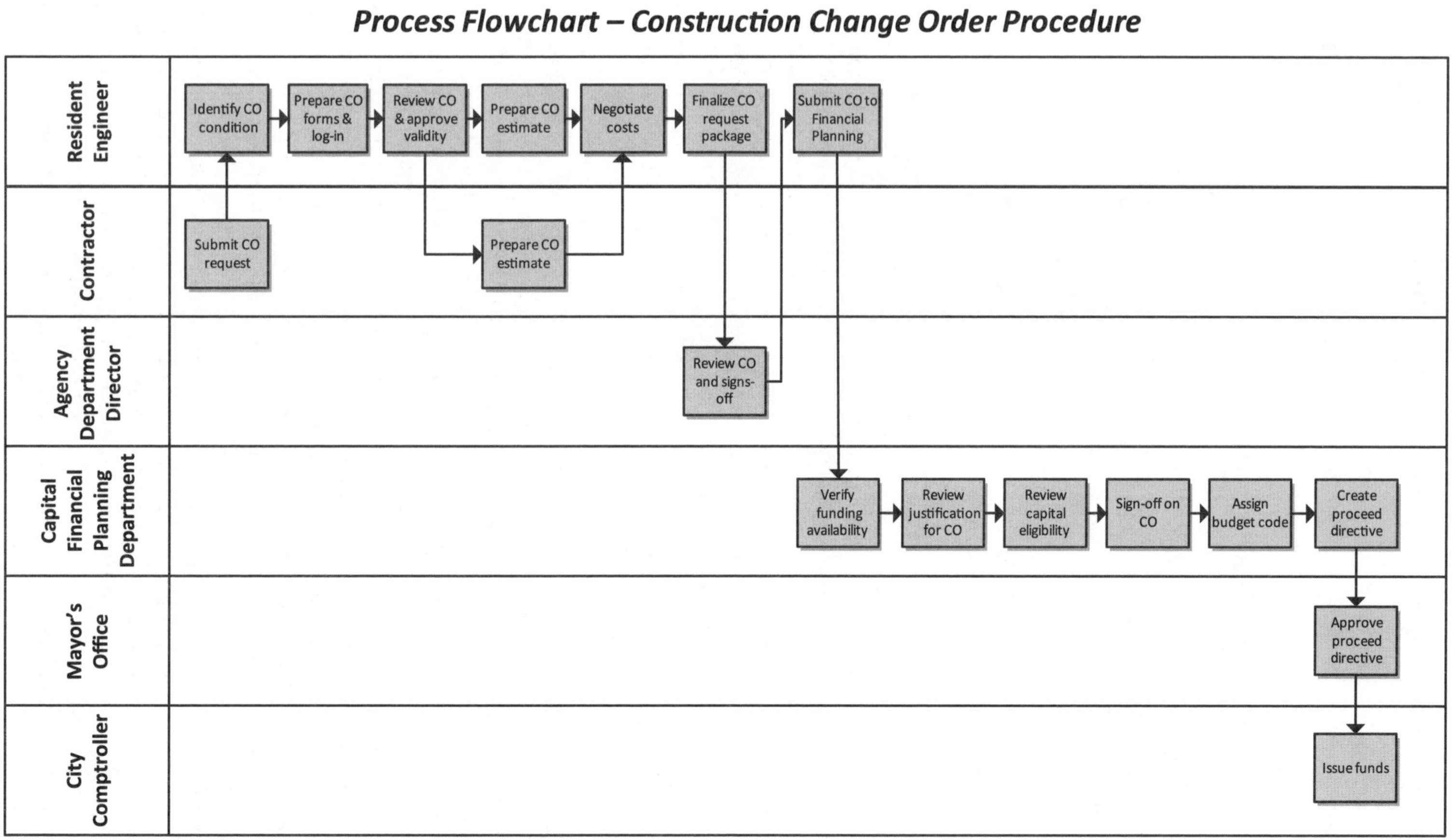

Process Flowchart – Construction Change Order Procedure

FIGURE 5.2 Process Flowchart

93

Gather and Analyze Project Cost Information

As mentioned in Chapter 4, the potential for achieving major savings in any project is greatest during the early phases of the project life cycle. It becomes increasingly expensive and time-consuming to make changes, regardless of benefits, as the project progresses toward completion. Finally, a point is reached where the cost to make a change exceeds any potential benefit; it is then simply "too late." Therefore, application of the Value Methodology at an early phase is important.

As one writer has put it, "Cost is the principal dimension in value analysis. Without cost for comparison, the analysis of value must necessarily be subjective—and consequently fall short of the full potential."[3] It is desirable to develop a cost estimate for each value alternative, which can then be compared to the baseline project concept. Yet in the early phases of a project, when the potential for savings is at a high point, many areas that are to be estimated are not yet clearly defined. Only after the project is well advanced and everything has been fully developed can the task of estimating project costs be made relatively easy and straightforward. Unfortunately, by this time, it may be too late to change and the cost to redesign will be too high and many value alternatives must be dropped by the wayside. It is essential, therefore, to look at methods by which the value specialist can gain an appreciation of costs very early in the project cycle.

Cost is one of the most misunderstood items in business today. The cost of a product under study may vary greatly, depending upon whom you ask and the level of cost with which they are familiar. Is the cost fully burdened? Does it include profit? Is it just material cost? Construction costs, while detailed parametric information and historical data is often available, are heavily influenced by the availability of skilled labor and vary widely from region to region. Finally, the true cost of procedures and processes within organizations is often unknown.

Cost Visibility

While a primary goal of many value studies is cost reduction, some organizations have their costing systems set up to determine whether cost and/or profit targets will be met and not necessarily answering the question of how much it costs to produce the product. As mentioned earlier, the cost of management procedures, policies, and processes may be unknown. In either case, the use of cost visibility techniques is essential in developing an understanding of project costs.

Cost visibility techniques establish costing ground rules to determine what is included in the project cost. This helps the value study team organize the cost and understand the current cost situation, including the cost-driving elements.

First, determine the appropriate level of cost for the project, depending on the stage of the project's life cycle. For example, a value study focusing on the construction of a new hospital early in the design process would probably use area costing (i.e., cost per square meter). A study focusing on an existing product would utilize detailed unit production costs (i.e., bill of materials). Once a level of costing has been decided on, it is important to maintain whatever level was chosen throughout the value study in order to maintain consistency and avoid confusion in communicating the cost of alternative concepts.

The following are several important items to consider as project cost data is analyzed:

- *Determine total cost.* Based on the costing ground rules, determine the total cost for the project. For goods, a product that retails to the customer for $18.29 may have a total production cost (material, labor, and some portion of overhead) of $12.79 for the purposes of the study. For construction projects, the total cost would include all design costs, contractor overhead and profit, design and estimating contingencies, real estate, and mitigation costs. For processes or services, the total cost would include direct and indirect labor costs, as well as any support costs (materials, transportation, office space, etc.).
- *Determine cost elements.* Break down the elements of total cost into major areas such as material, labor, and overhead. For construction studies, costs can be broken down through the use of a standard estimating format, such as *Uniformat* and *MasterFormat.*
- *Determine incremental unit costs.* This step identifies where costs are being created on a unit basis by component or elements of a process. This translates into cost per hour, cost per cubic meter, or cost per subassembly.
- *Determine annualized costs.* To establish a base for determining cost improvements, calculate the annualized cost of the study item by multiplying the unit cost by the number of units produced per year. For product studies, annualized costs will be used at the end of the study to determine annualized savings.
- *Determine life cycle costs.* Many projects will want to consider the long-term costs associated with the maintenance and operation of products, facilities, and processes. These are costs with which the customer and/or owner will be very concerned. Life cycle costs will be discussed in greater detail later in this chapter.

Cost Models

Upon receipt of the project cost information from the project team, the value specialist should prepare a cost model for the project. The first step in preparation of the cost model is to validate the cost information provided by the project team. The reason for verifying cost information is to ensure that both groups agree on the unit prices, quantity of materials, and/or labor that went into preparation of the cost estimate. If there are discrepancies in the cost, these should be identified early to avoid confusion or misunderstanding during the implementation phase of the project. To construct the cost model, the value specialist and/or the estimator on the value study team distributes cost by process, by trade, by system, and other identifiable areas. This helps the value team at the beginning of the value study to know where the major costs are to be found. Pareto's law of economics indicates that 80 percent of the cost will normally occur in 20 percent of the items being studied.

There are essentially three types of cost models that should be considered:

1. *Initial cost models.* Initial cost models provide a representation of the acquisition costs of a project. Such a model should include all costs associated

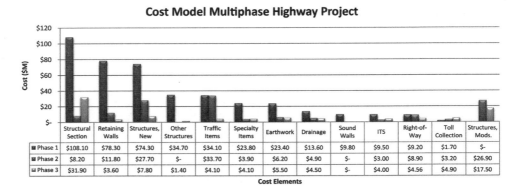

FIGURE 5.3   Cost Model (broken down by project phase)

with initial production, construction, or acquisition. This is the most common and immediately useful form of cost modeling. Pareto Cost Models are very useful, as described in Chapter 4. For projects involving multiple phases or segments, sometimes it is useful to organize the model differently (see Figure 5.3). The bottom line is that the cost information should be summarized in a concise and meaningful way so that the value study participants can develop an overview of the project costs and draw meaningful conclusions quickly and easily.

2. *Cost-worth models.* Based upon a standard initial cost model, a comparison can be made between the cost of any project element and its worth, as evaluated by the value specialist or value study team. As discussed in Chapter 2, "Value," worth is a subjective and mostly individual assessment of what one is willing to pay for an item. It is usually defined as the least cost means of reliably performing a function. The purpose of a cost-worth model is to identify areas having a cost considerably in excess of the evaluator's opinion of their worth (see Figure 5.4).

3. *Life cycle cost models.* This type of cost model is useful for illustrating the cost of ownership, especially for facilities and major durable goods. Such a model would include initial project costs, maintenance costs, energy costs, and other factors, such as financing, taxes, insurance, and so on (see Figure 5.5).

Sequence Flowcharts

Another tool for analyzing project costs for processes and procedure is the sequence flowchart. This technique graphically depicts the process being studied by showing the relationship of activities, costs, time, and responsibilities. This is a very useful technique for value teams studying a manufacturing process or administrative procedure. A well-prepared sequence flowchart details each activity that occurs in a process and the time and cost of those activities. To develop the chart, list the operations down the left side and identify those performing the tasks across the top. Indicate the flow of operations by placing circles in the appropriate locations.

Cost Worth Model Molded Lamp Socket

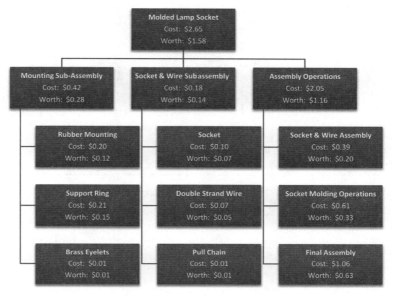

FIGURE 5.4   Cost-Worth Model

Life Cycle Cost Model Building

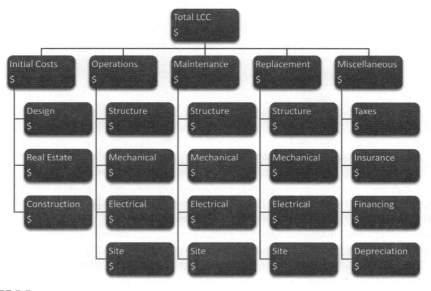

FIGURE 5.5   Life Cycle Cost Model

Project: Fan Assembly Process	Annual Volume:		6,000	Unit Cost:	$54.07		Annual Cost:	$324,420
	Material		Balance	Inspection	Activity	Total	Activity	Misc.
Activity	Handling	Assembly	Dept.	Dept.	Time	Time	Cost	Cost
Deliver components to assembly area	○				0.12	1.70	$ 1.65	
Assemble blades and hubs		○			0.37	0.80	$ 5.27	
Check torque		○			0.02	1.00	$ 0.29	
Move blade and hub assembly to balance area	○				0.09	1.50	$ 1.24	Bal. Ck.
Balance blade and hub assembly			○		0.60	2.00	$ 9.33	$ 3.23
Move blade and hub assembly to final assembly	○				0.07	1.00	$ 0.96	
Clean and touch-up blade and hub assembly		○			0.09	1.00	$ 1.28	Fix Ck.
Assemble blade and hub assembly into fan housing		○			1.33	3.50	$ 18.95	$ 2.17
Move assembly to inspection	○				0.11	3.00	$ 1.51	
Inspect and coat bolts				○	0.45	2.00	$ 7.09	
Move to dispatch area	○				0.08	1.00	$ 1.10	
				TOTAL:	3.33	18.50	$ 48.67	$ 5.40

FIGURE 5.6 Sequence Flowchart for a Manufactured Component

Insert the time (i.e., time per event and/or elapsed time) and cost (i.e., cost per event and/or miscellaneous costs) information in the appropriate columns (see Figure 5.6).

This document provides the team with easy to understand, current information regarding the project. The following are step-by-step instructions on preparing and costing a sequence flowchart:

1. Review the project scope. Clearly identify where the project begins and ends.
2. Walk through the process from the point the project begins until it ends. Ask questions of the people on the line to better understand the problems with the current process. Note that manufacturing routings usually contain only a portion of the information required.
3. Determine the number of times the process is accomplished per year. Use this lot size for all time and cost data during the study.
4. Start at the beginning of the project and identify each activity in the sequence that it occurs. List these steps down the left column of the sequence flowchart.
5. Identify each department or labor classification involved in the process. List this information across the top of the Sequence Flowchart.
6. Determine the average time to perform each task (per lot). This is the event time for that task. Also determine the total time for the task. The "total time" is the time from the start of one task until the start of the next task. This includes in-process storage and other manufacturing delay times. (*Note:* A time study is not required; however, *do not* rely on existing data such as manufacturing routings, as they may not represent what is currently occurring nor be as detailed as necessary.)
7. Identify any other related manufacturing costs such as packaging, inspection, scrap, rework, setup, and so on. Record this cost information in the "miscellaneous cost" column.

In the example in Figure 5.6, the time and cost detail reflect the cost for a single component. In many cases, the sequence flowchart is developed around a standard lot size for manufacturing processes. The appropriate lot size will vary with each project. The team should also understand the rationale for the current lot sizes and be sensitive to the effect of changes in that lot size.

Life Cycle Costing

There are many definitions of life cycle costing that are in use. The U.S. General Services Administration defines life cycle costing as follows:

> *Life cycle costing (LCC) is the development of all the significant costs of acquiring, owning and using an item, system or service over a specified length of time.*[4]

Life cycle costing is the total economic cost of owning and operating a facility, manufactured process, or product. The life cycle costing analysis reflects present and future costs of the project over its useful life. It allows an assessment of a given solution, and it is a tool for making comparisons. The underriding theme is that life cycle costing is a universal tool to express the multifaceted elements of cost and time in a uniform criterion of equivalent dollars.

The use of the life cycle costing technique has a broad range of applications. In the analysis of facilities, it can be applied during the conceptual, planning, design, construction, and operating stages for a facility or product. Its application as an aid for analyzing economic alternatives for purchases at home and in the marketplace has been used by all of us. Given the rise in the interest rates and inflation, the use of life cycle costing has been expanded. The impacts are astounding, as will be seen later in this chapter. Before explaining the applications of life cycle costing, facts about its application are addressed.

Most investors or owners want to know what the total ownership and/or operating costs will be for a given asset. In both the public and private sectors, an increasing interest is being manifested in knowing, to the greatest extent possible, what a project will cost throughout its entire lifetime. This involves both an estimate of construction or production costs and a forecast of the probable costs of energy, maintenance, taxes, and borrowed money.

If we consider a typical office building in the United States, operating expenses (e.g., electricity, water, maintenance, etc.) make up the largest cost of owning a building. First costs typically account for less than 10 percent of the money that must be spent on a facility over its life; as much as 85 percent of the building's real cost is related to operating the facility. Other costs include land acquisition, conceptual planning, renewal or revitalization, and disposal. An LCC analysis performed for a typical building would normally consider all of these factors that represent the owner's total costs.

What is usually not considered, however, are the costs to the end user. Personnel costs (e.g., salary and benefits) make up 78 percent of the total business expenses for tenants, according to a study conducted for the General Services

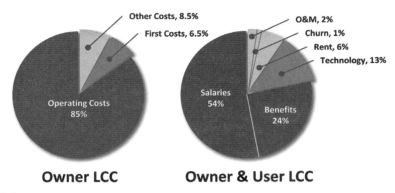

Owner LCC   **Owner & User LCC**

FIGURE 5.7   Total Life Cycle Costs—Office Building

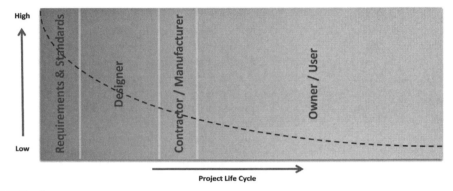

FIGURE 5.8   Impact of Major Decision Makers on LCC

Administration, while costs associated with the building itself account for only 9 percent (see Figure 5.7). This is a very important consideration to keep in mind and one that is difficult, if not impossible, to put a dollar value on. This shows that there are hidden life cycle costs that have a major impact on the user that we may not be able to effectively measure.[5] While an owner of a privately owned building that is rented out may or may not be interested in the costs incurred by his or her tenants, owners of public buildings (i.e., taxpayers) should be. Individuals and organizations are becoming increasingly aware of sustainable design and even landlords are beginning to think along these lines to ensure that their properties remain marketable and attractive to prospective tenants into the future.

Figure 5.8 is a generalized curve that shows whose decisions have the greatest impact on cost. If the area under each segment of the curve represents an impact on cost, it would be seen that the designer or project team has by far the greatest role to play. The initial contractor can only perform within the carefully defined limits of his contract, and once the design is completed, he or she can have little effect on total costs. The owner has even less influence, although the owner's total expenditures during the life of the facility are far greater than money spent on design. This figure illustrates that the best place to save money is during the design or project development phase. In short, good project management and design are worth every cent they cost.

Life cycle analyses are not limited to use only during the planning stage, but can be used at any time during the useful life of the facility. As an example, processing plants that are manufacturing a competitive product must know every element of cost from obtaining and processing raw materials to marketing, sale, and the distribution of the final product. A corporate owner of a sports complex uses life cycle analysis to account for building amortization, operating and advertising costs, and other expenses to know what it needs to make in order to break even. The use of life cycle analysis affects all facts of our economic livelihood.

Final analysis should account for noneconomic criteria that have intrinsic benefits that do not lend themselves to finite cost evaluations. Factors such as safety, reliability, operability, and environmental factors may be more important than monetary savings. The Value Metrics process presented in this book provides a method for considering these types of "soft" factors in considering performance and value.

While LCC provides an excellent tool for decision making, its application should be understood to avoid possible pitfalls in its use. Fiscal managers especially should appreciate that LCC dollars may not be the same as budget dollars. One of the problems is that cost estimates may not be applicable as budget estimates because they are expressed in constant dollars (excluding inflation) and all cash-flow dollars are converted to equivalent moneys at a common point in time. LCC estimates are not necessarily equivalent to the obligated amounts for each funding year.

Cost categories to be used in a life cycle cost analysis encompass a broad area. Funds for a project may be spent over a long time frame: from the years leading up to its completion to the time when the facility, product, or process has outlived its usefulness. The following are types of costs that might factor into a total project's life. This is not to say that these are all of the costs involved. However, this list serves as a reminder of the major cost factors to look for when performing life cycle comparisons. LCC considerations may include:

- *Investment costs.* The amount of money expended for the assessment of market potential, the time and expenses involved in analyzing site alternatives, and the expenses incurred for development of a financial plan. Investment costs may also include expenses for obtaining a line of credit and other financing alternatives. The preparation of stock and bond sales may be another type of investment cost.
- *Land acquisition costs.* Costs for realty fees, title searches, legal fees, deed filing fees, insurance, cost of land, and the interest on borrowed money for the purchase or leasing of land for use for a facility. In addition, the cost of environmental mitigation may need to be considered, depending upon regulatory requirements:
  - Property costs
  - Real estate fees
  - Environmental mitigation costs

- *Project development costs.* Costs associated with the planning, design, bidding, construction, inspection, and initial start-up of a facility, product, or process. Any anticipated future costs for design modifications should also be included:
  - Project management
  - Planning
  - Design and engineering
  - Project support (e.g., purchasing, marketing, accounting, etc.)
  - Redesign costs
- *Construction and manufacturing costs.* The cost of constructing, manufacturing, or implementing a facility, product, or service.
- *Replacement costs.* The future costs to modify or replace a portion of the project. Usually, specific pieces of equipment or parts are the major source of replacement costs. Based on the expected life of the components, several replacements may occur during the total project life.
- *Salvage costs.* The value of the project or product at some future time. Usually salvage value is the amount received from the sale at the end of the life cycle period. Conversely, it could reflect the costs for demolition and/or environmental remediation.
- *Operating costs.* The costs required to operate the facility, product, or process. These costs are the day-to-day costs of staffing; energy costs to create and maintain a working environment and to operate equipment; costs of outside services such as waste disposal, water and sewage costs; chemicals and other resources needed to manufacture or to process a product; and the costs of transportation from the source of raw materials to the final delivery point. These costs are often periodic costs falling at scheduled intervals:
  - Staffing
  - Fuel or energy
  - Chemicals and supplies
  - Operating schedule
  - Outside services
  - Resource recovery
  - Transportation
- *Maintenance costs.* Factors included in maintenance costs would include labor, cost of parts, materials, cleaning materials and equipment, and preventive maintenance. Also included are normal maintenance and repair of equipment, painting, and so on:
  - Material/parts/lubricants
  - Staffing/labor
  - Preventive maintenance
  - Cleaning
  - Durability of products
- *Miscellaneous costs.* Such costs could include insurance policies; federal, state, and local taxes; depreciation; and the effects of inflation:
  - Taxes
  - Insurance
  - Depreciation
  - Inflation
- *Time value of money.* Time has a high price tag when evaluating alternatives. The longevity of a project and the lifespan of individual components must be

considered in the decision-making process. The cost of money is the interest that is charged on borrowed money for the project.

Elements of cost in a life cycle cost analysis are for the total life of the product. Some costs are one-time expenditures that occur before the project is completed. Others are single expenditures that are amortized for periods up to and beyond its useful life.

The Time Value of Money

As money can produce earnings at a certain rate of interest by being invested for a period of time, it is important to know that one unit of money received at some future date does not produce as much earnings as the same unit of money received in the present. This relationship between interest and time forms the basis for the concept known as the "time value of money."

Money also has a time value, as the buying power of a dollar varies with time. The relationships between $1 in hand, $1 promised in the future, or a series of payments at specified times in the future are difficult concepts for many of us to grasp.

During periods of inflation, the quantity of goods and services that can be bought with a certain amount of money decreases as the purchase date moves into the future. Although this change in the buying power of money is important, the concept of the time value of money is even more so, in that it has earning power. It is necessary to know the different methods for computing interest in order to calculate the actual effect of the time value of money in the comparison of alternative solutions.

The following considerations must be kept in mind for application in calculations of investment alternatives:

- Present Value (P) is produced at the beginning of a period, at a time in the present.
- Future Value (F) occurs at the end of a future period, from a time considered as present.
- Annuity Amount (A) is a single payment within a series of equal payments made at the end of each period under consideration. This is akin to a monthly mortgage payment.
- Interest Rate (i) is the cost of money established by the organization or lending institution. The federal government's Office of Management and Budget (OMB) frequently updates interest rates per OMB Circular A-94.[6] The interest rate is also referred to as a discount rate.
- Life Cycle Period (n) being the total number of periods—usually expressed in years.

It is useful to think of the relationship of money at different points in time as a triangle where P equals a single present amount of money; F equals a future single sum of money; and A equals money expressed as a series of equal amounts (like the monthly mortgage payments). Figure 5.9 illustrates this interrelationship and includes the names of the financial equations involved in calculating the time value of money. These financial equations are provided in Table 5.1.[7]

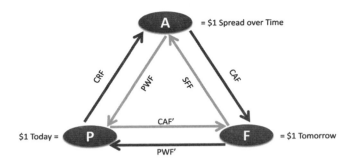

FIGURE 5.9 Time Value of Money

TABLE 5.1 Time Value of Money, Financial Formulas

Name of Factor	Abbreviation	Formula
Single Payment Compound Amount Factor	CAF′	$F = P(1 + i)^n$
Single Payment Present Worth Factor	PWF′	$P = \dfrac{F}{(1 + i)^n}$
Equal Payment Series Compound Amount Factor	CAF	$F = A\dfrac{(1 + i)^n - 1}{i}$
Equal Payment Series Sinking Fund Factor	SFF	$A = F\left(\dfrac{i}{(1 + i)^n - 1}\right)$
Equal Payment Series Capital Recovery Factor	CRF	$A = P\left(\dfrac{i(1 + i)^n}{(1 + i)^n - 1}\right)$
Equal Payment Series Present Worth Factor	PWF	$P = A\left(\dfrac{(1 + i)^n - 1}{i(1 + i)^n}\right)$

Inflation and Escalation

The terms *inflation* and *escalation* are often confused. Inflation refers to the persistent and appreciable rise in the general level or average of prices. Deflation has the exact opposite effect, or "negative inflation." Inflation reduces the purchasing power of money over time. Differential escalation refers to the annual change in the price of a specific commodity or service that is in addition to the general inflation rate.[8] Perhaps the best examples of this phenomenon are the prices of oil and steel, which tend to follow independent price fluctuations and cycles apart from the macroeconomic forces of more general inflation or deflation.

Since it is very difficult, if not impossible, to accurately predict inflation rates very far into the future, it is generally best not to consider the effect of future inflation when performing life cycle calculations unless the owner requests it. Similarly, it is not recommended that differential annual escalation be considered unless there are very good reasons to do so.

Inflation can be calculated by amending the preceding financial formulas where "j" equals the general rate of inflation. For example, calculate a future single sum "F" using the single payment compound amount factor as follows:

$$F = P(1 + i)^n(1 + j)^n$$

We can expand this equation by considering differential annual escalation where "e" the differential rate of inflation:

$$F = P(1 + i)^n(1 + j)^n(1 + e)^n$$

If constant dollars are used (i.e., inflation is not considered), then $(1 + j)^n$ would be eliminated if we were to consider only the effect of differential escalation.

This book is not intended to serve as a treatise on engineering economics and it is generally recommended that the reader refer to the other sources referenced in this section if a better understanding of these concepts is desired.

Life Cycle Costing Methods

Using life cycle costing will aid the decision-making process and increase the sensitivity to cost for operating and maintaining facilities, products, and processes. Life cycle costing is actually a series of computations applying economic factors to monetary expenditures as identified in the previous section. The validity of the comparison, like all estimates, is dependent on the quality of the cost estimates used in the analysis. There is no good substitute for sound cost figures. Therefore, before proceeding with a life cycle analysis, be certain of the quality and the validity of cost parameters to be sure of the accuracy of the results. The following steps outline the process for developing a LCC analysis:

- *State the problem.* As life cycle costing can be used as a decision-making tool, its first step involves identification of the problem to be solved. A problem statement will help to focus on the basis of the comparison. A description of the physical facilities and the alternatives to be compared should be defined thoroughly. Before going further into the analysis, check to see if the objectives will be met by the comparisons and the cost parameters in the analysis.
- *Establish the alternatives.* Next, the alternative concepts to be analyzed are documented with a listing of background information on physical components of alternatives and the corresponding differences. It is essential to establish basic cost and budgeting data of the owner's program at this time, as the data will form the criteria for life cycle input and guidelines for analysis of results.
- *Establish the parameters.* Life cycle analyses are impacted by *time, cost, and the cost of money.* Time factors include the project planning life, sometimes called the useful life of the project; equipment life; the owner's planning schedule; foreseeable major expansions; and deletions or changes to the total program. Project life estimates, especially for equipment replacement, are hard to predict, as the life of the equipment is dependent on the quality of the equipment and the maintenance performed to keep it in operating condition. The useful life is the time that the facility will be used. Often a facility will

have several major renovations during its useful life. Costs for additional renovation expenditures are planned by the owner and are usually included in life
cycle comparisons. Cost parameters have been outlined previously. Major
impacts are being felt by owners from escalating energy, labor, and maintenance costs above the normal inflation rates. These fluctuations in cost are
accounted for by the use of escalation rates. The cost of money is taken into
account by setting interest, inflation, and escalation rates. Monetary loans for
financing and tax benefits are part of the analysis.

The easiest way to model life cycle costs is to convert all costs to a present
worth amount. The Present Worth Method can be set up using spreadsheet software
like Excel, most of which include macros for the financial equations identified in
Table 5.1.

The Present Worth Method requires that all costs for the life cycle analysis,
present, annual, and future expenditures be brought back to today's baseline costs.
Initial costs are already expressed in present worth amounts. Operations and maintenance costs are usually estimates of annual costs, based on stated conditions of
use. The interest rate, life cycle period (useful life) should be established by the
owner and/or user. This method is illustrated in Figure 5.10.

This example compares two possible options for a new air-conditioning system.
The following is a step-by-step walkthrough of the Present Worth Method:

1. Input the Life Cycle Period (i.e., total length of time in years) and discount rate
   (i.e., cost of money). In this example, 20 years was the period established by
   the owner at a discount rate of 10 percent.
2. Input the initial capital costs to purchase and install the equipment. Note that
   the costs of the alternative system are approximately 40 percent higher than
   the original system. The initial capital costs are already expressed in present
   worth dollars, so it is not necessary to apply any of the financial factors here.
3. Input the annually recurring costs. In this case, we must consider the annual
   maintenance costs (i.e., servicing and operations) to run the two systems as
   well as their energy requirements. These costs are expressed in present worth
   dollars and do not consider inflation. These annualized costs (A) must be converted to present worth costs (P) by applying the Present Worth Factor (PWF).
4. Input the single future costs. In this example, the chiller bundles will need to
   be replaced before the end of the life cycle period that has been established
   (20 years). The cost to do this (which is based on the cost to do so in today's
   dollars) is identified for both the original and alternative systems. Note that the
   replacement costs are different and occur at different periods. The Present
   Worth Factor (PWF) is used to convert these future single amounts (F) to
   present worth costs (P).
5. Input the salvage costs. Salvage costs represent the residual value of the system
   at the end of the life cycle period (which is year 20). Salvage costs are akin to
   the single future expenditures identified in the previous step. However, since
   they typically represent money back to the owner, they are expressed as a
   negative number (in other words, a negative cost).
6. Calculate the present worth value of all costs. This step simply adds all of the
   present, future, and annual costs that have been converted into present worth

	LIFE CYCLE COSTS - PRESENT WORTH METHOD						
	New Office Building						
Title:	Air Conditioning System					**Alternative No.** 12.0	**Page No.** 6 of 6
	Life Cycle Period 20 Years					**ORIGINAL**	**ALTERNATIVE**
	Discount Rate 10 %						
A.	**INITIAL COST**					$540,000	$750,000
					INITIAL COST SAVINGS:		($210,000)
B.	**RECURRENT COSTS**						
	1. General Operations & Maintenance					$20,000	$12,000
	2. Energy Costs					$50,000	$21,000
	3. Supplies & Misc.						
					Total Annual Costs:	$70,000	$33,000
					PWF Factor:	8.5136	8.5136
				PRESENT WORTH OF RECURRENT COSTS:		$595,949	$280,948
C.	**SINGLE EXPENDITURES**	**Year**	**Amount**	**PWF' Factor**		**Present Value**	**Present Value**
	1. Chiller Replacement	10	$100,000	0.3855		$38,554	$0
	2. Chiller Replacement	15	$125,000	0.2394		$0	$29,924
	3.			1.0000		$0	$0
	4.			1.0000		$0	$0
	5.			1.0000		$0	$0
	6.			1.0000		$0	$0
				PRESENT VALUE OF SINGLE EXPENDITURES:		$38,554	$29,924
D.	**TOTAL RECURRENT COSTS & SINGLE EXPENDITURES (B+C)**					$634,504	$310,872
E.	**SALVAGE VALUE**	**Year**	**Amount**	**PWF' Factor**		**Present Value**	**Present Value**
	1. Residual Equipment Value	20	-$100,000	0.1486		($14,864)	$0
	2. Residual Equipment Value	20	-$200,000	0.1486		$0	($29,729)
F.	**TOTAL PRESENT WORTH VALUE (A+D+E)**					$1,159,639	$1,031,143
				TOTAL LIFE CYCLE SAVINGS:			$128,497

FIGURE 5.10   Life Cycle Cost: Present Worth Method

dollars and expresses them as a single total. The total alternative costs are subtracted from the total original costs to give us the total life cycle cost savings, which in this case is $128,497.

The alternative air-conditioning system, though 40 percent more expensive to install initially, ended up being the most economical option for the owner when considering the total cost of ownership over the life of the equipment. The value specialist must always consider life cycle costs in the search for improved value.

Gather and Analyze Project Risk Information

Risk is something that we deal with in our daily lives. For the most part, we assess it on an unconscious level, usually out of habit. Will I get hit by a car if I cross the street? Will I burn my hand if I take a pan out of the oven without a hot pad? Will I get sunburned today if I don't put on lotion? If you are reading this paragraph now, it is probably safe to assume that you are pretty good at dealing with these mundane risks. Most of us are. This type of risk analysis is intuitive and is built upon years of experience, observation, and instinct. Generally speaking, the decision making involved is pretty straightforward and seldom do we devote much time to our analysis. It seems that when we face risks personally, they are generally easier to deal with and we arrive at answers rather quickly.

By contrast, when risks are removed from us, they seem to take on additional complexity. This is especially true when considering decisions related to the development and delivery of projects. There are countless risks that a project can encounter at any point in its life cycle. What if the geotechnical information is wrong and the foundation collapses? What if the price of steel skyrockets two years from now when construction starts? What if it drops? What if the project's environmental document is held up in review and delays the construction bid date? The answers to these problems are not always clear, nor are the often complex interdependencies of how these problems relate to each other. The best we can do is make educated guesses about the probabilities of the larger risks and their potential impacts. It is doubtful that every potential project risk could even be identified no matter how much time is spent. Uncertainty is the fundamental nature of risk and although we can never know anything with 100 percent certainty, we can get reasonably close if we have a rationale structure with which to work.

Risk is one of the most insidious forces that a project can face and it can do an enormous amount of damage to project value if it is allowed to go unchecked. Value methodology can play a hugely important role in the management of risk by minimizing threats and maximizing opportunities. In light of this, the first step is to gather and review the project risk information. This includes the project's risk management plan, risk register, any qualitative or quantitative analysis, and the risk response plan.

As the discipline of project management becomes more sophisticated, the management of risk has drawn increasing attention. The tools, techniques, and training available to project managers and team members have been growing rapidly over the past few years. It is likely that some level of risk information will be available to the value team.

It is not the intent of this book to provide a comprehensive overview of the discipline of risk management; however, it will be summarized below so that at least those who are unfamiliar with it can develop a better understanding, especially as it relates to VM. Risk management can be thought of as a pyramid having multiple tiers. Each tier requires the one beneath it to be successful (see Figure 5.11).

Therefore, if we use this analogy, the process of Risk Management Planning forms the first crucial step in the management of risk. The following is a brief description of each level of the risk management pyramid:

- *Risk management planning.* This level is concerned with determining the general approach, or strategy, in dealing with project risk. It addresses who will be involved, what activities will be performed, and how risk will be dealt with in relation to other project development activities.
- *Risk identification.* This level focuses on identifying potential project risks and formally organizing them into a risk register. Risk identification includes the following steps:
  - Identify risk categories appropriate for the project
  - Brainstorm potential risks associated with each strategy
  - Organize, prioritize, and define key project risks
  - Set up the risk register
- *Qualitative risk analysis.* This level expands on the risk register by further elaborating upon potential risks. Risks are categorized according to their probabilities and impacts.
  - Identify the most critical risks by analyzing the Risk Register to permit appropriate focus on the Top 12 to 20 Risks.
  - Identify the event description: A detailed description concerning the nature of the risk, its trigger, and whether it may be a recurring event. Think SMART (SMART is an acronym for: Specific, Measurable, Attainable, Relevant, and Time bound).

FIGURE 5.11 Levels of Risk Management

- Specific. A good event description should answer the following questions:

  Who: Who is involved? Who is responsible?

  What: What will happen?

  Where: Where will it happen?

  When: When might it happen? Could it happen more than once?

  Why: Why will it happen? What causes it to happen?
- Measurable. Establish concrete criteria for how you will know when the risk occurs.
- Attainable. Think of "attainable" as "manageable." Can the risk even be managed or controlled? We talked about this earlier in the chapter; however, think about it in a little more detail. Sometimes risks that initially appeared to be manageable turn out not to be.
- Realistic. To be realistic, the risk must be something that at least has some probability of occurrence. For example, something like "Godzilla rises from the sea and destroys the job site" probably isn't very realistic. At least, let's hope not!
- Timely. A risk should be grounded within a time frame. With no duration of time assigned to it there's no sense of urgency. When in the project's life cycle might the event occur? During design? During environmental review? During construction?
- Develop a detailed description concerning the potential impact of the risk. Most risks can have a pretty broad range in terms of the degree of impact. This range should be discussed in greater detail.
  - Identify worst-case scenario
  - Best-case scenario
  - Most likely scenario
- Define the probability that the risk event (regardless of its degree of impact) will occur.

- *Quantitative risk analysis.* This level develops more specific information regarding the probabilities and impacts of risks and builds upon the work done during qualitative risk analysis. Often, mathematical models are constructed to develop a deeper understanding of the cumulative impacts of risks to a project's scope, schedule, and cost. Monte Carlo analysis is often used for this purpose. The Washington State Department of Transportation (WSDOT) has developed an Excel-based spreadsheet that provides a Monte Carlo risk model that is available to the public to download. It is called the Risk Based Estimate Self-Modeling (RBES) and is an excellent tool for projects related to design and construction.[9]
- *Risk response planning.* This level is concerned with identifying and developing strategies and action plans to deal with risks by reducing threats and enhancing opportunities.
- *Risk monitoring and control.* This level is where risk is actively measured. Identified risks are tracked, old risks are retired, new risks are added, response plans are executed, and the effectiveness of the risk management plan is monitored.

The project's risk management plan will provide an overview of how the project is addressing risk. The level of detail and complexity with which this is done will vary from project to project. Hopefully, the project will at least have a risk register available for the value team to peruse. A risk register will provide information on specific risks to the project and should include at least some qualitative analysis on them, including their probability and impacts (see Figure 5.12).

If no qualitative analysis has been performed, the value specialist should consider adding this activity to the value study agenda, either as part of the value study or as a separate activity performed prior to it. If the project team has not performed a qualitative analysis, then it is likely that they are unaware of what risks exist and how they could impact the project. If the risks are known and have at least passed through some degree of previous analysis, then the value team will be in a position to consider ways to mitigate threats and enhance opportunities as a part of the value study effort.

Assuming that the risks have at least been identified, risks can then be prioritized by utilizing a Probability and Impact (P&I) Matrix. This project team should discuss the various risks and determine their impact and probabilities. The P&I Matrix shown in Figure 5.13 includes a rating of 1 to 5 for both probabilities and impacts. A risk's probability and impact can then be cross-indexed and a total risk score assigned to it by multiplying the two ratings—the higher the risk score, the more critical the risk. Obviously, risks falling in the red zone should be considered during the value study. Those in the yellow or green zones can be addressed if time permits.

Conduct Value Study Kick-Off Meeting

The team portion of the value study should always begin with a kick-off meeting. The purpose of the kick-off meeting is to introduce the participants to the VM process and the value study schedule and objectives; provide an overview of the current state of the project; provide an opportunity for the value team to receive clarifications from the project team; and develop an understanding of how the project is performing relative to its scope statement. The kick-off meeting should focus on following activities:

- Introduce value study process, objectives, and schedule
- Present project overview
- Identify project constraints and stakeholder issues
- Identify project performance—*Value Metrics*
- Measure project performance—*Value Metrics*

The value study kick-off meeting should be attended by the value team, project team, project owner and/or sponsor, customer representative(s), and any other stakeholders who are not part of the project team but have a vested interest in the project.

Introduce Value Study Process, Objectives, and Schedule

It is likely that the majority of those present at the kickoff meeting will be totally unfamiliar with Value Methodology and may not understand what the

ID	Category	Type	Rank	Title	Description	Trigger	Prob. %		Impact
1	Environmental	T	3	Wetlands Mitigation	Lack of land availability for wetlands or habitat restoration. The environmental review has not yet been completed and it is possible that the extent and quality of the impacted wetlands has been underestimated. This could affect the mitigation ratios.	Required by USFWS	Medium 50%	Worst Case	Assume that another 65 acres of land are required. Cost would be $10 million (from Environmental Mitigation Program EMP). Schedule delay would be two years if notified at the time of the BO.
								Best Case	Assume that another 15 acres are required. Cost would be $2.25 million (from EMP). Schedule delay would be only a month because of early coordination with agencies.
								Most Likely	Assume that the best guess is that 20 acres will be required ($3 million from EMP). A 12-month schedule delay will occur.
2	Geotechnical	T	4	Differing Site Conditions	Lack of good soils data could result in incorrect assumptions about the foundation systems required for the building. This could affect the design, cost, and schedule of the foundation system.	Excavation reveals poor soils	High 75%	Worst Case	Assume that soils will require the installation of deep piles to compensate for poor soils. Assume a $2 million cost premium and a delay of one month to the project.
								Best Case	Assume that the current foundation design will only require minor modifications at a cost of $100,000 and no schedule delay.
								Most Likely	Assume that the current foundation design will only require moderate modifications at a cost of $500,000 and a two-week delay.

FIGURE 5.12 Risk Register

Probability		THREATS					OPPORTUNITIES				
Very High 95%	5	5	10	15	20	25	25	20	15	10	5
High 75%	4	4	8	12	16	20	20	16	12	8	4
Medium 50%	3	3	6	9	12	15	15	12	9	6	3
Low 25%	2	2	4	6	8	10	10	8	6	4	2
Very Low 5%	1	1	2	3	4	5	5	4	3	2	1
Impact		1	2	3	4	5	5	4	3	2	1
		Very Low	Low	Medium	High	Very High	Very High	High	Medium	Low	Very Low

FIGURE 5.13 Risk Probability and Impact Matrix

value is in conducting a value study. The value specialist must always keep in mind that the performance of a value study involves a significant allocation of time, money, and resources. There will be some individuals that question the need for conducting the value study in light of the cost. This is why it is important that the value specialist do an excellent job in communicating to the participants the value study process, objectives, and schedule. Copies of the value study schedule should be distributed to all participants, and an attendance sheet should be distributed to the group so that names and contact information can be documented.

After all the participants have been properly introduced, the value specialist should begin by clearly stating the objectives for the value study, which should have been identified in the prestudy meeting. Following this, the value specialist should refer everyone to the value study schedule and provide a brief overview of each major activity. It is important to stress that the value study will be considering all aspects of value, and not just cost. As cost cutting carries with it many negative connotations, it is best to emphasize the value improvement aspects of VM to maintain a positive and collaborative value study environment.

Often the value study's sponsor, who may be the project owner, will want to make a few statements regarding the study objectives and current state of the project. The importance of demonstrating the visible involvement of the study sponsor at this early stage of the process cannot be understated. The value specialist should always seek to encourage this, as it sends a very strong message to the participants. Management involvement is much better than management support.

Present Project Overview

An informational overview of the project should be presented by the project team. It is recommended that the project manager initiate this presentation by providing the value team with the project's history and objectives.

Following this introduction, a more detailed presentation of the project should be made by the project team members representing expertise in the various disciplines necessary to develop key project areas. This briefing should focus on a discussion of major project elements rather than finite technical details. For example, a project overview focusing on a new hospital should include input from the following project team members concerning the following project elements:

- Project manager—scope statement, project history, objectives, and budget
- Medical facilities planner—medical facility specifications, user requirements
- Architect—functional requirements, building layout, exterior and interior finishes
- Structural engineer—building structure
- Civil engineer—site work, vehicular circulation, site utilities
- Mechanical engineer—HVAC systems, plumbing, fire protection
- Electrical engineer—electrical distribution, lighting, data and communication systems

The point here is to acquaint the value team with the "big picture." Hopefully, each member of the value team will have had time to make a more detailed review of the technical documents.

Following this presentation, the value team should be afforded the opportunity to ask questions and receive additional clarifications concerning project information. The value specialist should ensure that the value team members utilize good human relations during this dialogue and that the questions are not phrased in a critical manner. The project team will be the value team's best source of information, and it is critical that a high level of professionalism be maintained in order to foster trust and openness during the VM process.

Identify Project Constraints and Stakeholder Issues

While all of the key participants are present, the value specialist should take the opportunity to ask the project team to identify constraints related to the project. Project constraints typically relate to issues beyond the control of the project team and may include political considerations, funding or revenue issues, regulatory requirements, and legal considerations. The value team must have a basic understanding of these constraints as they will have an impact on the types of alternatives they will generate later on in the value study process.

In addition to project constraints, there may be other concerns that external stakeholders will want the value team to consider. These may include issues related to indirect project impacts to the public. These types of issues are common with construction projects where there may be citizens and businesses that may be directly or indirectly affected by the project. This information should be solicited from the participants and documented.

It is recommended that the value specialist record these on a flip chart or white board, or utilize a multimedia projector so that all participants can be involved in the documentation of these constraints and issues.

Identify and Measure Project Performance—Value Metrics

Once the project overview has been completed, the value specialist should review the project's performance objectives with both the value team and the project team. Performance attributes and requirements should be identified and defined prior to the value study, as discussed in Chapter 4, "Preparation." For example, a project focused on making improvements to a 1.5-ton forklift truck might have identified the performance attributes and requirements shown in Figure 5.14.

Each of the performance attributes and requirements should also have been defined and documented (as discussed in Chapter 4), so the value specialist should confirm that the project team is still in agreement with them. The value specialist should now ask the project team to describe how the current project is meeting each performance attribute. The rationale provided by the project team should be recorded for each performance attribute, as identified in Figure 5.15. This information will establish a baseline understanding of how the current project is meeting the project's original scope statement.

When the project's current performance has been identified, the value specialist should ask the project team to identify specific parameters for each of the performance attributes. It is important to remember that performance requirements do not have parameters, but rather, they establish specific conditions that must be met

1.5-Ton Forklift Truck

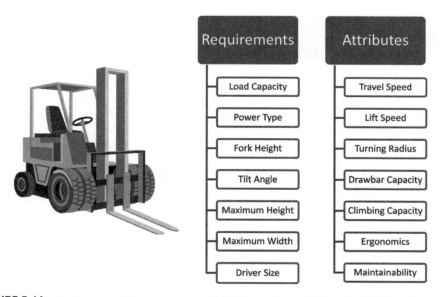

FIGURE 5.14 Performance Requirements and Attributes for a 1.5-Ton Forklift Truck

1.5-Ton Forklift Truck

Requirements	Attributes
Load Capacity • 3,000 lbs.	**Travel Speed** • 10.3 mph
Power Type • Gasoline	**Lift Speed** • 118 fpm
Fork Height • 130 in.	**Turning Radius** • 71.5 in.
Tilt Angle • 5 degrees	**Drawbar Capacity** • 1,540 lbs.
Maximum Height • 180" with raised mast	**Climbing Capacity** • 40% tan q, w/load
Maximum Width • 42"	**Ergonomics** • Finger tip steering, adj. seat, good visibility
Driver Size • Accommodate driver between 5' to 7' & 100 lbs. to 300 lbs.	**Maintainability** • Cushion tires, 6-gal. fuel tank, 5.3-gal. oil

FIGURE 5.15   Baseline Performance Levels for a 1.5-Ton Forklift Truck

in order to meet the project's scope statement. A maximum and minimum value should be established for each of the performance attributes. These should reflect the lowest acceptable and highest reasonable performance levels for each attribute and not necessarily the highest and lowest values that are achievable.

In the forklift example, the technology exists to create a forklift that can exceed 60 miles per hour; however, such high speeds far exceed the average forklift customer's needs. This is an excellent, if rather obvious, illustration of why parameters must be established using the customer's or user's requirements (see Figure 5.16).

The value team must have a clear understanding of the project's performance attributes and parameters if they are to improve value. The performance must be in line with the customer or user's needs, since unnecessary performance will not contribute to optimum value. The next step in the performance identification step is to begin the process of measuring project performance.

Develop Performance Attribute Scales

Having established the project's performance attributes and related parameters, the next activity in Value Metrics is to set up a system of performance measurement. This is accomplished by developing a rating scale based upon the parameters identified for each of the performance attributes.

For the sake of simplicity, it is recommended that scales based on values ranging from 0 to 1 be utilized. This, in essence, provides a simple ratio scale whereby a 0 indicates unacceptable performance, while a 1 would define the maximum amount of performance desired relative to fulfilling the project's purpose

1.5-Ton Forklift Truck

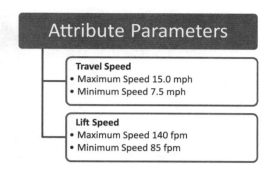

FIGURE 5.16 Example of Performance Attribute Parameters

TABLE 5.2 Example of a Quantitative Scale for a Performance Attribute

Travel Speed

Definition:	A measure of the travel speed of an unloaded forklift. The speed is measured in miles per hour.	
Verbal Rating	**Description of Performance**	**Numeric Rating**
Excellent	15.0 mph	(1.0)
Very Good	13.125 mph	(0.875)
Good	11.25 mph	(0.75)
Fair	9.375 mph	(0.625)
Meets Requirement	7.5 mph	(0.50)

and need. If we are constructing a scale based directly on numerical data (e.g., travel speed), then we can construct a ratio scale between 0 and 1 that represents the relative differences between the minimum and maximum values. Optionally, a scale of 0 to 10 or 0 to 100 could also be used. In any event, what is important to maintain is a ratio measure.

Building on the forklift example, we can identify a range of performance levels and assign their relative values (see Table 5.2). This example assumes that a linear scale is being used, meaning that there is a uniform distribution of measurement between the ratings. In this case, the minimum requirement for travel speed of 7.5 mph is assigned a numeric rating of 0.50. The maximum value, which is a top desired speed of 15.0 mph, is approximately double the minimum speed, is therefore assigned a numeric value of 1.0. The intermediate numeric ratings are distributed evenly between the high and low values on the scale.

However, it may not always be desirable to use a linear scale. For nonlinear scales, utility curves can be created for each performance attribute to graphically reinforce the logic of the rating scales. Both Fallon and T. Fowler[10] present good models for developing utility curves for this express purpose. Figure 5.17 illustrates a nonlinear utility curve reflecting customer preference for speeds between 10.5 to 12 mph. Ratings for speeds higher and lower than this range will thus have a smaller incremental effect on performance.

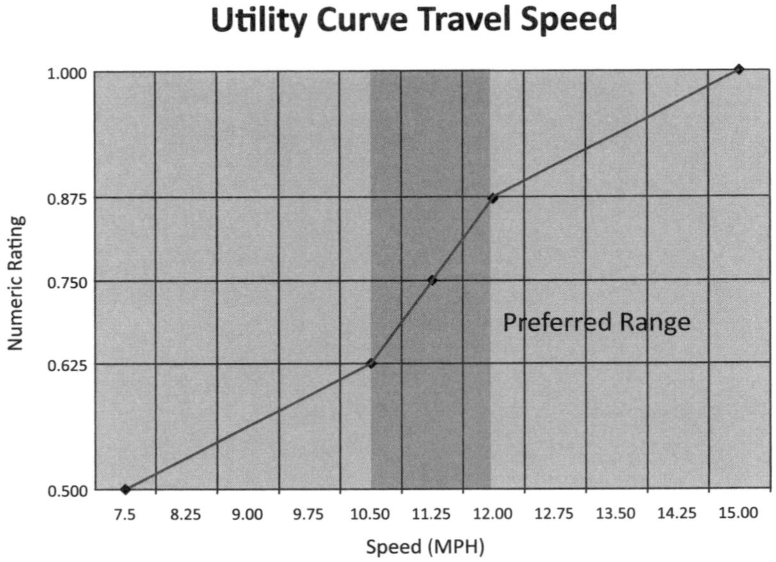

FIGURE 5.17   Nonlinear Utility Curve

Utility curves provide a graphical means of defining the relationship between the upper and lower parameters of the numeric scale. Figure 5.18 shows a range of potential utility curves, and their meanings, for a performance attribute called "travel speed."

There are two possible methods for calibrating the scales—quantitative and qualitative. Quantitative scales can be used where data is readily available. The previous examples illustrated for "travel speed" reflect quantitative scales.

Qualitative scales are useful for measuring performance attributes for which hard data does not exist, are subjective in nature, and/or are difficult to quantify within the time frame of a value study. An example of a qualitative scale is shown in Table 5.3.

Regardless of which type of scale is selected, it is important to define the performance quantification relative to each of the numerical ratings. This will become apparent later in the process when rating the alternative concepts.

Additionally, the value specialist may opt to move the performance identification process to the Preparation Phase. This often makes good sense and provides the owner, project team, and project stakeholders additional time to consider performance.

Determine Relative Importance of Performance Attributes

Individual rating scales will need to be developed for each performance attribute. Once this has been completed, the importance of the various performance attributes relative to the project's need and purpose should next be determined using an AHP paired comparison. AHP is an acronym for Analytic Hierarchy Process, which is a decision structure developed by Dr. Thomas Saaty in the 1970s while he was a professor at the Wharton School of Business. AHP is a very flexible and powerful

Utility Curves Travel Speed

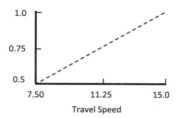

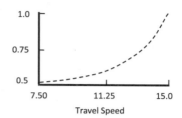

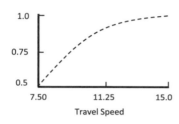

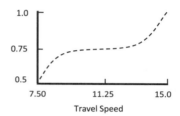

FIGURE 5.18 Examples of Different Utility Curves

TABLE 5.3 Example of a Qualitative Scale for a Performance Attribute

Ergonomics

Definition:	A measure of how well the vehicle can be adjusted to optimize the use of the machine to a specific user. This attribute considers comfort, ease of use, and productivity.	
Verbal Rating	**Description of Performance**	**Numeric Rating**
Excellent	Design provides excellent ergonomic performance in the following areas: *Seating *Steering *Cab dimensions *Features that reduce operator stress *Visibility *Controls *Cab ingress/egress	(0.95)
Very Good	Design provides very good ergonomic performance.	(0.75)
Good	Design provides good ergonomic performance.	(0.50)
Fair	Design provides fair ergonomic performance.	(0.25)
Meets Requirement	Design meets the minimum acceptable level of ergonomic performance.	(0.05)

system for group decision making that uses scaled paired comparisons based upon a fundamental scale. Value Metrics is predicated on the principles of AHP.

The first step is to determine the relative importance (referred to as priorities) of the performance attributes. There are two dimensions to consider in determining relative importance: (1) the importance of the performance attribute in meeting the project's need and purpose, and (2) the importance of the impacts relative to the ranges being considered in the rating scales. In other words, an attribute that is of high importance in meeting the project's need and purpose that has a high degree of impact in terms of its measurement would dominate an attribute that is also of high importance that has a low degree of impact. In the forklift example, it is highly unlikely that all seven of the performance attributes are of equal importance; therefore, we must have a means for determining this. The performance attributes are compared in pairs, asking, "Which of these two performance attributes is more important in satisfying the project's purpose and need?" In this method, a pair of attributes is compared using the Fundamental Scale as defined in Table 5.4.[11]

The Project Team and other stakeholders evaluate the relative importance of the performance attributes that are used to evaluate the baseline concept and value alternatives. The process for completing the Performance Attribute Matrix involves the following steps:

TABLE 5.4   AHP Fundamental Scale

AHP FUNDAMENTAL SCALE

Intensity of Importance	Definition	Explanation
1	Equal importance	The two attributes contribute equally to the project's need and purpose.
3	Moderate importance	Experience and judgment slightly favor one attribute over another.
5	Strong importance	Experience and judgment strongly favor one attribute over another.
7	Very strong importance	Experience and judgment very strongly favor one attribute over another.
9	Extreme importance	The evidence favoring one activity over another is of the highest possible importance.
2, 4, 6, 8	For compromises between the preceding values	Sometimes there is a need to compromise between the preceding values in which case these intermediate values can be used.
Reciprocals	If attribute x has one of the above nonzero numbers assigned to it when compared to attribute y, then y has the reciprocal value when compared with x.	Used to represent the reciprocal value of the dominant attribute for the weak attribute for a paired comparison.

- *List performance attributes.* Enter the names of all of the performance attributes into the matrix.
- *Discuss pairs.* Compare attribute pairs by asking, "Which of these two performance attributes is more important in satisfying the project's purpose and need?" The first step is to determine which attribute is more important. Once the dominant attribute has been identified, the next step is to apply the AHP Fundamental Scale to determine the degree of importance. An important thing to understand is the meaning behind the numbers in the AHP Fundamental Scale. In the example in Figure 5.19, the group discusses the importance of Travel Speed compared to Lift Speed. It is decided that Travel Speed is moderately more important than Lift Speed from the perspective of the customer, and in considering the importance of the impacts in the rating scales. Based on this assessment, an intensity of 2 is entered using the AHP Fundamental Scale. The intensities of 1–9 on the AHP Fundamental Scale represent orders of magnitude. In this case, the group is saying that the intensity of importance of Travel Speed is twice that of Lift Speed. If the two attributes were felt to be of equal importance, than a 1 would be assigned (i.e., 1:1).

The process is continued for all pairs until the matrix is completed. If additional sensitivity is desired, fractions can be used (i.e., 2.5 or 3.7). Once the intensity of the dominant attribute is assigned, the reciprocal must be assigned to the corresponding cell on the matrix. In the example above, the

PERFORMANCE ATTRIBUTE MATRIX								
1.5-Ton Forklift Truck								
Rate the relative importance of the attributes relative to the project's Need and Purpose.								
Performance Attributes	Travel Speed	Lift Speed	Turning Radius	Drawbar Capacity	Climbing Capacity	Ergonomics	Maintainability	PRIORITIES
Travel Speed	1	2	0.5	4	3	2	2	0.208
Lift Speed	0.5	1	0.333	3	0.5	0.5	0.5	0.082
Turning Radius	2	3	1	3	2	1	1	0.205
Drawbar Capacity	0.25	0.333	0.333	1	0.25	0.333	0.333	0.044
Climbing Capacity	0.333	2	0.5	4	1	2	0.2	0.116
Ergonomics	0.5	2	1	3	0.5	1	0.2	0.112
Maintainability	0.5	2	1	3	5	5	1	0.234
SUB TOTALS	5.08	12.33	4.67	21.00	12.25	11.83	5.23	1.000

FIGURE 5.19 Performance Attribute Matrix (using AHP paired comparisons)

reciprocal of 2 is 1/2 or 0.5. This value is entered into the corresponding cell. Be sure to enter the values in the correct cells. Reading the values in the cells by rows will always tell you how an attribute in that row was rated as compared to the attribute listed in the column. Therefore, it is easiest if the comparisons are made row by row rather than column by column. In other words, perform all of the comparisons on Row A first, followed by Row B, and so on.

- *Total scores.* The Performance Attribute Matrix utilizes what is called a normalized eigenvector. The process for determining the priorities of the performance attributes involves the following steps:
  1. Total the intensities for each column. In the example, we would add the intensities in the first column (Travel Speed) first: $(1 + 0.5 + 2 + 0.25 + 0.333 + 0.5 + 0.5 = 5.08)$. Do this for each column.
  2. Determine the priorities of the attributes. This is calculated by taking the intensity value in each cell, row by row, and dividing it by the sum of that column's total and then adding them all together. In the example, to calculate the priority of Travel Speed, we would take each value in the first row and divide it by the column total (i.e., Subtotal). We would then add these quotients together and divide them by the total number of attributes: $[(1/5.08) + (2/12.33) + (0.5/4.67) + (4/21) + (3/12.25) (2/11.83) + (2/5.23)]/7 = 0.208$. This process would be repeated for each attribute, row by row, until all priorities are established. The total of all priorities should, of course, equal 1. By this process, we have established the relative importance of the attributes in contributing to the performance of the project's need and purpose.

When the Performance Attribute Matrix has been completed, the results should be reviewed with the group to ensure that there is consistency in logic. At first glance, the mathematics involved can seem a little overwhelming. It is recommended that paired comparisons be made using specialized software (which is discussed further below) or by constructing a matrix with spreadsheet software such as Excel. The use of software will automate the calculations and allow the value specialist and the group to focus on eliciting the performance preferences.

The psychology behind the AHP merits further discussion. It must be remembered that AHP is being used to synthesize priorities (or preferences, if you like) for performance based upon judgments elicited from a group. Judgments are an expression of opinion and therefore are subjective in nature. By establishing which judgments are dominant, we are making a statement about what is more important. Further, we are using intensities as a means of how strongly we prefer one attribute or another. From this, we are able to derive mathematical priorities that give us a numeric representation of the relative measures of importance. The human brain is very good at comparing the relative difference between things.

To further illustrate this, we will consider a simple example initially presented by Saaty.[12] Assume we have three apples and wish to compare them using the AHP paired comparison method. Apple A is 12 cubic inches, Apple B is 6 cubic inches, and Apple C is 2 cubic inches. If we use their relative sizes as intensities (i.e., Apple A is 2 times larger than Apple B and 6 times larger than Apple C, while Apple B is 3 times larger than Apple C) and plot them on an eigenvector (see Figure 5.20),

Size Comparison	Apple A	Apple B	Apple C	Priorities
Apple A	12/12 = 1	12/6 = 2	12/2 = 6	0.600
Apple B	6/12 = 0.5	6/6 = 1	6/2 = 3	0.300
Apple C	2/12 = 0.167	2/6 = 0.333	2/2 = 1	0.100
Subtotal	1.667	3.333	10	1.000

FIGURE 5.20   AHP Paired Comparison of Apples

we derive priorities that are exactly proportional to the actual sizes of the apples. The cognitive sciences continue to present data collected from a variety of studies that further supports the hypothesis that humans make comparisons based upon the relative differences between things and not on absolute values.

Rate Performance of Baseline Concept(s)

Assuming the Performance Attributes, and their associated scales, have been defined and their priorities have been derived, the next step is to establish the performance of the Baseline Concept. The Project Team should take the lead in this process. Using the performance scales, each attribute should be rated accordingly. It is essential that a detailed description for the rating rationale be developed and recorded. Table 5.5 shows an example of how the baseline concept was rated by the project team based upon the scales that were developed to assess performance.

Some projects may have multiple design concepts; this is typical on public transportation and infrastructure projects where multiple design concepts are initially developed to satisfy environmental review processes. If this is the case, it is important to rate all of the design concepts and define their rating rationale. Once this has been completed, we can compare the performance ratings of the baseline concept and any other competing concepts. Figure 5.21 shows an example of a performance profile comparing the initial performance ratings of an existing forklift (Baseline Concept) and a new prototype (Design Option A). Both concepts were rated by the project team and we can see a side-by-side comparison of how they performed. The "Change in Performance" line gives us information on the net change in performance of Design Option A as compared to the Baseline Concept.

We can also consider performance another way by developing a performance profile that shows the contribution of each performance attribute to total performance. This is achieved by multiplying the performance ratings (illustrated in

TABLE 5.5 Performance Rating Rationale for Baseline Concept

Performance Rating—Baseline Concept (1.5-Ton Forklift Truck)

Performance Attribute	Rating	Rationale for Rating
Travel Speed	0.7	Current top travel speed is very good at 10.3 mph.
Ergonomics	0.6	Ergonomics are generally good. Key features include: *Seating is adjustable *Power steering has tilt adjust *Cab dimensions are roomy and will accommodate larger drivers *Excellent visibility with minimal obstructions *Controls are backlit and easy to reach/see
Maintainability	0.6	Maintainability is rated as fair due to limited gas tank capacity, and service hatches that are difficult to access. Service life on hydraulic components is excellent but current engine and drivetrain reliability could use improvement based on warranty service data for the current model.

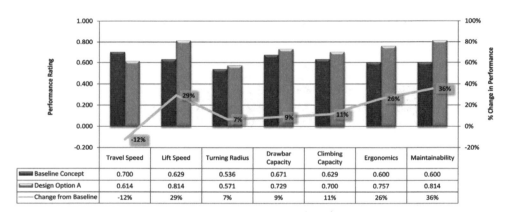

	Travel Speed	Lift Speed	Turning Radius	Drawbar Capacity	Climbing Capacity	Ergonomics	Maintainability
Baseline Concept	0.700	0.629	0.536	0.671	0.629	0.600	0.600
Design Option A	0.614	0.814	0.571	0.729	0.700	0.757	0.814
Change from Baseline	-12%	29%	7%	9%	11%	26%	36%

FIGURE 5.21 Performance Profile of Design Concepts (Forklift)

Figure 5.21) by the priorities developed for the attributes (see Figure 5.19). The raw data is summarized in Table 5.6.

Figure 5.22 provides us with the big picture, and in this example we can see that Design Option A (0.70) provides greater overall performance than the Baseline Concept (0.617).

One of the software programs available to organizations today is called Decision Lens.[13] Decision Lens fully utilizes the AHP method and follows a structure very similar to the one presented here for Value Metrics. Although it was designed to provide an interactive structure for complex decisions, such as strategic investment and portfolio planning, it also works well for assessing project performance. One of the major advantages of Decision Lens is its use of interactive remote control

TABLE 5.6 Summary of Performance Scores

Performance Attributes	Priorities	Baseline Concept		Design Option A	
		Rating	Score	Rating	Score
	P	R	(P×R)	R	(P×R)
Travel Speed	0.208	0.700	0.146	0.614	0.128
Lift Speed	0.082	0.629	0.052	0.814	0.067
Turning Radius	0.205	0.536	0.110	0.571	0.117
Drawbar Capacity	0.044	0.671	0.030	0.729	0.032
Climbing Capacity	0.116	0.629	0.073	0.700	0.081
Ergonomics	0.112	0.600	0.067	0.750	0.084
Maintainability	0.234	0.600	0.140	0.814	0.190
Total Performance Scores			0.617		0.700

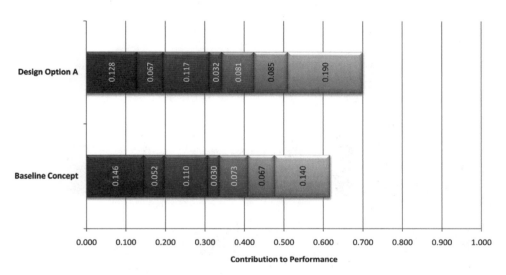

■ Travel Speed ■ Lift Speed ■ Turning Radius ■ Drawbar Capacity ▨ Climbing Capacity ▨ Ergonomics ▨ Maintainability

FIGURE 5.22 Aggregated Performance Profile of Forklift Concepts

keypads. This allows all participants to key in their individual preferences and priorities without requiring a facilitator to develop consensus. As a result, this approach results in a much more accurate and representative assessment of performance. This is particularly useful when there are multiple stakeholders that hold opposing viewpoints. Figure 5.23 displays a screen shot of an AHP paired comparison using Decision Lens during an actual value study.[14] Note that all participants are able to express their preferences directly and the system automatically calculates the average intensities.

Figure 5.24 displays another screen shot from the Decision Lens software. This chart on the right-hand side is similar to the one presented in Figure 5.22, which provides a side-by-side comparison of the performance of competing design

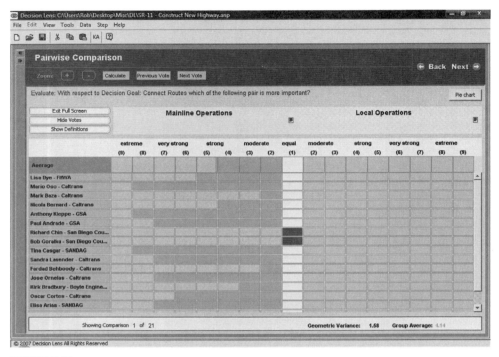

FIGURE 5.23   Paired Comparisons—Decision Lens

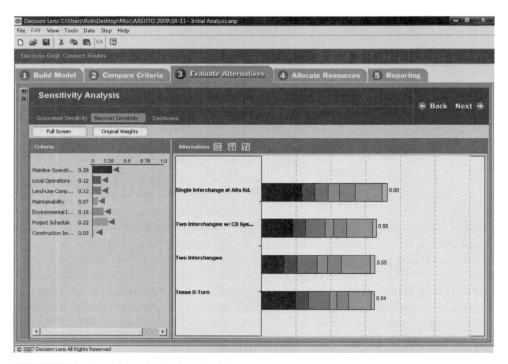

FIGURE 5.24   Sensitivity Analysis—Decision Lens

concepts. Decision Lens permits sensitivity analysis to be performed by the group after the fact. The relative priorities of the attributes can be adjusted to see how they influence the total performance of the competing concepts. This is a very powerful function and is extremely useful in testing the group's assumptions and revealing additional information about the impact of performance.

Another important advantage in utilizing specialized software is that allows more complex hierarchies to be considered while maintaining a reasonable degree of simplicity. For example, a performance attribute could be broken down into multiple subattributes and assigned relative priorities. Using the forklift example, "Ergonomics" could be broken down into subattributes like "Comfort," "User Interface," and "Visibility" to describe different aspects of ergonomic performance. Doing so requires a separate paired comparison of the subattributes to derive their relative priorities with respect to the parent attribute, "Ergonomics." The trade-off is greater sensitivity in attribute measurement in exchange for a more complex analytical structure. It is generally not recommended to use this approach without using the appropriate software unless there is sufficient time to perform the analysis as the additional complexity could significantly increase the time requirements for the analysis.

Determine Value of Baseline Concept(s)

The priorities that are derived from the Performance Attribute Matrix are utilized in measuring total project performance. All of the information developed on the baseline project's cost and performance at this point can be summarized using the Value Matrix.

The Value Matrix facilitates the comparison of competing concepts and/or value alternatives by organizing and summarizing the data developed for performance, cost, and schedule (and potentially risk) into a matrix format. A value index is derived based on one of the equations selected for functional value (see Chapter 2).

All competing concepts are compared to the baseline concept for the all attributes in order to compare and contrast the potential for value improvement. The matrix is essential for understanding the relationship of cost, performance, and value of the project baseline and of the concepts developed during the VM process. Comparing the performance and cost suggests which alternatives are potentially as good as or better than the project's baseline concept in terms of overall value. Comparison at the value index level suggests which alternatives have the best performance versus cost, or provides the project with the "best value."

For Table 5.7, we will assume that the simple algorithm of performance over cost will be used to derive the value index. The variables of schedule and risk will be discussed in greater depth later in this chapter.

The total performance scores for each concept (which is calculated by multiplying the performance rating by the performance priority for each Performance Attribute) are divided by the total cost. To maintain consistency, costs are converted into a ratio scale. It is not absolutely essential that this be done, and if cost is the only element on the input side, then the raw costs could also be utilized. To convert costs into relative scores, add the costs for the various concepts together and then divide the cost of each option by the total to develop a relative score

TABLE 5.7   Converting Costs of Concepts to a Relative Score

Concepts	Total Cost	Relative Score
Baseline Concept	$15,000	0.484
Design Option A	$16,000	0.516
Total	$31,000	1.000

TABLE 5.8   Value Matrix Comparing Baseline Concept and Design Option

Concepts	Performance Score	Cost Score	Value Index	Change in Value
Baseline Concept	0.617	0.484	1.275	N/A
Design Option A	0.700	0.516	1.357	6%

expressed as a ratio. The result expresses cost in the same 0 to 1 ratio used for performance.

For our example, we are ready to calculate the relative value of the forklift concepts. Because we are only considering the variables of performance and cost, the value index is derived by dividing the performance score by the cost score (see Table 5.8).

The results show that Design Option A, although being more expensive, offers the best value (6 percent more than the Baseline Concept) when considering performance. This has been expressed graphically in Figure 5.25.

Depending on which value equation is used (which depends on how project schedule will be considered), the following steps are needed to determine the value index for the Baseline Design Concept and each value strategy:

- If schedule is assessed as an output (i.e., like performance), then $V_f = \dfrac{(P+T)}{C}$

  is used. In this method, time has already been calculated and included as part of the total performance score.

- If schedule is assessed as an input (i.e., like cost), than $V_f = \dfrac{P}{(C+T)}$ is used.

  In this case, time must be converted into a ratio scale as well (similar to the above example for cost) and the relative importance (i.e., priority) of cost and schedule must be determined. As there are only two input variables (cost and time), the priorities are easily achieved by directly assigning weights to them. Let us assume that for our forklift example the Project Team decides that cost is more important than schedule (in this example, assume production time is being assessed independent of cost and that there is no "double counting"). Based on internal discussion, they decide that cost should represent 0.8 (80 percent) and schedule 0.2 (20 percent) of the total inputs (see Table 5.9).

  If the value matrix is recalculated to consider the composite effect of both time and cost, we can see how the value indices change (see Table 5.10).

- If a quantitative risk analysis was performed, the resulting data could be included in the totals for cost and schedule when computing the value indices.

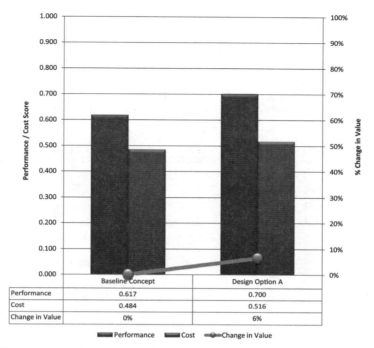

FIGURE 5.25 Comparison of Value—Forklift Concepts

TABLE 5.9 Converting Schedules of Concepts into Relative Scores

Concepts	Total Time	Relative Score
Baseline Concept	42 days	0.600
Design Option A	28 days	0.400
Total	70 days	1.000

TABLE 5.10 Value Matrix Considering Both Cost and Schedule

Strategies	Outputs Performance Score		Inputs Cost Score		Schedule Score		Total Score	Value Index	Change in Value
Priorities	1.0		0.8		0.2				
Baseline Concept	0.617	0.617	0.484	0.387	0.6	0.12	0.507	1.216	N/A
Design Option A	0.700	0.700	0.516	0.413	0.4	0.08	0.493	1.420	17%

Regardless of which equation is selected, the Value Matrix is essential for understanding the relationship of cost, performance, schedule, and risk as well as the value of the Baseline Concept and of the Value Strategies. The comparison of these elements in this manner exposes the trade-offs between the inputs and the outputs and provides useful information to decision makers in acting upon the information developed during the value study.

Conduct Site Visit

Depending on the type of project being studied, a site visit may be scheduled and can be an important part of the Information Phase. When possible, site visits should always be conducted for projects dealing with the design and construction of facilities. Site visits are also strongly recommended for product studies. An incredible amount of valuable information can be gathered through this firsthand view of the existing site and conditions.

Site visits conducted for construction projects should provide enough time to survey the entire site. Ideally, the project manager or project engineer will lead the site visit and identify the location of key project elements. Existing utilities, site circulation, construction staging, and property issues can be discussed on a firsthand basis. If conducting a site visit is not practical or feasible, consideration should be given to obtaining a video survey of the site, or barring this, aerial photographs of the site.

Site visits for product studies may include a walkthrough of the current manufacturing operations. This will help the team gain a better understanding by visualizing the existing process. Many times, the value team members will pick up on small details of manufacturing processes that will open the door to a series of questions. It is surprising how much creativity can be stimulated through this process.

If the study is focusing on an existing product, at least one completely assembled unit should be available for the value team to study. The various parts should also be made available for closer inspection. It is also useful to see the product itself operate. This is not always possible at the factory location, so consideration should be given to visiting a customer or user site to witness the operation of the product. If the product is large in scale, it is recommended that the value study be physically located near or adjacent to an assembled unit. The ability of the value team to get close to and study the product will again help stimulate creativity and develop a better understanding of the product's functions. If competing products exist, then these should be obtained, or rented in the case of large durable goods, for study and review by the value team.

Summary

During the Information Phase, the value team must gain a sound understanding of the project's scope, schedule, cost, and risks. The value team develops an understanding of project scope through a thorough review of project documents, listening to and engaging with the project team, identifying the constraints and issues of the project stakeholders, and conducting a site visit. The application of Value Metrics will help the value team develop a much deeper understanding of project performance through the identification of performance attributes and the establishment of a system for measuring performance. The utilization of cost models and the application of life cycle costing methods will allow the value team to develop an understanding of project cost, while the application of project scheduling techniques and software will provide them with a solid grounding with respect to understanding project schedule. Finally, developing an understanding of project risks can unearth a treasure trove of opportunities for the value team to enhance project value.

The flow of information requires careful management as the value team must digest an immense quantity of information in a relatively short period. Every effort must be made to make the best use of the information at hand. The techniques and methods discussed in this chapter are presented toward achieving this objective.

Appendix 5A: Case Study

In the weeks between the time of the prestudy meeting and the start of the value study, the value specialist selected the value team members, coordinated the distribution of project documents to them, and began reviewing and analyzing this information in greater detail. What follows is a summarized account of this information and analysis.

Project Drawings

The project's design had completed the Predesign phase, which is roughly equivalent to 10 to 15 percent of design completion. As part of the Predesign Report, drawings were included that provide details concerning the Technical High School. These drawings (see Figure 5.26) and the supporting cost and schedule information constitute the "baseline" concept for the project to which the alternatives developed during the course of the value study would be compared.

Cost Information

The value team reviewed the Predesign Concept Cost Estimate. A summary of the estimate for both Phase 1 and Phase 2 is presented in Table 5.11. Based on this information, a simple Pareto cost model was prepared (see Figure 5.27).

One of the observations made by the value team in analyzing the cost data was surprisingly that the cost of transforming the existing Supermarket Building into the Technical Building was relatively high. In fact, this cost was nearly as high as the cost of the new Classroom Building, which was to be entirely new construction. Most of the individuals involved on the project had assumed that the cost of utilizing the existing structure would be significantly less. Further, the strategy of splitting the renovation of the Supermarket Building into two phases seemed to be fraught with inefficiencies. Clearly, this information indicated to the value team that

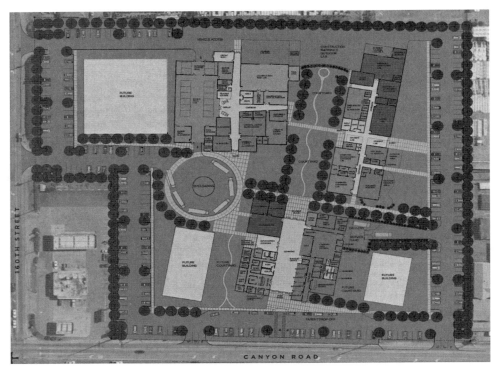

FIGURE 5.26   Site Plan, New Technical High School

both the phasing approach and the adaptation of the Supermarket Building should be a major focus of the value team's efforts.

Educational Program

The value team reviewed the Predesign Concept Report and additional information. The project's educational program was distilled and summarized into the following table in order to better understand the size, location, and costs of the various educational components (see Table 5.12).

The analysis of the project's educational program raised further questions about the adaptation of the Supermarket Building. One of the misleading features in the way the cost estimate was broken down between the two phases was that all of the shell upgrades were being accomplished along with only one-third of the interior renovations in Phase 1. In order to arrive at a true area cost, the Phase 1 interior renovations should include the cost of the shell upgrades as well. Once this was calculated, the total SF costs of renovating the existing Supermarket Building into the Technology Building exceeded the cost of both the Classroom and the Administration Buildings!

Further, the value team began to develop a better understanding of what types of activities were being supported in various program spaces. Questions began to arise regarding the necessity for some of the programs and the value study team's

TABLE 5.11 Cost Estimate, New Technical High School

New Technical High School
Predesign Concept Cost Estimate

Design Phase:	Predesign
Date of Estimate:	7/29/2008
Month of Cost Basis:	Jul–08

Phase 1 Construction

	Size	Unit	Unit Cost	Total
Administration Building	25,017	SF	$343.62	$8,596,342
Classroom Building	25,348	SF	$292.23	$7,407,446
Tech. Bldg.—Shell Upgrades	35,830	SF	$33.03	$1,183,465
Tech. Bldg.—Interior Improvements	8,016	SF	$203.51	$1,631,336
Tech. Bldg.—Exterior Canopy	1	LS	$391,145.00	$391,145
Sitework	1	LS	$4,756,014.00	$4,756,014
Off-Site Improvements	1	LS	$120,085	$120,085
			Subtotal	$24,085,833

Project Soft Costs	% of Construction		Total
State Sales Tax	8.80%		$2,119,553
Architect/Engineer Fee	12.00%		$2,890,300
Permits	0.70%		$168,601
Testing and Inspection	lump sum		$110,000
Construction Contingency	5.00%		$1,310,312
Building Furnishings and Equipment	lump sum		$2,360,026
Builders Risk Insurance	0.50%		$120,429
Construction Management	1.00%		$240,858
Utility Connections	lump sum		$240,000
Legal Services	lump sum		$50,000
Overall Project Contingency	0.80%		$192,687
		Subtotal	$9,802,766
		Total Phase 1 Project Cost	$33,888,599
Phase 1 Add-Alternate Item: Multipurpose Room			$2,131,818

Phase 2 Construction	Size	Unit	Unit Cost	Total
Tech. Bldg.—Additional Renovations	27,814	SF	$263.73	$7,335,386
Sitework	1	LS	$862,068.00	$862,068
			Subtotal	*$8,197,454*

Project Soft Costs	% of Construction		Total
State Sales Tax	8.80%		$721,376
Architect/Engineer Fee	12.00%		$983,695
Permits	0.70%		$57,382
Testing and Inspection	lump sum		$110,000
Construction Contingency	5.00%		$409,873
Building Furnishings and Equipment	lump sum		$827,425

(Continued)

TABLE 5.11   (Continued)

Builders Risk Insurance	0.50%	$40,987
Construction Management	1.00%	$81,975
Utility Connections	lump sum	$240,000
Legal Services	lump sum	$50,000
Overall Project Contingency	0.80%	$65,580
	Subtotal	$3,588,292
	Total Phase 2 Project Cost	$11,785,746

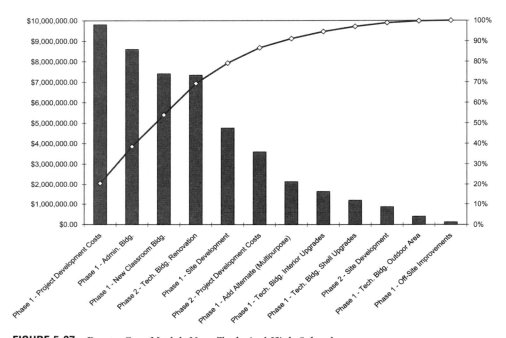

FIGURE 5.27   Pareto Cost Model, New Technical High School

educational planner and technical high school principal began making notes regarding their observations.

Schedule Information

The project's schedule information was limited at this early stage of the design. A high-level GANTT chart had been developed (see Figure 5.28).

Project Opportunities

The value team members were asked to provide the value specialist with their questions, comments, and observations concerning their review of the project

TABLE 5.12 Educational Program, New Technical High School

SUMMARY OF EDUCATIONAL PROGRAM

Technical High School Project

Program Spaces	Building	Phase	Total SF	% Bldg. Area	Cost/SF	Total Cost
Engine Tech.	Technology	2	11,655	28.7%	$296.76	$3,458,738
Commons/Circulation	Technology	2	4,960	12.2%	$296.76	$1,471,930
Criminal Justice	Technology	2	3,500	8.6%	$296.76	$1,038,660
Creative Design	Technology	2	2,660	6.6%	$296.76	$789,382
Engine Tech.—Outdoor	Technology	2	2,000	4.9%	$76.17	$152,340
General Classrooms	Technology	2	1,900	4.7%	$296.76	$563,844
Student Lounge	Technology	2	385	0.9%	$296.76	$114,253
Staff Work Room	Technology	2	260	0.6%	$296.76	$77,158
Restrooms	Technology	2	60	0.1%	$296.76	$17,806
Construction Tech.	Technology	1	6,800	16.8%	$236.54	$1,608,472
Construction Tech. —Outdoor	Technology	1	5,135	12.7%	$76.17	$391,145
Mech/Elec	Technology	1	700	1.7%	$236.54	$165,578
Restrooms	Technology	1	565	1.4%	$236.54	$133,645
Materials Engineering	Classroom	1	6,250	23.8%	$292.23	$1,826,438
Computer Labs	Classroom	1	4,150	15.8%	$292.23	$1,212,755
Circulation	Classroom	1	3,260	12.4%	$292.23	$952,670
Veterinary Asst.	Classroom	1	1,350	5.1%	$292.23	$394,511
Large Laboratory	Classroom	1	2,700	10.3%	$292.23	$789,021
Therapeutic Lab	Classroom	1	2,500	9.5%	$292.23	$730,575
General Classrooms	Classroom	1	2,300	8.7%	$292.23	$672,129
Materials Eng.—Outdoor	Classroom	1	1,310	5.0%	$76.17	$99,783
Student Lounge	Classroom	1	900	3.4%	$292.23	$263,007
Restrooms	Classroom	1	625	2.4%	$292.23	$182,644
Mech/Elec	Classroom	1	550	2.1%	$292.23	$160,727
Staff Work Room	Classroom	1	400	1.5%	$292.23	$116,892
Culinary Arts	Administration	1	8,200	28.2%	$343.62	$2,817,684
Commons/Circulation	Administration	1	6,575	22.6%	$343.62	$2,259,302
Administrative Offices	Administration	1	4,500	15.5%	$343.62	$1,546,290
Teaching Academy	Administration	1	2,400	8.3%	$343.62	$824,688
Multipurpose and Testing	Administration	1	2,000	6.9%	$343.62	$687,240
Restrooms	Administration	1	1,400	4.8%	$343.62	$481,068
Information Commons	Administration	1	1,200	4.1%	$343.62	$412,344
Mech./Elec.	Administration	1	900	3.1%	$343.62	$309,258
Deli	Administration	1	800	2.8%	$343.62	$274,896
Shipping/Receiving	Administration	1	560	1.9%	$343.62	$192,427
Custodial/Storage	Administration	1	500	1.7%	$343.62	$171,810
		TOTAL	**95,910**			**$27,361,105**

Breakdown by Phase	Total SF	Total Cost
Phase 1	68,530	$19,676,996
Phase 2	27,380	$7,684,109

Breakdown by Building	Total SF	Total Cost
Admin. Bldg.	29,035	$9,977,007
Classroom Bldg.	26,295	$7,401,149
Tech. Bldg.	40,580	$9,982,949

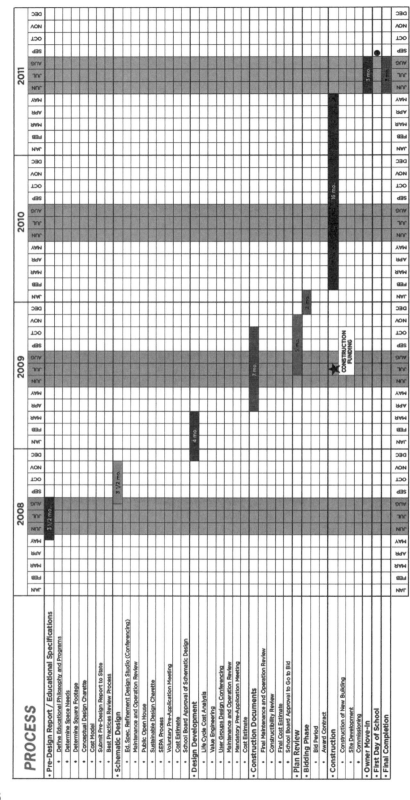

FIGURE 5.28 Project Schedule, New Technical High School

136

documents. These comments were shared among the team members prior to commencement of the value study and helped prepare the team in thinking about opportunities for value improvement.

- It is unclear from the Predesign Concept where the data is that supports the specific programs being included in the Skills Center. Are there specific forecasts for the number of anticipated students for each program?
- Some programs will require significantly more space and/or expensive equipment than others. Do the enrollment forecasts warrant the expense of these programs? Is this a good investment?
- Is Travel/Tourism a viable vocation in this day and age? This industry has all but vanished with the advent of Internet travel planning.
- The emphasis for most private technical high schools is medical technology, information technology, and criminal justice. Looking at the program, these are among the smallest program spaces. Does this make sense?
- What is the rationale for splitting up this program into multiyear construction? It appears there is a $10 million premium in project escalation to do this.
- The culinary arts program appears to include both catering and food service curriculum. Generally, the food service curriculum is by the far the most popular among students. It is recommended that the value team explore reconfiguring this space.
- Does the phasing of program spaces match vocational demand patterns?
- The collision and engine repair shops are the most expensive and equipment-intensive programs. Do the student forecasts and vocational demands warrant this expense?
- The cost of renovating the Supermarket Building exceeds the cost of constructing new buildings. It is unclear what is driving these costs up.
- The costs for the Supermarket Building shell renovations do not appear to include enough money for seismic upgrades to meet code.
- The construction phasing plan should be revisited. There are opportunities to improve efficiency and the delivery of the educational program by rethinking this.

Kick-Off Meeting

The kick-off meeting for the value study began with introductions and an overview of the VM process by the value specialist. This was followed by an overview of the project's history and development by the principal of the new technical high school. The design team then presented the Predesign Concept plans and the educational program. The value team asked many questions related to their observations during their review of the project documents and the project team provided clarifications.

Following the presentation of the Predesign Concept, the value specialist focused the group's attention on project performance. Those present reviewed the list of performance requirements and attributes to ensure that there was still a consensus that they described the project's performance accurately. A few minor edits to some of the definitions were made, but otherwise the group felt comfortable with the development of the performance information.

During the interim period between the prestudy meeting and the first day of the value study, the value specialist had prepared preliminary performance scales for the six performance attributes. These scales were now presented to the group and discussed. The following scales were agreed upon and applied for the remainder of the value study effort (see Table 5.13).

The value specialist led the group through the process of determining the relative importance of the performance attributes. Emphasis was placed on eliciting the information first from the School District personnel, who represented the end users. AHP-paired comparisons were made via the performance attribute matrix (see Figure 5.29). The value specialist asked the question for each of the attribute pairs, "Which performance attribute provides the greatest benefit to the project relative to its need and purpose?" A lively discussion ensued concerning the strength of the group's preferences for performance. The value specialist worked carefully with the group to arrive at an intensity rating that best reflected their preferences. It was decided that "Program Compatibility" was clearly the most important aspect of performance as it had the greatest impact on the project's primary objective of providing facilities that supported the educational program. This was followed by "Building Organization" and "Site Organization," both of which were of great importance in influencing how efficiently the buildings and the campus as a whole worked to support the project's educational objectives. "Maintainability" followed the first three attributes and was considered to be important in ensuring the viability operations and maintenance of the campus over the course of its life. Finally, "Aesthetics" was considered to be of greater importance than "Phaseability," which reflected the thought that the appearance of the campus would be of concern throughout the life of the campus, while construction phasing issues were only of a limited duration. In light of this information, the value team's initial observations related to the construction phasing strategy were further reinforced as it was adding a great deal of cost to the project without contributing much in the way of performance.

The value specialist next led the group through the process of rating the performance of the Predesign Concept. As there were no additional design concepts being considered, it was only necessary to rate the one concept that serves as the baseline for comparing value alternatives against.

The performance of the Predesign Concept was discussed at length for each attribute, again focusing on the responses from the School District personnel who represent the users of the project. Table 5.14 summarizes this information. Each attribute was then rated relative to the performance scales.

Overall, the School District staff felt that the Predesign Concept provided a good overall level of performance, but it highlighted areas that could still be improved. Specifically, there were concerns expressed about the construction phasing approach as well as a number of program and organizational issues that could be improved on. The Value Metrics process had already proved to be of great benefit to both the value team and the design team because it provided insight into the user's preference for performance and opinions on how well the baseline concept achieved this.

The value specialist concluded the kick-off meeting by asking the project team to make a decision as to the relative importance of cost and time in the value equation. This was a simple decision; however, it generated a significant amount

TABLE 5.13 Performance Attribute Scales

Program Compatibility

Verbal Rating	Definition	Number Rating
Excellent	The size, shape, characteristics, and amenities of the interior spaces provide the highest level of performance and compatibility with the program and functioning of the building. The design greatly exceeds the original program and provides the highest desired level of performance in delivering the educational program.	(0.95)
Good	The size, shape, characteristics, and amenities of the interior spaces provide a greater than satisfactory level of performance and compatibility with the program and functioning of the building.	(0.75)
Fair	The size, shape, characteristics, and amenities of the interior spaces provide a satisfactory level of performance and compatibility with the program and functioning of the building.	(0.50)
Poor	The size, shape, characteristics, and amenities of the interior spaces provide a less than satisfactory level of performance and compatibility with the program and functioning of the building. Delivery of the educational program will be negatively affected by the design.	(0.25)
Very Poor	The design of the building is highly incompatible with the program. There are numerous and significant problems that greatly diminish the delivery of the educational program.	(0.05)

Building Organization

Verbal Rating	Definition	Number Rating
Excellent	The building(s) has been organized in a manner that provides the highest level of performance with respect to adjacencies of interior spaces, the efficiency of interior circulation, and ease of way finding.	(0.95)
Good	The site has been organized in a manner that exceeds expectations for performance with respect to adjacencies of interior spaces, the efficiency of interior circulation, and ease of way finding.	(0.75)
Fair	The site has been organized in a manner that provides a satisfactory level of performance with respect to adjacencies of interior spaces, the efficiency of interior circulation, and ease of way finding.	(0.50)

(Continued)

TABLE 5.13 (Continued)

Building Organization

Verbal Rating	Definition	Number Rating
Poor	The site has been organized in a manner that provides a less than satisfactory level of performance with respect to adjacencies of interior spaces, the efficiency of interior circulation, and ease of way finding.	(0.25)
Very Poor	The site has been organized in a manner that results in numerous and significant challenges related to adjacencies of interior spaces. the efficiency of interior circulation, and ease of way finding.	(0.05)

Site Organization

Verbal Rating	Definition	Number Rating
Excellent	The site has been organized in a manner that provides the highest level of operational efficiency with respect to site circulation, orientation of the building(s), and adjacencies of site elements and access to/from the site.	(0.95)
Good	The site has been organized in a manner that exceeds the major design objectives and will provide a greater than satisfactory level of operational performance.	(0.75)
Fair	The site has been organized in a manner that meets the major design objectives and will provide a satisfactory level of operational performance.	(0.50)
Poor	The site has been organized in a manner that does not meet some of the major design objectives and will provide a less than satisfactory level of operational performance.	(0.25)
Very Poor	The site has been organized in a manner that results in numerous and significant challenges related to circulation, access, adjacencies, and/or the orientation of the buildings. The design will significantly reduce operational efficiency for the post.	(0.05)

Aesthetics

Verbal Rating	Definition	Number Rating
Excellent	Overall project aesthetics are of the highest level of appropriateness and compatibility.	(0.95)
Good	Overall project aesthetics are of a greater than satisfactory level	(0.75)
Fair	Overall project aesthetics are of a satisfactory level	(0.50)
Poor	Overall project aesthetics are of a lower than satisfactory level.	(0.25)
Very Poor	Overall project aesthetics are inappropriate.	(0.05)

TABLE 5.13   (Continued)

Maintainability

Verbal Rating	Definition	Number Rating
Excellent	The project provides the highest possible level of maintainability and far exceeds expectations when compared to comparable facilities within the district.	(0.95)
Good	The project provides a high level of maintainability. The facility utilizes many low-maintenance features and is better than average in terms of expected maintenance.	(0.75)
Fair	The project provides a satisfactory level of maintainability and is typical of district facilities of this nature.	(0.50)
Poor	The project is expected to require greater than normal maintenance due to existing site conditions or materials selection.	(0.25)
Very Poor	The project is expected require maintenance that far exceeds the norm for a district facility of its kind.	(0.05)

Phaseability

Verbal Rating	Definition	Number Rating
Excellent	The project can be phased in a manner that will have no impact to ongoing operations and will not incur a cost premium.	(0.95)
Good	The project can be phased in a manner that will have only minor impacts to ongoing operations and cost.	(0.75)
Fair	The project can be phased in a manner that will have minor to moderate impacts to ongoing operations and cost.	(0.50)
Poor	The construction phasing approach will create significant operational and cost impacts.	(0.25)
Very Poor	The construction phasing approach will create major and disruptive operational impacts. Cost impacts will also be significant. Requires extraordinary mitigation measures and creates major inconveniences to the campus.	(0.05)

of discussion by the members of the design team and the School District staff. It was decided that at this point in the project, cost was definitely more important, especially considering the fact that the project was significantly over budget by nearly $9 million. After much debate, the project team decided that the distribution between cost and schedule was approximately 0.8 (cost) and 0.2 (schedule). Of course, the project milestone of initiating construction was a performance requirement and would have to be met regardless.

PERFORMANCE ATTRIBUTE MATRIX							
New Technical High School							
Rate the relative importance of the attributes relative to the project's Need and Purpose.							
Performance Attributes	Program Compatibility	Building Organization	Site Organization	Aesthetics	Phaseability	Maintainability	PRIORITIES
Program Compatibility	1	2	3	4	5	4	**0.360**
Building Organization	0.5	1	2	3	4	3	**0.231**
Site Organization	0.3333	0.5	1	3	3	2	**0.153**
Aesthetics	0.25	0.3333	0.3333	1	2	0.25	**0.068**
Phaseability	0.2	0.25	0.3333	0.5	1	0.2	**0.047**
Maintainability	0.25	0.3333	0.5	4	5	1	**0.141**
SUB-TOTALS	2.53	4.42	7.17	15.50	20.00	10.45	**1.00**

FIGURE 5.29   Performance Attribute Matrix, New Technical High School

The kick-off meeting was adjourned and the value team reconvened after lunch to conduct the site visit.

Site Visit

The value team was accompanied by the design team's project manager on the site visit. The team surveyed the existing conditions of the Supermarket Building and the surrounding area. The building itself was in reasonably good condition, but it required significant renovations in order to be usable for the educational programs that it would later support. The high-bay space was suitable for a number of technological programs involving machinery and heavy equipment; however, it was less suitable for some of the classroom-oriented programs that were also planned to be located there.

The existing parking lot was in need of repair and access from the adjacent streets would need to be redeveloped, considering other transportation improvement projects that were being planned by the city that would affect traffic patterns. Of these improvements, the major street running east-west was planned to be modified to separate traffic with a landscaped median. This would affect traffic turning into and out of the site and would force the main vehicular entrance onto the minor roadway running north-south.

TABLE 5.14 Baseline Concept Performance Evaluation, New Technical High School

Performance Attributes	Performance Rationale for Baseline Concept	Rating
Program Compatibility	The current concept provides adequate space to support all 12 programs. Most ancillary and supporting spaces are currently being provided for. There could be a need for additional locker, display, and breakout space. Some of the spaces in the Technical Building have been "forced" a little in order to fit the available space.	0.70
Building Organization	The buildings have been organized by like functions. The Technical Building (i.e., existing Supermarket Building), which is a high-bay space, has been allocated to industrial/construction programs. The Administration Building includes the Catering Program to support student activities. The use of three separate buildings allows some of them to be closed during off-hour adult learning times. The internal corridors could be laid out more efficiently, but the circulation appears to be adequate.	0.70
Site Organization	The campus is arranged as a pedestrian-friendly campus with a central axis running off the indoor commons area to an outdoor commons area. Circulation will be accommodated around the site perimeter. There are separate entrances for buses and cars. The county is placing some limits on parking spaces. Separate service entrances are provided for the buildings.	0.80
Aesthetics	Building materials currently include block masonry, clerestory windows, and metal siding on new buildings. The Supermarket Building will have a new matching veneer installed. Stained concrete floors in commons, carpet in classrooms. Landscaping is included for the commons area. There is a high-bay commons space in the Administration Building. The aesthetic development appears to be quite good at this stage in the development and	0.75
Phaseability	Phase 1 includes both new buildings; rehabilitation of the Supermarket Building shell and interior renovation of about 7,000 SF for Construction Tech. There is bid alternate for the Teaching Academy/Multipurpose (which would not be included in the event that the construction bids come in too high). Phase 2 finishes interior renovation of the Technical Building and the remainder of the site development (parking and landscaping). The Phase 2 renovations will create significant disruptions to the Phase 1 programs being supported in the Technical Building.	0.40
Maintainability	The State's Sustainable Schools Protocol (SSSP) for High Performance Schools is the project goal. Typical building materials for high school construction. The buildings are oriented to take advantage of day lighting and natural ventilation. Overall, the systems and materials selected should be maintainable and offer a good service life.	0.75

The design team had clearly done an excellent job of aligning the new buildings to take advantage of desirable view sheds toward a nearby mountain range. The orientation of the Supermarket Building posed access concerns along the north side of the site due to grade issues and tight property lines.

The site visit was very helpful in establishing a visual reference point in thinking about the project. The team members took digital photographs of the site to help them think about it during the course of the value study.

CHAPTER 6

Function

© Magixl 2009, www.magixl.com

The function of muscle is to pull and not to push.

—Leonardo da Vinci

The illegitimate son of a 25-year-old notary and a peasant girl, Leonardo was born on April 15, 1452, in Vinci, Italy, just outside Florence. Growing up in his father's Vinci home, Leonardo had access to scholarly texts owned by family and friends. He was also exposed to the city's longstanding painting tradition, and when he was about 15, his father apprenticed him to the renowned workshop of Andrea del Verocchio in Florence. Even as an apprentice, Leonardo demonstrated his colossal talent. His genius seems to have seeped into a number of pieces produced by Verrochio's workshop from the period 1470 to 1475. Leonardo stayed in the Verrocchio workshop until 1477, when he struck out on his own.

In 1482, he entered the service of the duke of Milan. He spent 17 years in Milan, leaving in 1499. It was during these years that Leonardo hit his stride, reaching new heights of scientific and artistic achievement. The duke kept Leonardo busy painting and sculpting and designing elaborate court festivals, but he also put Leonardo to work designing weapons, buildings, and machinery. From 1485 to 1490, Leonardo produced studies on a wide variety of subjects, including nature, flying machines, geometry, mechanics, municipal construction, canals, and architecture (designing everything from churches to fortresses). His studies from this period contain designs for advanced weapons, including a tank and other war vehicles, various combat devices, and even a submarine. Also during this period,

Leonardo produced his first anatomical studies. His Milan workshop was a veritable hive of activity, buzzing with apprentices and students.

After leaving Milan in 1499, Leonardo traveled throughout Italy for a period of about 16 years for a number of employers. In about 1503, Leonardo reportedly began work on the *Mona Lisa*. Following the death of his patron Giuliano de' Medici in March of 1516, he was offered the title of Premier Painter, Engineer and Architect of the King by Francis I of France. His last and perhaps most generous patron, Francis I provided Leonardo with steady and comfortable employment, including a stipend and manor house near the royal chateau at Amboise. Leonardo died on May 2, 1519, in Cloux, France. Legend has it that King Francis was at his side when he died, cradling Leonardo's head in his arms.

Leonardo da Vinci has been dubbed by history as the original Renaissance man due to his broad range of intellectual and artistic pursuits. In fact, the term *Renaissance* refers to the central theme of the period, that of the vigorous renewal of intellectual and artistic achievement. Central to Leonardo's personal experience was his deep-seated desire to understand the workings, or functions, of things. This included his fantastic inventions, scientific studies, and his detailed analysis and illustrations of human anatomy. Leonardo da Vinci's drive to understand how things function sets the stage for this chapter dedicated to the Function Phase.

Function Phase

The functional approach embodies that group of techniques within the Value Methodology that sets it apart from traditional cost reduction and problem solving efforts. The Function Phase consists of three distinct yet interrelated techniques:

1. Defining functions
2. Classifying functions
   - Basic versus secondary functions
   - Work versus sell functions
3. Evaluating functions
   - Levels of abstraction
   - Numerical Evaluation Technique
   - FAST diagrams
   - Dimensioning FAST diagrams—*Value Metrics*

These techniques are tied together into a system known as function analysis. This system is perhaps the single most important and useful technique in Value Methodology; however, it is the most difficult to explain and also the most difficult to grasp and put into practice.

Defining Functions

Function, the specific purpose or intended use for any product, process, or facility, is the characteristic that makes it work or sell. In short, it is the reason why the owner, customer, or user needs a particular thing. Function is closely related to

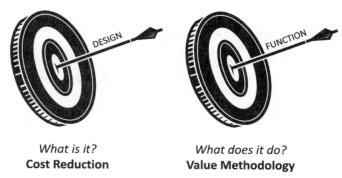

What is it?
Cost Reduction

What does it do?
Value Methodology

FIGURE 6.1 Focus of Cost Reduction versus Value Methodology

use value or the properties and qualities that satisfactorily and reliably accomplish a use.

Preliminary attempts to define the function(s) of a product will usually result in many of its work or sell concepts described in multiple sentences. While this method could conceivably describe an individual function satisfactorily, it is neither concise nor workable enough for the functional approach. Value Methodology determines function by consideration of the user's actual need. The traits or performance characteristics that justify a product's existence, in terms of the particular owner, client, or user, are determined.

The first principle in defining a function is that it be accomplished by using only two words—a verb and a noun.

The verb portion of this should answer the question "What does it do?" This question focuses attention on the function rather than the product or its design and leads straight to the heart of the functional approach. This is a radical departure from the typical cost reduction effort where the first question is "What is it?" followed by a second question of "How do we make it cheaper?" This more traditional emphasis on making the same product less expensive gives little thought to the more vital considerations of the project's functional components or the user's need and purpose (see Figure 6.1).

After answering the question "What does it do?" with a verb that defines the item's required action (it may, for instance, generate, control, pump, enclose, protect, or transmit), the second question, "What does it do this to?" must be answered with a noun that tells what it is acted upon (electricity, temperature, liquids, light, surfaces, space, sound, and so on). This noun portion of the two-word abridgement must be measurable or at least understood in quantifiable terms, since a specific measurement must be assigned to it during the later evaluation process that relates cost and performance to function. A measurable noun together with an active verb provides a description of a work function (e.g., insulate energy, transmit load, support object, and so on). Such verb-noun abridgments establish quantitative statements and are called *work functions*.

The following are examples of work functions for various types of value studies:

- In product design studies, electric motors *produce torque,* lightbulbs *emit light,* fuel tanks *contain liquid,* heating elements *produce heat.*

- In design and construction studies, structural columns *transfer load,* interior walls *separate space,* doors *control access,* clerestory windows *admit light,* and ceiling tile *attenuates sound.*
- In manufacturing process studies, a machining or casting process is designed to *shape material,* while a material handling procedure is designed to *deliver material,* and a QA/QC process is to *verify quality.*
- In business process studies, a payroll system is designed to *distribute money,* an inspection report procedure is designed to *identify condition,* and a change order approval procedure is designed to *authorize change.*

Simple statements such as these ensure clarity of thought and communicate the work function with little confusion.

Functional definitions containing a passive verb and a nonmeasurable noun are classified as "sell functions." They establish qualitative statements; that is, demonstrate approval, enhance satisfaction, improve convenience, and so on. Tables 6.1 and 6.2 provide sample lists of verbs and nouns for work and sell functions.

TABLE 6.1   Verbs and Nouns for Work Functions

Active Verbs		Measureable Nouns	
Actuate	Impede	Acceleration	Liquid
Amplify	Interrupt	Air	Load
Apply	Limit	Contamination	Object
Change	Locate	Current	Particles
Collect	Modulate	Data	Polarity
Conduct	Move	Density	Protection
Contain	Prevent	Energy	Radiation
Control	Protect	Flow	Solids
Emit	Reduce	Fluid	Sound
Enclose	Rotate	Force	Space
Fasten	Secure	Friction	Speed
Filter	Store	Insulation	Torque
Ignite	Transfer	Light	Voltage

TABLE 6.2   Verbs and Nouns for Sell Functions

Passive Verbs		Nonmeasureable Nouns	
Allow	Facilitate	Aesthetics	Form
Characterize	Improve	Acceptance	Gratitude
Communicate	Maintain	Appearance	Happiness
Constitute	Manage	Approval	Identity
Convey	Offer	Beauty	Pleasure
Demonstrate	Present	Comfort	Prestige
Describe	Provide	Convenience	Satisfaction
Display	Represent	Effect	Status
Enhance	Request	Features	Style
Exemplify	Show	Feelings	Symmetry

Of course, it is possible to combine active verbs and nonmeasurable nouns and passive verbs and measurable nouns. However, it is important for the value team to concentrate its efforts on just what it is they are trying to articulate with the function statement. Care must be exercised to provide the correct level of functional definition. For example: The function of a water service line to a building could be defined as *provide service*. In this example, "provide" does not give us any useful information on the manner in which water is being provided, and "service" is not readily measurable and does not enable us to intelligently seek alternatives. On the other hand, if we define the function of the water line as *conduct fluid*, the noun in the definition is measurable, and acceptable alternatives, being dependent upon the quantity of water being transported, can be more easily determined. When the noun used is a measurable noun (e.g., the water volume in terms of "Q" factor in the fluid flow equation), we are a step closer to being able to establish a cost-to-function relationship.

Let us expand on this point further. As we will see in the chapters that follow, function statements serve as our focus for creativity. If we were handed the statement "provide service" on a scrap of paper and were told to brainstorm as many different ways as possible to "provide service" without knowing what it was intended to describe, then the types of ideas we would come up with would differ radically from a similar scrap of paper that instead had the words "conduct fluid." It is therefore important to consider our words very carefully when we define functions.

The system of defining a function in two words, a verb and a noun, is known as two-word abridgement. Advantages of this system are that:

- It forces conciseness by defining a function in two words. If with two words, the functional component is still too large to be defined or to be understood by the team, then this is a sign to drill deeper and to provide a more detailed two-word definition.
- It avoids combining functions and defining more than one simple function. By using only two words, you are forced to break the problem into its simple elements.
- It aids in achieving the broadest level of dissociation from specifics. When only two words are used, the possibility of faulty communication and misunderstandings is reduced to a minimum.

Functions and Functional Value

Functions serve as the foundation for value. An owner, customer, or user wants a function, or group of functions performed. He or she may select from a variety of physical manifestations that deliver the particular function(s) desired. The criterion employed in selecting which of these to utilize is value. In Chapter 2 the four variables of performance, cost, time, and risk were presented as the primary variables of functional value. If we think about these in terms of questions, we arrive at the following:

- Function: "What does it do?"
- Performance: "How well does it do it?"

- Cost: "How much does it cost?"
- Time: "How long will it take?"
- Risk: "How certain are we?"

Unless we are able to answer all five of these questions, we cannot fully understand value. Ultimately, people seek to perform functions rather than to acquire things. Functions take precedence; without them, technology loses its meaning. If they are not fully understood, then our ability to innovate is diminished.

Classifying Functions

There are several classifications of functions:

- Basic functions
- Secondary functions
- Higher-order functions
- Assumed functions

Basic Functions

The basic function(s) is the specific purpose for which a project exists. The basic function answers the question "What must it do?" Basic functions have value (use and functional value). An item may possess more than one basic function. This is determined by considering the customer's needs. A non-load-bearing exterior wall might be initially defined by the functional description *enclose space*. However, further functional analysis determines that for this particular wall two basic functions more definitive than the above exist (e.g., *secure area* and *restrict view*). Both answer the question "What must it do?"

The four rules that govern the selection of basic functions are:

1. Once defined, a basic function cannot change.
2. The cost contribution of a basic function is usually a fraction of the overall cost of the project.
3. Basic functions cannot be sold alone; however, the secondary functions that support the basic function cannot be sold without satisfying the basic function.
4. The loss of the basic function(s) will cause a loss in value.

Secondary Functions

Secondary functions answer the question "What else does it do?" For VM purposes, all secondary functions are considered to have no value. Secondary functions are support functions and usually result from a particular design configuration or approach. Generally, secondary functions contribute greatly to cost and may or may not be essential to the performance of the basic function. Secondary functions that lead to esteem value (convenience, user satisfaction, and appearance) are permissible only insofar as they are necessary to permit the item to buy or sell. Therefore, while secondary functions have zero use value, they may sometimes play an important part in the marketing and acceptance of a design or product. Value Methodology attempts to separate the costs required for basic functional performance from those incurred for nonessential secondary functions. Once identified, it becomes easier to reduce the cost of secondary functions, while still providing the appeal necessary to permit the design to sell. By concentrating on only what is essential to the project's need and purpose, Value Methodology can successfully eliminate many unnecessary secondary functions.

Higher-Order Functions

Higher-order functions represent the specific need(s) that the basic function(s) exists to satisfy. This function(s) identifies the overall need of the customer and generally relates to the "need" statement of a project's need and purpose. For example, the basic function of a classic mousetrap is to *kill mice*. The higher-order function would be to *eliminate mice*.

Assumed Functions

Assumed functions describe functions that lie beyond the scope of the study. They are generally not part of the function analysis process unless the level of abstraction changes the scope of the problem. Levels of abstraction will be discussed in greater detail later in this chapter.

Examples of basic and secondary functions include:

- *Multimedia projector.* Its basic function is to *project image*. In addition, the projector has many required secondary functions, such as *convert energy, generate light, focus image, enlarge image, receive current, transmit current, support weight*, and so on. Unwanted functions such as *generate heat* and *generate noise* and the sell function of *enhance convenience* also exist.
- *Shopping center.* Its basic function is to *attract customers*. In addition, the shopping center has many secondary functions such as *enclose space, condition air, control access, park vehicles*, and so on. Sell functions such as *enhance appearance* may also exist.
- *HVAC system.* The basic function of the HVAC System is to *condition air*. The other functions such as *heat air, cool air, move air, control humidity, distribute air*, and so on, are secondary functions. Unwanted functions such as *generate noise* also exist.
- *Manufacturing process.* Its basic function is to *assemble product*. In addition, the manufacturing process has many secondary functions, such as *form shape, move material, attach components, inspect product*, and so on. *Generate scrap* is an unwanted function that plagues most manufacturing processes.
- *Hiring procedure.* Its basic function is to *fill vacancy*. In addition, the hiring procedure has many secondary functions, such as *create announcement, interview candidates, review résumés, conduct orientation, evaluate application, select candidate*, and so on. While administrative procedures may have unwanted functions, sell functions are rare.

The value team should first seek to randomly identify project functions. The value specialist should initiate this exercise. Functions should be first written down without respect to classification. It is a good idea to begin by starting at the project's purpose and need and then work downward toward the primary project elements, and then toward specific details as necessary. Once a reasonable list of functions has been prepared, the next step is to begin thinking about function classification. A basic example is provided in Figure 6.2. This approach to function classification was the one originally developed by Miles, which he referred to as *Random Function Determination*. In this process, we make a list of the components of the system and then identify the functions associated with it. Consider the functions of a hammer.

Levels of Abstraction

Determination of the basic function(s) is not always an easy process. For instance, the most offered basic function for a hammer is *drive nails*. This definition, however, immediately stumbles over an obvious question: "What about the other uses of a hammer?" Can't hammers be used for purposes other than driving nails, such as those suggested in Figure 6.3?

The hammer doesn't actually drive the nail; it transmits force from a person's hand and arm to the head of the nail. It doesn't matter to the hammer whether it's

COMPONENT	VERBS	NOUNS
Head	Drive	Nails
	Transmit	Force
Claw	Remove	Nails
	Increase	Leverage
Handle	Improve	Grip
	Absorb	Shock
Label	Identify	Brand

FIGURE 6.2   Functions of a Hammer

FIGURE 6.3   Uses of a Hammer

FIGURE 6.4 More Uses of a Hammer

a chisel or a cobbler's tack. So *transmit force* would appear to be a better definition of its basic function. Force can be quantified. But wait! Aren't there still other common uses for hammers, as suggested in Figure 6.4?

A judge's gavel *conveys authority.* A croquet player's mallet *moves ball.* A doctor's hammer *tests reflexes.* Aren't these also basic functions? Well, there is a simple way to check by asking a single question: "If the hammer were unable to transmit force, would it still fulfill its reason for being?" For each of the six uses of a hammer displayed in Figures 6.3 and 6.4, all must transmit force in order to fulfill the associated higher order functions. Here are the answers to the questions posed above for each use of the hammer:

- A carpenter's hammer must *transmit force* to drive a nail into a board.
- A sculptor's hammer must *transmit force* to strike the chisel, which chips the stone. In this case, the chisel also *transmits force.*
- A cobbler's hammer must *transmit force* to drive the tack into the sole of the shoe.
- A judge's gavel must *transmit force* in order to create noise and convey his or her authority to the courtroom.
- A croquet player's mallet must *transmit force* to move the ball through the wickets.
- A doctor's hammer must *transmit force* to the patient's knee in order to test his or her reflexes.

It appears then that transmit force is indeed the correct basic function. In each case the desired effect is quantifiable. The hammer, depending upon its application, may have a radically different higher-order function associated with it. It becomes apparent that a forcing process in either one direction or another in order to develop a multiplicity of two-word abridgements from which one or more levels may be chosen as the level of the primary function to be studied. This is referred to as the *ladder of abstraction.*

Building on the previous example, let us consider the functions of a forklift using Random Function Determination (see Table 6.3). Here we have a multitude of functions. In fact, if we wanted to consider every system down to the last nut, washer, and bolt, the list could include hundreds or even thousands of functions.

The ladder of abstraction method has been developed as a thought-forcing process. To drive one's thinking up the ladder, we ask, "Why?" To force the thought

TABLE 6.3 Functions of a Forklift Using Random Function Determination

Component	Verbs	Nouns	Type
Forklift	Store	Objects	
	Relocate	Objects	
	Move	Objects	
	Supply	Objects	
	Move	Vehicle	
Fork Arms	Lift	Objects	
	Engage	Objects	
	Support	Objects	
	Balance	Objects	
Counterweight	Counterbalance	Objects	
Hydraulic System	Pump	Fluid	
	Contain	Fluid	
	Create	Pressure	
	Control	Pressure	
	Move	Arm	
	Tilt	Arm	
Engine	Generate	Power	
	Ignite	Fuel	
	Generate	Torque	
Fuel System	Contain	Fuel	
	Transfer	Fuel	
Drive Train	Transfer	Torque	
Wheels	Transfer	Torque	
Tires	Increase	Friction	
Steering System	Control	Direction	
Foot Pedals	Control	Speed	
Seat Assembly	Position	Operator	
Roll Cage	Protect	Operator	

processes down the level of abstraction, we must ask, "How?" Figure 6.5 illustrates the functions of a forklift using the ladder of abstraction.

Obviously, from the ladder of abstraction, the two-word abridgements on the upper rungs of the ladder are fairly abstract when thinking about the nature of a pencil. Conversely, the functions on the lower rungs of the ladder are much more concrete. If *relocate objects* was the level of abstraction selected for focus during the next step in the VM Job Plan, the Speculation Phase, then the value team might identify other ways of relocating objects such as hand trucks, pallet jacks, conveyor systems, and cranes. If the team focused on a function higher up on the ladder of abstraction, such as *store objects*, then the team might identify concepts such as warehouses, storage yards, shipping containers, and flatbed trucks.

The real value of the ladder of abstraction is that more creative ideas can be generated by using more than one definition. It leads to greater fluency (more ideas), greater flexibility (more variety of ideas), and an improved functional understanding of the problem. This forcing technique can also help team agreement on the level of abstraction or basic function to be analyzed. From this forcing

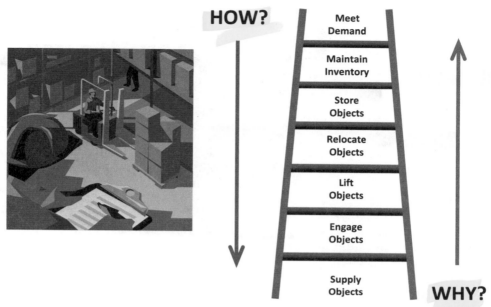

HOW?

Meet
Demand

Maintain
Inventory

Store
Objects

Relocate
Objects

Lift
Objects

Engage
Objects

Supply
Objects

WHY?

FIGURE 6.5   Ladder of Abstraction (Forklift)

process has evolved the technique known as FAST (Functional Analysis System Technique).

Evaluating Functions

In the earlier example concerning the functions of a simple object or system, determining which function is the basic function and which are the secondary functions may appear to be obvious. This is not always the case, however, especially when considering more complex projects. Classifying the functions listed in the forklift example will be much more challenging than considering those of a simple tool like a hammer. It takes time and experience to train the mind to think using the functional approach, and sometimes the classification of functions requires more careful analysis and evaluation. There are other techniques for classification in addition to the random function determination process identified above. The one most commonly used is called the Function Analysis System Technique, or FAST diagram.

Function Analysis System Technique

The Function Analysis System Technique, commonly referred to by the acronym FAST, is a powerful diagramming technique for analyzing the relationship of functions. FAST diagrams have the following uses:

- Show the specific relationships of all functions with respect to one another
- Test the validity of the functions under study

- Help identify missing functions
- Broaden the knowledge of all team members with respect to the project

The Function Analysis System Technique was developed by Charles W. Bytheway of the Sperry Rand Corporation and was first introduced in a paper presented at the 1965 National Conference of the Society of American Value Engineers. Subsequently, FAST has been widely used by governmental agencies, private firms, and value consultants.

FAST builds on the verb-noun rules described earlier in this chapter. It is an excellent communication technique in that it allows value team members to contribute equally and communicate with one another while addressing the problem objectively and without bias or preconceived conclusions. FAST has also proven to be a useful tool for project planning and a good way to present complex concepts to decision makers.

FAST distinguishes between basic and secondary functions, which make it a natural for classifying functions. However, it does this in a way that provides a means of graphically illustrating the intuitive logic used to determine and test function dependencies through the development of a diagram that, at first glance, appears to resemble a flowchart or network diagram.

The major difference between the Random Function Determination process first described by Miles and the FAST process is in its ability to analyze a system as a whole, rather than analyzing the individual parts of a system. When studying systems, it becomes apparent that functions do not operate in a random fashion. A system exists because functions form dependencies with other functions, just as parts form a dependency link with other parts to make the system work.

It is important to understand that there is no "correct" FAST diagram, as in comparing it to an accepted norm, but there is a "valid" FAST model. The degree of validity is directly dependent upon the talents of the value team members and their adherence to the rules of function-logic as defined in the remainder of this chapter. The FAST diagram must be constructed using team consensus, as the discussion the diagram generates is just as important as the diagram itself. A FAST diagram is "complete" only when consensus among its creators is reached.

In the previous section dealing with levels of abstraction, the concept of "How?" and "Why?" logic was introduced; this intuitive logic forms the basis in constructing FAST diagrams. The directional references of the HOW and WHY questions remain the same. HOW is read from left to right and WHY is read from right to left. Using the examples below, if the function were addressed and the question asked, "How are objects stored?" the answer, in the form of a function could be *relocate objects* (see Figure 6.6).

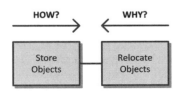

FIGURE 6.6   "How?—Why?" Logic (two functions)

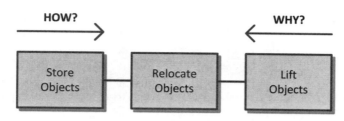

FIGURE 6.7   "How?—Why?" Logic (three functions)

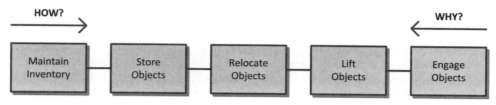

FIGURE 6.8   "How?—Why?" Logic (five functions)

Continuing in the HOW direction, the question is asked, "How are objects relocated?" The answer could be *lift objects* (see Figure 6.7).

To test the logic of the example above, the functions can read in the reverse WHY direction. "Why are objects lifted?" "To *relocate objects*." Why are objects relocated?" "To *store objects*." If the team agrees with the answers they can continue to expand the FAST model, either in the WHY or HOW direction. In the WHY direction the question is asked: "Why are objects stored?" "To *maintain inventory*." Switching to the HOW question in the opposite direction, the question is asked: "How are objects lifted?" "*Engage objects*." Examining the function inputs thus far, the FAST model would look as follows (see Figure 6.8).

The example was constructed with the intent of describing a forklift; however, the same function model could have been applied to an automated palletizing system, a bridge crane, or even a warehouse worker. This shouldn't be too surprising because all of these things perform the functions described, in the same dependency order. The differences occur when additional secondary functions are added and when the model is dimensioned in terms of time, performance, or other measurements that reflect the problem under study.

The Importance of Nouns

The previous three figures have considered the functions of a forklift. Forklifts act upon pallets, which are essentially wooden trays that allow the arms of the forklift to easily pick them up off the ground without damaging the materials placed on top of them. Because forklifts are specifically designed to pick up pallets, which are generally uniform in size throughout the world, wouldn't the word "pallet" be an appropriate noun to use in function statements? On the face of things, this seems like a logical choice.

The selection of nouns is worth discussing in greater detail at this point. The word "pallet" conjures up a very precise image in our head. Further, when "pallet" is used as the noun in function statements, it is really describing a series of activities rather than functions. *Lift pallet*, although stated in functional verb-noun syntax, describes an activity. When visualizing the statement *Lift pallet*, it is easy to imagine a forklift lifting a wooden pallet and placing it on a warehouse shelf. The word "pallet" is leading our thinking to focus on the current state of things rather than on the function. A more general noun to use in place of "pallet" should be found.

What is a pallet? A pallet is a wooden tray that has specific physical properties. It is an object that has standard dimensions, weight, capacities, and tolerances. Further, the forklift just doesn't lift pallets; it also lifts things placed on top of the pallets such as boxes or crates. Therefore, we could use the word "object" to describe a pallet and whatever is placed on top of it. The word "object" is non-specific and suggests a physical thing. "Object" is a measurable noun, as we can describe an object physically in terms of its size and weight. Alternatively, we could use the word "load," which more specifically refers to its weight, which is also measurable. However, because the size (i.e., dimensions) of a pallet is just as important as the weight of the pallet, "object" is probably a better choice.

The simple substitution of "object" for "pallet" has transformed our understanding of the functions of a forklift. The change may seem subtle at first; however, when the value team moves into group creativity in the Speculation Phase, they will have laid the foundation to greatly expand their thinking. Try brainstorming different ways to *lift objects* as opposed to ways to *lift pallets*. Far more ideas will be generated using the former statement than the latter.

Reverse Logic?

Many individuals, when first introduced to FAST diagrams, find it counterintuitive, especially those accustomed to flowcharts and network diagrams. They appear to be backward! This is one of the most important aspects of FAST and it is what forces those involved in constructing FAST diagrams to think about a project differently. Unlike these more common diagramming techniques, FAST appears to read from finish to start if viewed from left to right. There are a number of reasons for this difference:

- The FAST diagram begins with the goal or objective, which focuses our attention where it should be. When beginning any endeavor, we usually know what we want to achieve, so why not begin there? Addressing functions on the FAST diagram with the question WHY, the function to its left expresses the goal of that function. The question HOW is answered by the function on the right, and describes the approach being utilized to perform the function to the left.
- Changing a function on the HOW-WHY path affects all of the functions to the right of that function. This is a domino effect that only goes one way, from left to right. Starting with any place on the FAST diagram, if a function is changed the goals are still valid (functions to the left) but the method to accomplish that function, and all other functions on the right, are affected. Functions to the right of another function are called "dependent functions" because the way that a function performs is dependent on the function to its left.

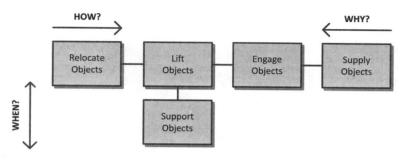

FIGURE 6.9 "When?" Logic

- Reading the goal, or the left side of the diagram, to the beginning, on the right end (in the HOW direction), goes against our system paradigm. Because it seems strange, building the model in the HOW direction, or function justification, will focus the team's attention on each function element of the model. On the other hand, reversing the FAST model and building it in its system orientation will cause the team to leap over individual functions and focus on the system, leaving function "gaps" in the system.

Another way of thinking about building FAST diagrams is that they are built in the HOW direction and the logic is tested in the WHY direction.

When Logic

The "when" direction is not part of the intuitive logic process but it supplements intuitive thinking. In terms of FAST logic, "when" is not necessarily time related, but indicates cause and effect. Referring to Figure 6.9, "when you *lift objects*, you *support objects.*" *Support objects* is a supporting secondary function that supplements the function "lift objects." As a supporting secondary function, it can be expanded in the HOW-WHY directions to create a minor logic path and build a subsystem FAST diagram. Since the independent function is not on the major logic path, changing the function would not significantly affect the basic function. Another helpful way to think of a "when" function is to add the qualifying statement "caused by." For example, *support objects* is also "caused by" *lift objects.*

Structure of the FAST Diagram

The FAST diagram is built upon the left-right logic of HOW and WHY and the up-down logic of WHEN. There are several additional elements that are necessary to further communicate the functional relationships. The basic elements of the FAST Diagram are illustrated in Figure 6.10.[1]

SCOPE LINES Scope lines represent the limits of the value study and are shown as the two dashed vertical lines on a FAST diagram. The scope lines demarcate the "scope of the study," or that element of the problem with which the value team is concerned. The basic function will always be the first function to the immediate

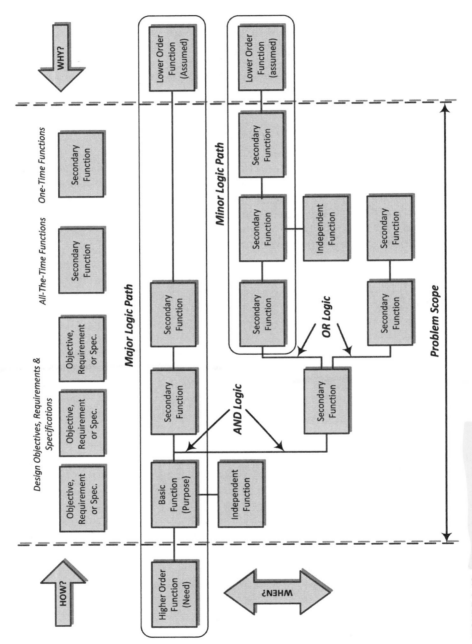

FIGURE 6.10 Structure of a FAST Diagram

160

right of the left scope line. The function to the immediate left of the left scope line is the higher order function, or output. The right scope line identifies the beginning of the value study and separates the assumed function, or input, from the scope of the study.

HIGHEST ORDER FUNCTION(S)

Higher Order Function(s) represent the need(s) for the project and is located to the left of the basic function and outside of the left scope line. Any function to the left of another function is a "higher order function" relative to that function. However, when considering Higher Order Functions, the reference is generally directed to the reasons for why the project exists.

LOWER ORDER OR ASSUMED FUNCTION(S)

Functions to the right and outside of the right scope line represent the input side that initiate the subject under study and are known as lower order functions. Functions that lie to the right of the rightmost scope line are also sometimes referred to as "assumed" functions. This is because these functions are generally left up to the customer or user to determine, so an assumption is being made as to what they are.

It is important to note that the terms "higher" or "lower" order functions should not be interpreted as meaning relative importance, but rather as the input and output side of the process. As an example, if we were analyzing a purchase order processing procedure, the function *receive order* could be the lowest order function, with the function *receive product* being the highest order function. How to accomplish the highest order function, *receive product*, describes the need for the procedure and helps prioritize our thinking to address the purpose of the procedure, or basic function, as *ship product*.

BASIC FUNCTION(S)

Basic Functions, which represent the purpose of the project under study, are located to the immediate right of the leftmost scope line and are directly connected to the higher order function. Once determined, the basic function will not change. If the basic function is not performed, the project loses its value.

SECONDARY FUNCTIONS

All functions to the right of the basic function portray the conceptual approach (i.e., design) selected to satisfy the basic function. The concept describes the method being considered, or elected, to achieve the basic function. The concept can represent either the current conditions (as is) or proposed approach (to be). Which approach to use (current or proposed) in creating the FAST model is determined by the value team and the definition of the problem under study. Conceptually, all functions to the right of the basic function are treated as "secondary" functions and are subject to change. Unwanted secondary functions can optionally be highlighted by using a double, or bold, line around the box.

Value studies focused on improving a design or concept that is currently in progress should first begin by constructing a FAST diagram based on this initial concept. Doing so will reveal potential problems or areas for study. Constructing a FAST diagram based on a design in progress will also be useful for the next step in the functional approach, which involves correlating cost and performance to the identified functions. Once this is accomplished, it may be useful, time permitting, to construct a FAST diagram based on how the value team believes the solution should look. If the value study is focusing on a project that has not begun design or formal planning, then the FAST diagram should be constructed based on what the solution could or should be.

OBJECTIVES, REQUIREMENTS, AND SPECIFICATIONS   Design objectives represent important issues that the project is trying address. For example, one of the design objectives for a forklift might be to "Ensure Reliability." Such a statement is global in nature and could apply to all of the functions that appear on the diagram. Requirements and specifications are issues relevant to the project that affect either how it operates or describe the qualitative aspects relevant to its design. These items must be achieved to satisfy the highest order function of the project in its normal operation. These can be stated using functional terminology or, in the case of a specification, it can be stated directly. For example, a specification stating "Support 1.5 tons" could be written in one of the boxes. Although these types of issues may not even be functions, they influence the concept selected to best achieve the basic function, and satisfy the customer's or user's expectations. These types of issues are generally included as part of the FAST diagram and are displayed above the diagram and are not connected directly to the main body of the diagram. It is suggested that these special issues be labeled as such or a graphic key (e.g., dashed box, shadow box, etc.) be used to distinguish them from the other functions that are part of the FAST diagram.

LOGIC PATH FUNCTIONS   Any function on the HOW or WHY logic path is a logic path function. If the functions along the WHY direction enter the basic function, it is a major logic path. If the WHY path does not lead directly to the basic function, it is a minor logic path. Changing a function on the major logic path will fundamentally alter or destroy the way the basic function is performed. Changing a function on a minor logic path will disturb an independent (supporting) function that enhances the basic function.

DEPENDENT FUNCTIONS   As discussed previously, starting with the first function to the right of the basic function, each successive function is "dependent" upon the one to its immediate left (or higher order function) for its existence. That dependency becomes more evident when the HOW question and direction is followed. If any function on a minor or major logic path is changed, it will affect all the functions to the right of the changed function. Therefore, those functions affected are dependent functions, because their existence depends on the functions to their left.

INDEPENDENT FUNCTIONS   Independent functions generally represent an augmentation to the function they are connected to on the logic path. They are said to be "independent" because they do not depend on other functions for their performance. Independent functions may be located above or below the logic path and are always considered to be secondary in nature.

AND/OR LOGIC   In some cases, it may be desirable to differentiate how functions may be connected. One way to do this is through AND/OR logic. The AND connection is represented by showing a split or fork between functions (see

Figure 6.11) and indicates that both paths must be followed. The AND lines can also indicate that the connecting functions are of equal or lesser importance, depending on how they are drawn.

The OR connection is represented by lines emanating from the root function at different locations (see Figure 6.12) and indicate a choice in the function path. The OR lines may also indicate function paths of equal or lesser importance similar to AND lines. The AND/OR lines may also be drawn in the vertical, or WHEN direction.

Types of FAST Diagrams

The following are three types of FAST diagrams that are commonly understood today:

1. *Classical FAST.* Classical FAST is used to describe the original FAST diagramming that was developed by Charles Bytheway. In his book *FAST Creativity & Innovation*, Bytheway presents the first FAST diagram that he presented in 1965. It was of an incandescent lightbulb. Bytheway states that the procedure he used at that time did not concentrate on creativity. It was primarily devoted to organizing the functions into a diagram that focused on "How?—Why?" logic. At this early stage, many of the features commonly included in FAST diagrams did not exist (see Figure 6.13).[2]

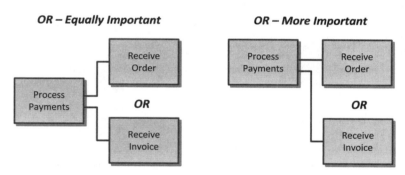

FIGURE 6.11   "Or" Logic

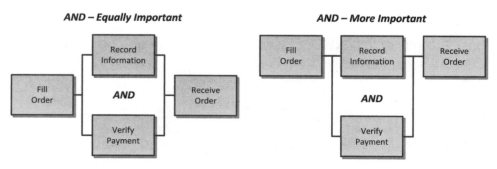

FIGURE 6.12   "And" Logic

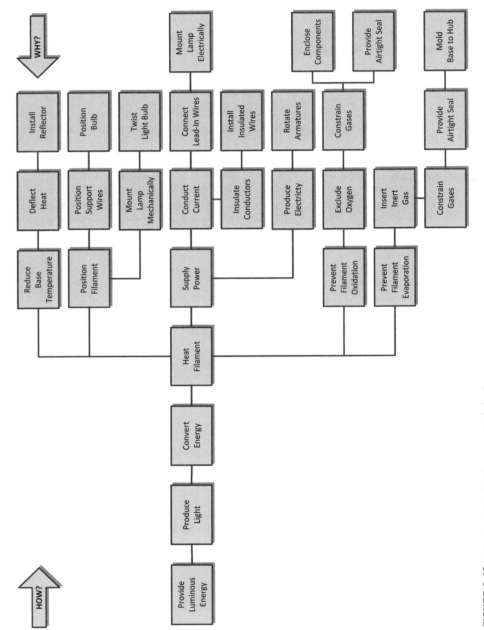

FIGURE 6.13 Classical FAST Diagram, Lightbulb

2. *Technical FAST.* Technical FAST represents an evolution of Bytheway's "classical" FAST diagram. Technical FAST includes all of the elements that have been discussed so far. Technical FAST is the most prevalent form of FAST diagramming practiced today.

3. *Customer-oriented or customer FAST.* Customer FAST was developed by Thomas Snodgrass and Theodore Fowler in 1972 to address what they felt were shortcomings with Technical FAST. Their approach was to consider the relationship of functions from the customer's or the user's perspective rather than from the designer's. A Customer FAST is structured such that the design-related (or technical) functions are located on the top of the diagram and the supporting functions (or customer based) are located on the lower portion. The Customer FAST Diagram in Figure 6.14 is taken from Snodgrass and Fowler's original paper.[3]

It is important to emphasize that while all three types described here are valid approaches, the most widely used and accepted type is the Technical FAST diagram, which is also the approach recommended by this book. With the advent of FAST dimensioning techniques, Technical FAST diagrams can be structured in a manner that addresses the customer's or user's supporting functions. Namely, these can be described through the dimension of performance. These techniques will be discussed further later in the chapter.

Examples of FAST Diagrams

Examples of "Technical" FAST diagrams for projects in design and construction, manufacturing, and processes have been included on the following pages for reference. It is important to emphasize that there are many ways to construct a FAST diagram; however, they must all follow the same structural guidelines. The differences usually relate to the verbs and nouns used to define the functions and differences in the degrees of abstraction used. The following six examples of FAST diagrams are provided:

1. *Forklift.* This FAST diagram represents the functions of a 1.5-ton forklift truck. This diagram demonstrates how the functions that were identified in Random Function Determination were assembled into a FAST diagram. This diagram represents the major systems and assemblies of the forklift. Note that there are two basic functions. Obviously, this diagram could be expanded to include the hundreds of other secondary functions that exist if each major system or assembly were to be broken down into subassemblies and individual component parts (see Figure 6.15).

2. *Roadway improvement project.* The purpose of this project was to perform a variety of improvements to a major city street that included improving traffic operations, improving bicycle and pedestrian safety, replacing aging utility lines, and enhancing the corridor's aesthetics. This FAST diagram represents the baseline design concept for the project and cost information (shown in $ millions) has been included (see Figure 6.16). The addition of cost information is an example of dimensioning FAST diagrams and is discussed in greater detail later in the chapter.

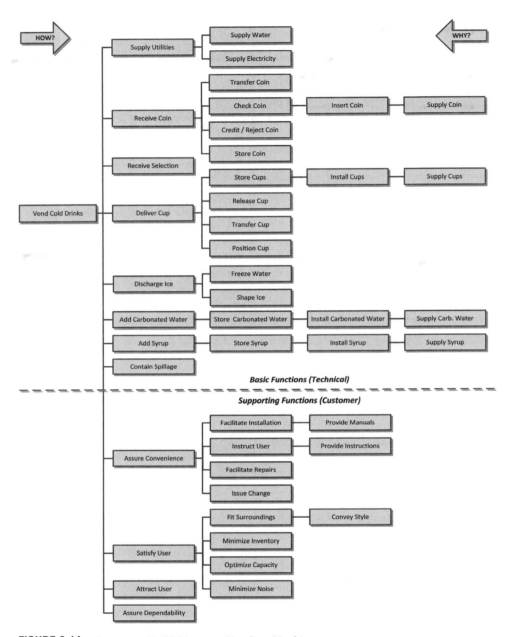

FIGURE 6.14 Customer FAST Diagram, Vending Machine

3. *Hiring procedure.* This FAST diagram represents the existing hiring procedures of a company. The assumed function, or input, to the procedure begins with an analysis of the company's workforce. The higher order function, or intended output, is that the newly hired employee will be assigned to staff a new project.

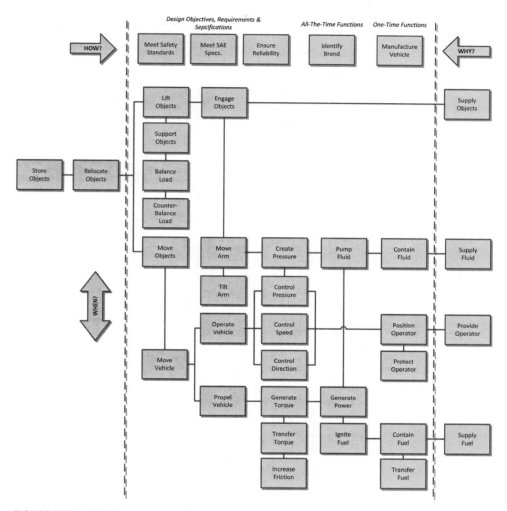

FIGURE 6.15 FAST Diagram, Forklift

Note the large number of functions arrayed in the WHEN direction. This is a common phenomenon of FAST diagrams related to procedures, where many activities may occur simultaneously and represent various steps that support an overarching function (see Figure 6.17).

4. *Recycled water system.* This project involved the design and construction of a citywide recycled water system that will supply recycled water to several landscape irrigation users and groundwater recharge facilities. This system will reduce overall water demands by utilizing treated effluent that would otherwise be discharged into a local river. The project includes an extensive pipeline, reservoirs, and modifications to an existing water pollution control plant. This FAST diagram represents the baseline design concept for the new system (see Figure 6.18).

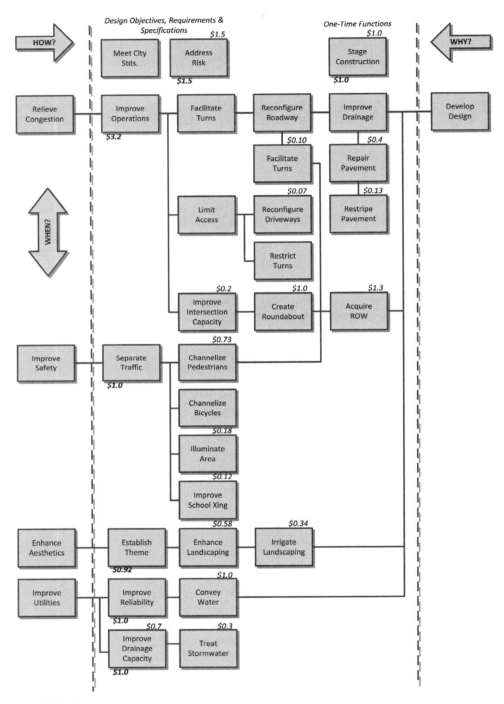

FIGURE 6.16 FAST Diagram, Roadway Improvement Project

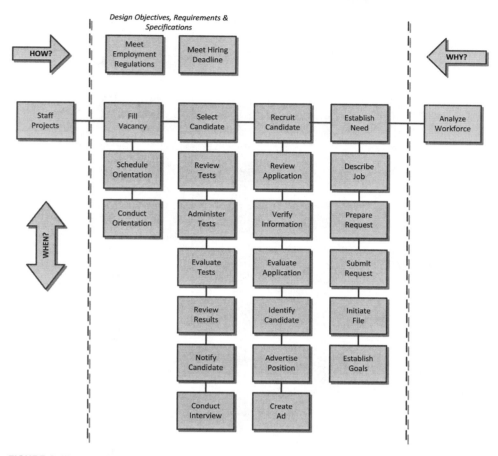

FIGURE 6.17 FAST Diagram, Hiring Procedure

5. *Manufacturing process.* This FAST diagram illustrates the functions involved in the assembly of an automotive component. The input to the study scope begins with the delivery of the required materials to the factory and concludes with the shipping of the completed component to the manufacturer that will incorporate the part into the production of a new automobile. Although this is a relatively simple diagram, the value of the FAST diagram will become obvious when labor and material costs, as well as performance attributes, are referenced to the functions, revealing activities that yield poor value (see Figure 6.19).

6. *Medical records management system.* In this example, we have a FAST diagram that illustrates an existing medical records management system that deals with sensitive patient health history information. In this example, one of the functions has been identified as an "unwanted" secondary function, *Discard Records.* The value team would obviously want to focus on generating ideas that would eliminate this function from the system (see Figure 6.20).

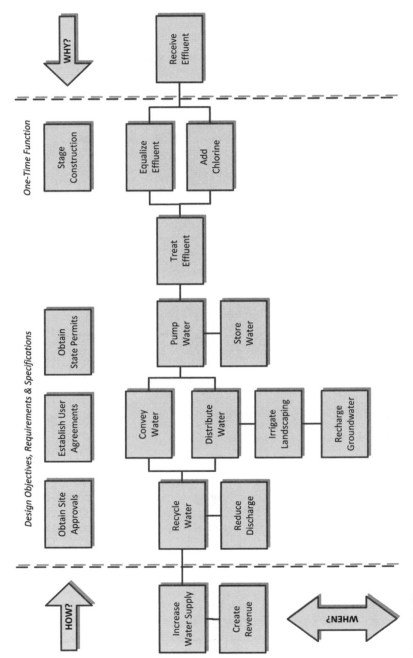

FIGURE 6.18 FAST Diagram, Recycled Water System

170

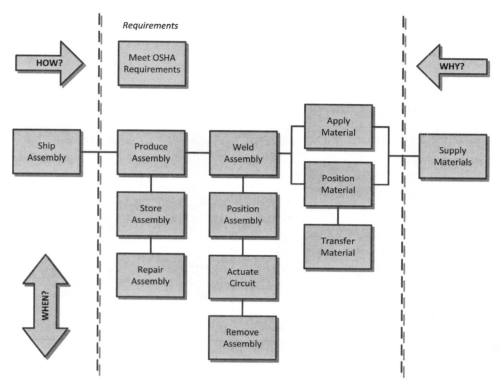

FIGURE 6.19 FAST Diagram, Manufacturing Process

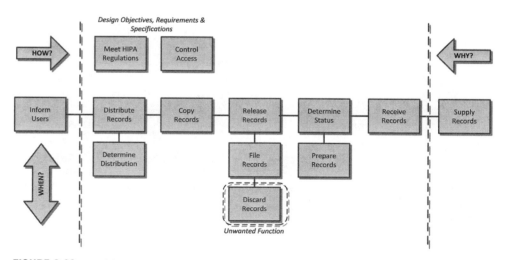

FIGURE 6.20 FAST Diagram, Medical Records Management System

FAST Diagrams versus Flowcharts

Some may believe that value studies of processes and procedures do not require the application of FAST diagramming because a process flowchart essentially represents the same thing. The fact is, however, that there are a number of critical differences between FAST diagrams and flowcharts (or network diagrams, if you prefer).[4]

The *functions* of a process or procedure represent the intended objectives, whereas the *activities* are the physical means of achieving those objectives. A FAST diagram arranges functions in a logical manner to answer questions like "How?" and "Why?" with the aim of defining the *purposes* for which the process or procedure exists. The process flowchart, on the other hand, specifies what *actions* occur by people and/or equipment to accomplish the intended functions.

Referring to the Merriam-Webster dictionary, consider that the definition of "analysis"—which is performed as part of the Function *Analysis* System Technique diagram—is "an examination of a complex system, its elements, and their *relations*." Kaneo Akiyama, in his book *Function Analysis*,[5] states, "Things that are static, fixed, and apparent can be defined in terms of shapes and colors. This is not the case with functions, which are dynamic, *relative*, and process-oriented." In terms of a value study, FAST diagrams are used to break down a project or process into its individual elements, and graphically represent how they *relate* to one another. A flowchart, on the other hand, is defined as "a diagram that shows step-by-step progression through a procedure or system." The flowchart is simply the graphical representation of a sequence of activities.

To further illustrate these differences using an example, a flowchart for an IT Equipment Deployment process for a large public agency was analyzed in order to understand why, on average, it took over 100 hours to deploy 20 computer workstations to employees (see Figure 6.21). The flowchart includes a great deal of information concerning the specifics of the activities. Indeed, there is so much information that it makes it very difficult to understand what is actually going on and how the activities are really interrelated.

The value team was charged with finding ways to reduce the deployment time. A FAST diagram was developed that was based on the flowchart. The value team then calculated the times to conduct each of the activities on the flowchart, based on information provided by the IT Department, and then assigned these times to the corresponding functions identified in the FAST diagram (see Figure 6.22).

A quick comparison of the original flowchart and the FAST diagram reveals the fundamental differences between the two techniques. First, it is much easier to understand what is actually going on when the functions related to the activities have been distilled. Further, because many activities are repetitious, they can be expressed as a single function and the time and/or cost needed to perform them can be included on the FAST diagram. This greatly simplifies the search for solutions as concise function statements, as opposed to long-winded activities, provide the focus for brainstorming.

Another way to think about these two graphic techniques is that a FAST diagram describes the system and the flowchart describes the actual activities involved in implementing the system. FAST is also a good method for identifying

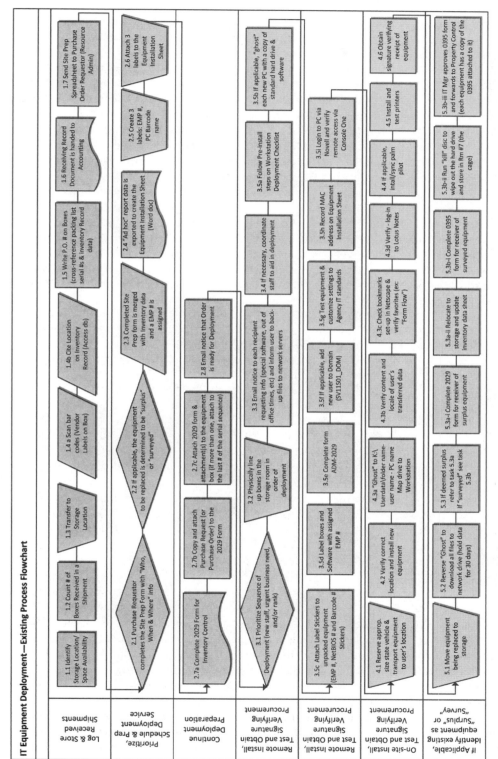

IT Equipment Deployment—Existing Process Flowchart

Log & Store Received Shipments	1.1 Identify Storage Location/ Space Availability → 1.2 Count # of Boxes Received in a Shipment → 1.3 Transfer to Storage Location → 1.4.a Scan bar codes (Vendor Labels on Box) → 1.4b Cite Location on Inventory Record (Access db) → 1.5 Write P.O. # on Boxes (cross-reference packing list serial #s & Inventory Record data) → 1.6 Receiving Record Document is handed to Accounting → 1.7 Send Site Prep Spreadsheet to Purchase Order Requestor (Resource Admin)
Prioritize, Schedule & Prep Deployment Service	2.1 Purchase Requestor completes the Site Prep Form with "Who, When & Where" Info → 2.2 If applicable, the equipment to be replaced is determined to be "surplus" or "surveyed" → 2.3 Completed Site Prep form is merged with Inventory data and a EMP # is assigned → 2.4 "Ad hoc" report data is exported to create the Equipment Installation Sheet (Word doc) → 2.5 Create 3 labels: EMP #, PC Barcode name → 2.6 Attach 3 labels to the Equipment Installation Sheet
Continue Deployment Preparation	2.7a Complete 2029 Form for Inventory Control → 2.7b Copy and attach Purchase Request (or Purchase Order) to the 2029 Form → 2.7c Attach 2029 form & attachment(s) to the equipment box (if more than one, attach to the last # of the serial sequence) → 2.8 Email notice that Order is ready for Deployment
Remote Install, Test and Obtain Signature Verifying Procurement	3.1 Prioritize Sequence of Deployment (new staff, urgent business need, and/or rank) → 3.2 Physically line up boxes in the storage room in order of deployment → 3.3 Email notice to each recipient requesting info (special software, out of office times, etc) and inform user to back-up files to network servers → 3.4 If necessary, coordinate staff to aid in deployment → 3.5a Follow Pre-install steps on Workstation Deployment Checklist → 3.5b If applicable, "ghost" each new PC with a copy of standard hard drive & software
Remote Install, Test and Obtain Signature Verifying Procurement	3.5c Attach Label Stickers to unpacked equipment (EMP #, NetBIOS # and Barcode # Stickers) → 3.5d Label boxes and Software with assigned EMP # → 3.5e Complete form ADM-2029 → 3.5f If applicable, add new user to Domain (SV11501_DOM) → 3.5g Test equipment & customize settings to Agency IT standards → 3.5h Record MAC address on Equipment Installation Sheet → 3.5i Login to PC via Novell and verify remote access via Console One
On-site Install, Test and Obtain Signature Verifying Procurement	4.1 Reserve approp. size state vehicle & transport equipment to user's location → 4.2 Verify correct location and install new equipment → 4.3a "Ghost" to K:\ Userdata\folder name- user name - PC name Map drive to Workstation → 4.3b Verify content and locale of user's transferred data → 4.3c Check bookmarks set-up in Netscape & verify favorites (ex: "Form Flow") → 4.3d Verify – log-in to Lotus Notes → 4.4 If applicable, intall/sync palm pilot → 4.5 Install and test printers → 4.6 Obtain signature verifying receipt of equipment
If Applicable, Identify existing equipment as "Surplus" or "Survey"	5.1 Move equipment being replaced to storage → 5.2 Reverse "Ghost" to download all files to network drive (hold data for 30 days) → 5.3 If deemed surplus refer to task 5.3a If "surveyed" see task 5.3b → 5.3a-i Complete 2029 form for receiver of surplus equipment → 5.3a-ii Relocate to storage and update inventory data sheet → 5.3b-i Complete 0395 form for receiver of surveyed equipment → 5.3b-ii Run "kill" disc to wipe out the hard drive and store in rm #7 (the cage) → 5.3b-iii IT Mgr approves 0395 form and forwards to Property Control (each equipment has a copy of the 0395 attached to it)

FIGURE 6.21 Process Flowchart, IT Equipment Deployment

flaws in the system, in that it enables the team to determine where unneeded or unwanted functions are included, and/or where needed or wanted functions are missing.

Charles Bytheway, the originator of the FAST method, used the system to stimulate creativity. He emphasized the use of what he called "thought-provoking questions" as opposed to focusing on completion of the FAST diagram, believing that success was defined by developing creative alternatives (solutions) based on the functions derived from answering the leading questions. This approach brings up a very big difference between a FAST diagram and a flowchart: Although it is not imperative for the FAST diagram to be complete, a flowchart must be completed to represent the entire process being defined.

FAST diagramming is arguably the most powerful technique used in the Value Methodology, and it is extremely effective for getting a multidisciplined team to reach consensus on the scope of the process or project being analyzed. At the same time, a FAST diagram must not be misinterpreted to represent activities on a flowchart. FAST reflects the divergent opinions and feelings of people. It is a subjective, albeit collective, representation of a project's scope. The flowchart, on the other hand, is the objective representation of what actually happens to accomplish the required functions.

Dimensioning FAST Diagrams—Value Metrics

There have been several examples so far in this chapter (Figures 6.16 and 6.22) that have combined various data (cost in the former and time in the latter) with FAST diagrams. The term commonly used to describe this technique is *dimensioning*. Dimensioning FAST diagrams allows pertinent data about a project to be linked directly to functions. Doing so magnifies the power of FAST by allowing powerful correlations to be made.

The following is a list—by no means all inclusive—of the type of project data that can be used in dimensioning FAST diagrams:

- Cost data (e.g., construction costs, labor costs, etc.)
- Time (e.g., construction days, FTE hours, process time, etc.)
- Performance (e.g., performance attributes)
- Risk (e.g., P&I risk ratings, categories of risks, etc.)
- Responsibilities (e.g., RACI, contracts, divisions, departments, etc.)

There are essentially two conventions for dimensioning FAST diagrams with the type of data listed above. These include direct dimensioning and/or utilizing a sensitivity matrix.

FAST DIMENSIONING: DIRECT METHOD   The first is to write the data directly in or above the function boxes, as was done in Figures 6.16 and 6.22. This is a simple and effective approach. When dimensioning cost data for construction or product studies, it is generally fairly easy to take the project cost estimate and begin allocating costs to the functions on the diagram from right to left. The functions on the right-hand side of the diagram are typically far more specific and finite in nature

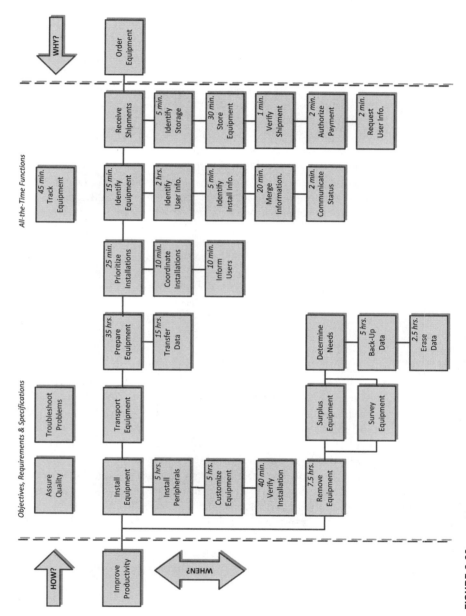

FIGURE 6.22 FAST Diagram, IT Equipment Deployment

than those appearing on the left (a feature of the ladder of abstraction discussed previously).

In Figure 6.16, the cost of each function is recorded above it on the right-hand side. The costs of the supporting secondary functions can be rolled up to the level of basic functions or to secondary functions that constitute major project elements or assemblies. In Figure 6.16, the total cost to perform the basic functions has been identified below them and on the left-side in bold print. Using this approach, it is very easy to see what the costs of the five basic functions are as well as their constituent functions. Time can be handled in a manner similar to cost as is the case in Figure 6.22. If desired, both time and cost information could be included in this manner on the same diagram. Such information will greatly assist the value team during the Speculation Phase.

Alternatively, a cost-function or time-function matrix can be developed to assist the team in allocating time and/or costs to functions. The functions within scope are listed across the top of the matrix. Then the major cost groups are listed down the left-hand side of the form with the associated incremental costs in the total-cost column. The value team will need to use its best judgment in splitting up the cost of a single element or component among multiple functions. Costs should be extracted from existing project data where available, such as a construction cost estimate, bills of material, or labor/time estimates. Next, the function impacted by each project element is identified. Once this is done, the team must estimate how much of the cost of each element belongs to each function. This need not be a precise estimate. Finally, all columns are added vertically to determine how much cost is allocated to each function. Typically, three or four functions will be responsible for 60 to 80 percent of the total cost. Table 6.4 shows an example of a cost-function matrix.

FAST DIMENSIONING: SENSITIVITY MATRIX   A sensitivity matrix can be used to correlate a variety of different types of information. It is particularly useful when there is too much information to display effectively using the direct method. Sensitivity matrices are particularly well suited for the dimensioning of performance, risk, and responsibility information.

A sensitivity matrix is constructed by listing the data that is desired to be displayed vertically below the FAST diagram. The functions on the FAST diagram are then numbered sequentially and the numbers arrayed along the horizontal axis creating a grid. The functions can then be cross-referenced using a symbol on the matrix to indicate the level or degree of correlation and/or impact.

Figure 6.23 illustrates an example using this technique where the functions on the FAST diagram have been numbered and cross-referenced with a breakdown of the performance attributes of the item's components, in this case a steering column assembly from the forklift example. The cost information from Table 6.4 has also been added using the direct method of dimensioning.

In this example, several functions indicating a potential for value improvement include *Direct Fluid*, which has a relatively high cost with a low contribution to total performance, and *Adjust Length*, which has a relatively low cost, but a high contribution to total performance. It is important to remember that a function indicating a high contribution to performance does not necessarily mean that the function is performing well. These cost-performance mismatches should

TABLE 6.4 Cost-Function Matrix

Item	Total Cost	Transmit Force	Convert Energy	Transmit Torque	Direct Fluid	Receive Torque	Contain Pressure	Restrict Travel	Dampen Shock	Adjust Length	Allow Attachment	Protect Components	Receive Fluid
Valve Assembly	23.53		5.25	3.75	4.88	1.65	4.5				3.5		
Housing Assembly	35.86	20.45			11.85			1.8			0.8	0.1	0.86
Tie Rod Assembly	27.49	20.39						0.6		3	3.5		
Tube Assembly	7.26	2.9	2.56								0.6	1.2	
Rack	14.78	5.33	9.45										
Bellows	1.9											1.9	
Rod Bushing	3.21		2.9									0.31	
Rack Guide	3.59	2.75						0.7	0.14				
Housing Cover	1.19											1.19	
Final Assembly	8.82	1.75	2.2	0.75	1.37	1.8	0.2	0.2		0.25	0.15	0.15	0.9
Scrap	3.44	0.15	1.93		0.05		0.18			0.3	0.08		0.08
TOTAL	131.07	53.72	24.29	4.5	18.15	3.45	4.88	3.3	0.14	3.55	8.4	4.85	1.84
% of TOTAL		41.0%	18.5%	3.4%	13.8%	2.6%	3.7%	2.5%	0.1%	2.7%	6.4%	3.7%	1.4%

lead the value team to focus further on these functions during the Speculation Phase.

Another use of the sensitivity matrix is illustrated in Figure 6.24. In this example, the functions of a large highway construction project have been correlated based on the project's construction contract matrix, which identifies which portions of the

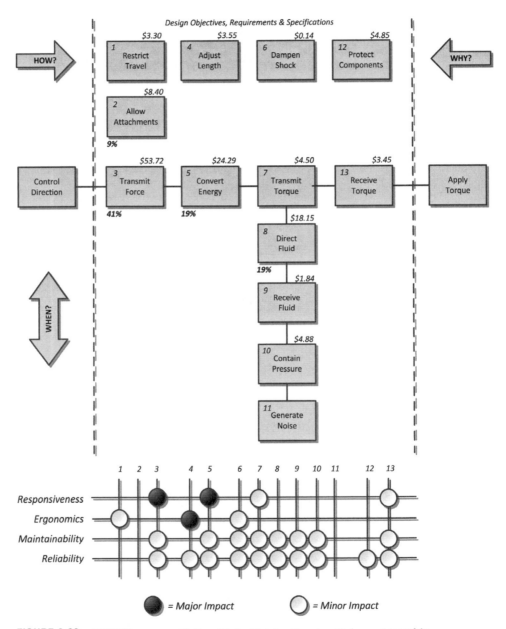

FIGURE 6.23 FAST Diagram with Sensitivity Matrix, Steering Column Assembly

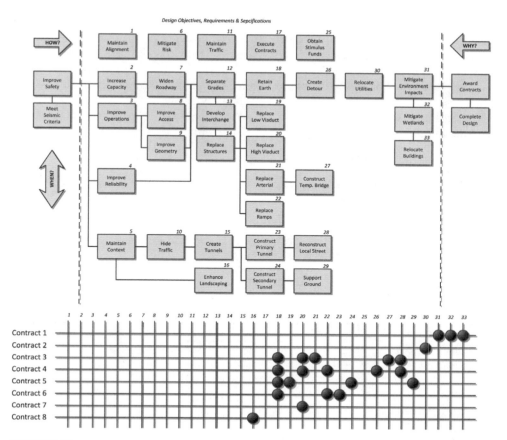

FIGURE 6.24 FAST Diagram with Sensitivity Matrix, Highway Construction Staging

project will be built by contract bid package. This FAST diagram was used to focus on constructability issues and the sequencing of construction work by function.

The technique of FAST dimensioning provides a highly effective tool for considering the relationship of function to the components of value: performance, cost, time, and risk. Value team members will be able to see not only high cost functions, but also performance, time, and risk critical functions. It is at this point that the direct consideration of these factors can begin focusing a value team's efforts on performance improvement and, ultimately, total value improvement.

Summary

The Function Phase is what helps people to better understand projects and what makes Value Methodology truly unique. As has been stated elsewhere in this book, understanding the problem is at least half the battle in coming up with solutions that will ultimately contribute to an improvement in project value.

Developing a mastery of the functional approach takes practice. A solid comfort level will be developed only through repeated application. All value practitioners must strive to develop these skills, especially the powerful technique of FAST diagramming.

Anyone who professes to employ the Value Methodology should be asked if they utilize Function Analysis and, if so, how they apply it. This is the primary test in determining whether VM is truly being applied. If the concepts and techniques of function analysis are neither understood nor employed properly, then it can be said with absolute certainty that whatever process it is claimed is being used, it is not Value Methodology.

Appendix 6A: Case Study

Following the site visit, the value team reconvened and began the Function Phase of the VM Job Plan. The value specialist facilitated the process of Random Function Determination by breaking the project into its primary components and identifying their related functions. These functions were then transferred onto a software program (Microsoft Visio) and a FAST diagram was developed while displaying it to the team by using a multimedia projector (see Figure 6.25). The value team identified the basic function of the project as being "Support Vocational Education." This in turn was supported by a host of required secondary functions that describe the specifics of the educational program. The value team then dimensioned the FAST diagram with both cost and performance information. Due to the size of the diagram, functions were organized on the diagram in a manner that allowed them to be highlighted in groups and linked to performance directly rather than developing a sensitivity diagram.

Using this dimensioning approach, the utility of FAST is enhanced. Beginning with the project's purpose, which is described by the basic function, "Support Vocational Program," a performance hierarchy emerges. First comes the delivery of the specific programmatic elements; these are linked to the performance attribute "Program Compatibility." These are in turn supported by the performance attributes of "Building Organization" and "Site Organization." What is interesting to note here is that the three buildings are internally organized to support the educational program, which is in turn organized on the site to create specific spatial relationships. These building forms are then supported on a technical level by the materials and systems that constitute the structure of the buildings, which in turn directly affect long-term operations and maintenance (i.e., "Maintainability"). "Aesthetic" performance is identified as a functional objective and applies to all of the functions on the diagram below it. Last, the issue of "Phaseability" is identified as a one-time function, as the phasing is planned to occur only once during the school's life span. This performance hierarchy directly corresponds to the priorities that were assigned to the individual attributes and further demonstrates the inherent logic of the diagram.

This function-performance hierarchy is fairly common to most projects involving buildings. It gives further credence to the age-old architectural axiom "Form follows function." A common problem with construction-related FAST diagrams is that the scope line is drawn too far to the right—in this case, imagine the scope

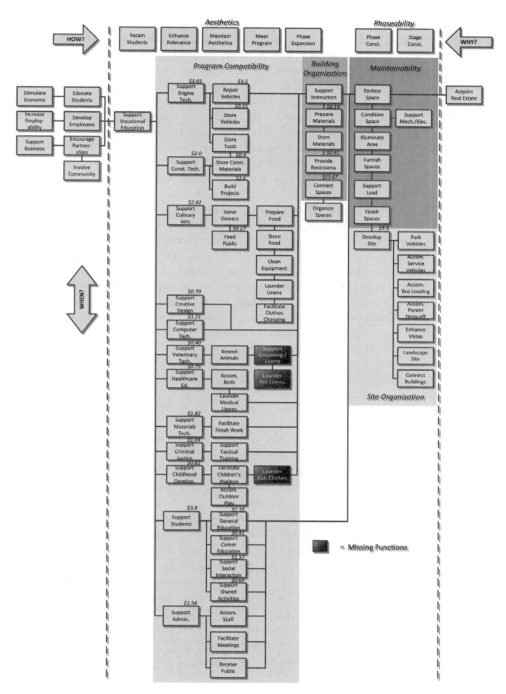

FIGURE 6.25 FAST Diagram, Technical High School

line drawn just to the left of the function *enclose space*. At this level, the scope of the problem is reduced to building materials and systems and tells us nothing about why we are enclosing the space. This is why value studies for construction projects should be performed at a conceptual level, such as in this case study example. It is critical to understand the reason why the space exists in the first place and why it must be enclosed.

The FAST diagram was dimensioned with cost data extracted and correlated from the project cost estimate. Due to the conceptual nature of the design, the value team took the total area costs for the various program areas (which included all materials and systems costs) and linked them directly to the functions describing them. This is a very quick and convenient way to dimension a FAST diagram for construction projects that are being performed early on in the design process and allows the relationships between cost and function to be clearly made.

The value team also identified several functions that had been omitted from the baseline concept. These were noted as such by shading the functions darker and keying them to a legend.

The value team determined that it would focus first on the functions that described the major program elements (i.e., those functions located in the column to the immediate right of the basic function) first and then address other key functions during the team brainstorming session in the Speculation Phase.

CHAPTER 7

Speculation

© Magixl 2009, www.magixl.com

Imagination is more important than knowledge.

—Albert Einstein

Albert Einstein was born on March 14, 1879, in Ulm, Germany. His father was a manufacturer of electrical equipment. There were no early indications of Einstein's intellectual capabilities; in fact, there was even some concern on the part of his parents when he was a small child that he might be somewhat challenged. During his school years, he showed no special aptitude because of his dislike for rigid methods of instruction, and he was cited by school officials as being disruptive. Einstein was fascinated by mathematics and science, subjects that he studied on his own. He became a high school dropout when he left school to join his family in Milan.

In 1896, he was able to enroll at the Swiss Federal Institute of Technology in Zurich after making up a number of subject deficiencies. At the institute, the academic fare did not suit him either; he managed, however, to pass the required examinations for his degree. In the two years following his graduation, in 1900, he subsisted on odd teaching jobs. By 1902, he had secured a position as patent examiner at the Swiss patent office in Bern, where he worked for the next seven years.

The year 1905 was a momentous year for science, for without any academic connections, Einstein published, at the age of 26, four papers in the journal *Annalen der Physik*—papers that were to alter the course of twentieth-century physics. The first dealt with the random thermal motions of molecules in colloidal solutions, called Brownian motion, first noted in 1827 by the English botanist Robert Brown. Einstein's second paper reinforced the quantum theory of light developed by Max Planck in 1900. Within it, Einstein established the photon nature of light by accounting for the photoelectric phenomenon discovered in 1902. For this contribution, Einstein was awarded the Nobel Prize in physics in 1921. The third and most famous of Einstein's 1905 papers dealt with the special theory of relativity: "Zur Electrodynamik bewegter Korper" ("On the Electrodynamics of Moving Bodies"). And the final paper of that year introduced the now famous equivalence between mass and energy in the equation $E=mc^2$. Because of this work, Einstein received his first academic post in 1908 at the University of Bern, which was followed by several others in Europe before he settled at the Institute for Advanced Study in Princeton in 1933.

Einstein thought of himself more as philosopher than as scientist, and in many ways he was from the same mold as the Greek natural philosophers, such as Plato and Aristotle, in trying to understand the natural world through mental concepts instead of experimentation. His success did draw on the insights of his predecessors and the powerful analytical tools of mathematics, but most of all it was the result of an unerring intuition, the likes of which have been equaled by very few.

Albert Einstein embodies the concept of creativity and imagination through his ability to release himself from the limitations of conventional thinking. His life and times serve as an excellent lead into this chapter's discussion of the Speculation Phase.

Speculation Phase

The purpose of the Speculation Phase is to produce new ways to perform project functions. In other words, it is all about creativity. In this chapter, the concept of creativity will be explored and techniques for fostering creativity will be presented.

Creativity

What is creativity? The *American Heritage Dictionary* defines the word "creative" as:

1. *Having the ability or power to create:* Human beings are creative animals.
2. *Productive; creating.*
3. *Characterized by originality and expressiveness; imaginative:* creative writing.

This is a pretty simple definition, though rather uncreative! If you asked this question of some very creative people, you might be surprised by what they have to say about the subject:

I am enough of an artist to draw freely upon my imagination. Imagination is more important than knowledge. Knowledge is limited. Imagination encircles the world.

—Albert Einstein, physicist

Sometimes I think the human mind is like a compost pile. It contains a variety of ingredients all stewing together toward the ultimate end of producing something useful. Some ingredients aid the process, some hinder it, and others are inert.

—Roger von Oech, Ph.D., creativity consultant

All children are artists. The problem is how to remain an artist once he grows up.

—Pablo Picasso, artist

When I am working on a problem I never think about beauty. I only think about how to solve the problem. But when I have finished, if the solution is not beautiful, I know it is wrong.

—Buckminster Fuller, architect

The best way to have a good idea is to have lots of ideas.

—Linus Pauling, chemist, Nobel Prize winner

Creativity takes courage.

—Henri Matisse, artist

Much has been written concerning creativity by history's greatest artists, scientists, architects, and inventors. Hundreds of quotes could easily be added to those listed above; however, what is interesting about these perspectives on creativity is that they all follow a number of basic themes:

- *Problem sensitivity.* Being aware that a problem exists combined with the ability to state the problem so that it does not limit or confine thinking. The ability to make keen observations, be inquisitive, maintain healthy skepticism, and appreciate the contributions of others.
- *Idea fluency.* Being able to produce ideas in copious quantities, closely coupled with the ability to restrain judicial thinking.
- *Flexibility.* Effecting quick and frequent reorientation of approaches. The ability to toy with elements and concepts, formulate wild hypotheses, and express the ridiculous.
- *Originality.* The ability to associate unrelated ideas and things and synthesize them into new solutions to a problem.
- *Constructive discontent.* To be dissatisfied with existing conditions and possess an attitude of mind that seeks to improve conditions.
- *Imagination.* The ability to confront and deal with reality by using the creative power of the mind. There are two general categories of imagination—controllable and uncontrollable. Creative ability is a byproduct of the controllable category.
- *Innovation.* The ability to build on or improve the ideas of others.
- *Fundamental knowledge.* To be well grounded in basic laws and concepts, well read, and conversant with many fields of thought. Knowledge provides a foundation from which creativity can draw upon.

- *Curiosity.* Possessing a wide range of interests. To be curious to know how things work and to be fearless in asking "Why?"
- *Self-confidence.* Developing the proper frame of mind toward creativity and to be sure of one's own ability to find new and better solutions. To have the courage to present new ideas to others.
- *Motivation.* Possessing a strong inner drive to work through a problem solution. Constructive motivation is considered essential to basic creative performance.
- *Emotional balance.* The creative process is fraught with generalization, freewheeling ambiguities, and disorder that are often frightening and uncomfortable. A high level of tolerance during the creative phase is absolutely essential in maintaining a team's enthusiasm and performance.
- *Permissive environment.* It is always easier to work in an environment that encourages new ideas. The characteristics of a permissive environment include:
  - Freedom of expression
  - Effective communication
  - Mutual respect and encouragement
  - Job satisfaction

Roadblocks to Creativity

In his groundbreaking book on creativity, *A Whack on the Side of the Head*, Roger von Oech identified a number of "mental locks" that inhibit creativity. These mental locks exist for one of two reasons. The first is that we usually don't need to be creative for most of the things we do. This is where our individual habits and routines come into play. Thus, most of the time we really have no incentive to be creative. The second reason is that when we really do need to be creative, the very habits, routines, and attitudes that we rely upon to get us through our daily lives literally lock down our creative side. What follows are the 10 mental locks identified by von Oech.[1]

1. "The right answer."
2. "That's not logical."
3. "Follow the rules."
4. "Be practical."
5. "Avoid ambiguity."
6. "To err is wrong."
7. "Play is frivolous."
8. "That's not my area."
9. "Don't be foolish."
10. "I'm not creative."

These mental locks, or *roadblocks*, act to stifle creativity unless they are recognized and overcome. The value specialist must take the lead in doing this. A discussion of each of these roadblocks is provided in the following sections as well as some strategies that can be applied to counteract them, regardless of what creativity approach is being used.

"The Right Answer" and "Follow the Rules"

It could be argued that we are most creative the day we are born. As infants, we have absolutely no knowledge of the world. Therefore, we do not know what is possible or impossible. We have not yet formed any habits, routines, or attitudes— nor do we have any concept of what these things are. We are purely creatures of imagination.

As we mature and begin to develop the ability to think critically, the first limits to our creativity are set, much like fence posts. Eventually, we hear the word "No!" directed at us for the first time by a concerned parent. Over a period of time, and a constant litany of "No's!" we begin to develop an understanding of right and wrong, good and bad, yes and no.

Slowly, and insidiously, this assault on our creative thinking increases as we learn the rules. If the change in our preference for creative versus critical thinking were plotted on a graph, it might look something like the one shown in Figure 7.1.

In Vincent Ruggiero's *Becoming a Critical Thinker*, he distinguishes the functions of creative and critical thinking:

> *Thinking is sometimes regarded as two harmonious processes. One process is the production of ideas (creative thinking), accomplished by widening your focus and looking at many possibilities. The key to this process is to resist the temptation to settle for a few familiar ideas. The other process is the evaluation of ideas (critical thinking), accomplished by narrowing your focus, sorting out the ideas you've generated, and identifying the most reasonable ones.[2]*

Larry Miles recognized this phenomenon, and his understanding of critical versus creative thinking led him to separate these two types of thinking by doing them at different times in the job plan, which is why the Speculation and Evaluation Phases are separate, distinct steps.

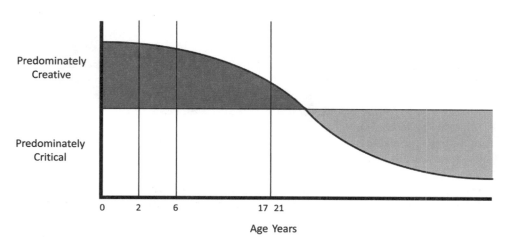

FIGURE 7.1 Creative versus Critical Thinking

By the time we have completed our primary education, we have been taught that there is generally only one right answer to any given problem and that the right answer is the one that is commonly accepted. This emphasis on critical thinking dominates our educational system. We are given only fleeting opportunities to exercise creative thinking during our education and most of these are limited to art, music, and writing classes.

In any event, regardless of whether we are developing our creative or critical thinking skills, we are taught to do so within the context of school, which is in turn governed by countless rules, regulations, and expectations of behavior. By the time we have established our professional careers, we have established a lifetime of mental conditioning from which it is very difficult to escape.

In beginning a creativity session, the value specialist should do two things in addressing these roadblocks:

1. Communicate to the value team that *there are no "right" answers*. The primary objective of the Speculation Phase is to generate as many different ideas as possible. In order to do this, no criticism will be allowed! The ideas will be evaluated in the following phase, so everyone will have an opportunity to voice their opinions about the ideas later.
2. Make it clear that *there are no rules*. *Ideas* should be focused on addressing the function or functions that the value team has identified for value improvement during the Function Phase. Once this first condition has been met, there should be no other rules that might inhibit the creative thinking process.

"That's Not Logical," "Avoid Ambiguity," and "Be Practical"

The emphasis of our educational system on critical thinking places greater value on thinking that is logical, orderly, and practical than on thinking that is ambiguous, chaotic, and abstract. This "left brain" or "hard" method of thinking tends to subordinate our "right brain" or "soft" thinking, and as a result, our creativity tends to suffer.

Individuals involved in professions such as marketing, advertising, and design are generally more adept at right brain or soft thinking because they are more concerned with developing creative concepts and ideas. On the other hand, individuals engaged in technical disciplines such as engineers, programmers, and analysts are particularly predisposed to left brain or hard thinking because they are more concerned with turning concepts into concrete reality (see Figure 7.2).

Obviously, we need to use both the left and right parts of our brain to be successful; however, during a creativity session, it is the right side that needs the extra stimulation. The value specialist should consider the following in breaking through these roadblocks:

- *Use metaphors to soften up thinking*. The use of metaphor is one of our greatest creative gifts and is used extensively by artists, musicians, writers, and poets. Try using metaphors to change your perspective on things. Try asking questions like "How is this review process a trip to the movies?" The answers may be surprising and can lead to valuable insight on the problem as well as spark

Left Brain Critical **Right Brain Creative**

Logical   Intuitive
Sequential   Random
Rational   Holistic
Analytical   Synthesizing
Objective   Subjective
Looks at parts   Looks at whole

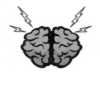

FIGURE 7.2   Left Brain versus Right Brain

the group's creativity. This technique is also useful in understanding how functions work. During a product study of a hammer, the question might be posed, "I am a hammer, what do I do?" "Imagine somebody picked you up and swung you at a nail, what would happen?" The concept of empathy that is conveyed by these questions stimulates all of our senses and forces us to think about problems differently.

- *Encourage "what-iffing."* Simply asking the question "What if?" can give creativity a jump-start. What-iffing is a great way to change paradigms. "What if we didn't have that funding deadline to meet?" "What if we could make it out of plastic?" "What if the customer didn't care how the thing looked?" "What if we didn't need management approval?" This is a very important strategy that often pays great dividends because it challenges assumptions and conventional wisdom. As discussed in Chapter 2, assumptions and wrong beliefs are pernicious when it comes to value. Far too many assumptions are made concerning projects and this is a great mechanism to challenge them during creativity.

- *Think ambiguously.* The VM process provides an excellent means to utilize the concept of ambiguity through the functional approach. A simple way to expand our creativity is to simply focus on ways of accomplishing the higher-order function (i.e., the function immediately to the left of the one on which we are focusing our creativity). Climbing the ladder of abstraction is a surefire way to do this. Instead of asking "How else do we control access?" we might ask "How do we enforce security?" Instead of asking "How do we transmit force?" we could ask "How do we drive nails?" These simple questions completely change the dynamic of the problem, and therefore multiply the number of potential solutions.

"To Err Is Wrong," "Play Is Frivolous," and "Don't Be Foolish"

Creativity takes courage, as pointed out by the famed painter Henri Matisse, who is credited with fathering the Fauvist movement around 1900. The reason creativity takes courage is that there is the possibility that any new or original idea may result in failure. It is important to recognize that failure, in and of itself, is not necessarily a bad thing. It is not the fear of failure, but rather the fear of embarrassment that is at the root of this particular roadblock. Mistakes are a natural part of the learning process and are an essential part of the creative process.

The value specialist will at some point be faced with a group of participants during a creativity session where nobody will have the courage to suggest anything.

This may be happening for a number or reasons. It may be that a manager or "boss" is in the room and that there is a general fear among subordinates of contradicting or embarrassing themselves in front of a superior. It may be that some of the participants are shy or introverted by nature. It may be that some are genuinely bored or uninterested. Whatever the case, one of the best things the value specialist can do is to lighten up the group's mood. Humor can work wonders, especially when people feel they can laugh at themselves. Humor, in and of itself, requires creativity and is an excellent means of stimulating the imagination. You do not need to be a trained comedian to instill a sense of levity. A few tips for breaking through these roadblocks include:

- *Don't be afraid to laugh.* The value specialist can get the ball rolling by throwing out a few goofy ideas to loosen the participants up a bit. Self-deprecation is an excellent way to demonstrate a willingness to laugh at oneself. If the value specialist can show everyone that he or she is not afraid of embarrassment, it will go a long way in making the others in the group feel safe in sharing their ideas.
- *Failure is an option.* The value specialist should ensure that criticism will be dealt with harshly at this point in the job plan. It is surprisingly difficult for most to keep their mouths shut when they have a reason for why something won't work. Don't give in to this temptation. There are a number of clever and amusing tactics that can be applied to this end. A colleague once brought a foam stick to a creativity session that she would use to whack over the heads of those who couldn't keep from making critical remarks. Another method is to have anyone who makes a critical remark contribute a quarter to the kitty.
- *Avoid "groupthink."* There will usually be many "sacred cows" for most projects. These often prove to be particularly troublesome areas to get people's creative input on. There is a tendency for people to conform to the standard way of thinking in these situations. The value specialist should take this as an excellent opportunity to play the fool and shake things up a bit. Challenge the group's established notions of thinking: "So what if the bridge falls down!" "Who cares about profit; let's just give them away!" "Who needs emergency lighting? Just give everyone flashlights!" I guarantee you will get a response.

"That's Not My Area" and "I'm Not Creative"

The value team will most likely include individuals representing a variety of disciplines who have expertise in several specific areas. Although specialized knowledge is essential for the success of most projects, it can also create mental roadblocks by limiting thinking to known solutions. In fact, some of the best ideas and solutions are conceived by others in the group that come from entirely different areas of expertise than the one being focused on. Often this is because these individuals do not know any better.

Another interesting fact is that creative people think that they are creative, while people who are not creative think that they are not. This phenomenon is known as the Self-fulfilling Prophecy, or the Pygmalion Effect. In 1971, Robert Rosenthal, a professor of social psychology at Harvard, described an experiment in which he told a group of students that he had developed a strain of super-intelligent rats that could run mazes quickly. He then passed out perfectly normal rats at random, telling half of the students that they had new "maze bright" rats and the other half that they got "maze dull" rats.[3]

The rats that were believed to be "bright" improved daily in running the maze—they ran faster and more accurately. The "dull" rats refused to budge from the starting point 29 percent of the time, while the "bright" rats refused only 11 percent of the time. Rosenthal concluded that this boost in performance was attributed to the fact that the students with the "bright" rats treated the animals more gently, showed greater enthusiasm for the experiments, and were more relaxed. Those with the "dull" rats essentially communicated feelings that were the opposite of these. In essence, the Pygmalion Effect is a phenomenon in which perceptions about performance have a direct impact on the outcome of that performance. Identified below are a few thoughts on changing your perspective during creative exercises:

- *I'm not a doctor but I play one on TV.* One technique that seems always to produce results is to give team members a pen and ask them to go up to the whiteboard and draw a sketch of a solution. An accountant may draw a very interesting sketch for a carburetor because she isn't an automotive engineer. A construction engineer may create a revolutionary flow chart for a change order administrative process. Anyone who has played the game Pictionary will appreciate how a little right-brained thinking can bring out the artist in all of us.
- *Try hitchhiking.* Einstein was once quoted as unabashedly saying, "The secret to creativity is knowing how to hide your sources." What he probably meant was that most ideas are built upon the ideas of others. Despite not being an expert in a given field, one should not be afraid to throw out an idea. Any idea from any source may provide the creative spark that others, including the experts, need to break through their mental roadblocks.
- *Believe in yourself.* As silly as it may sound, how people feel about themselves does indeed influence outcome. The value specialist should encourage others throughout the creativity session by instilling confidence in themselves and their team. You've got to believe the worth of ideas and have faith in the creative process, because pessimism is not going to get the job done.

Creativity Techniques

There are literally hundreds of creative techniques that have been developed, most of which have sprung up during the past fifty years. Regardless of the technique chosen, it is recommended that the value specialist begin by targeting those functions that were identified as having a high potential for value improvement. This will help keep the value team's creative thinking focused on areas that will yield the best return on their efforts.

This book will introduce only those creative techniques that the author has had direct experience with and that have proven to be the most compatible with the VM process. These techniques are:

- Classic brainstorming
- Brain writing
- Brain sketching
- Creativity checklists

Classic Brainstorming

This technique is probably the most widely used creative technique, as it is relatively simple and takes advantage of a group's creative synergism. It works best with smaller groups (typically four to ten people, the size of most value teams). Here is how it is done:

- Write the function to be brainstormed on a flip chart, whiteboard, or other system where everyone can see it. Make sure that everyone understands the problem or issue.
- Review the ground rules with the group:
  - Suspend judgment and avoid criticizing ideas. Each idea is as valid as any other.
  - The emphasis should be on generating a large quantity of ideas. If you limit the number of ideas, people will start to judge the ideas and only put in their "best" or more often than not, the least radical and new.
  - Freewheeling. In order to keep the flow of the meeting going, don't censor any ideas.
  - Listen to other ideas and try to piggyback on them to other ideas if possible.
  - Avoid any discussion of ideas or questions, as this tends to stop the flow of ideas.
- The value specialist should enforce these simple rules and write down all of the ideas as they occur.
- Clarify and conclude the session. Ideas that are identical can be combined; all others should be kept. When finished with one function, move on to the next.

Brain Writing

Brain writing (also called trigger sessions) is a good way of getting numerous ideas from untrained or reluctant participants. Here is how it works:

- Identify the function to be focused on.
- Each member of the group writes down his or her ideas using brief statements (five minutes only).
- One member reads out his or her list—others cross out the ideas on their own lists that have been read out loud and write down new "hitchhiked" ideas.
- The second member reads out his or her list of ideas not already covered, and this process is repeated until everyone has shared their list.
- The last member reads out his original list and his or her "hitchhiked" list, and the procedure is repeated in the opposite direction.

A good group will be able to manage at least a half-dozen passes. Everyone's paper is then collected and can be combined into a single list of ideas—all duplicates should have been crossed out during the process. The value specialist may want to write down the "surviving" ideas on a flip chart or whiteboard as the brain writing session evolves.

In a variation on this technique, everyone writes down their ideas on Post-it notes or small cards and places them in the center of the table. Everyone is then free to pull out one or more of these ideas for inspiration. Team members can create new ideas, variations, or piggyback on existing ideas.

Brain Sketching

A technique similar to brain writing, brain sketching utilizes evolving sketches rather than written lists of ideas to foster creative idea generation. As usual with most brain writing techniques, only limited facilitation skill is needed.

- A group of four to ten people sit around a table, or in a circle of chairs. They need to be far enough apart to have some privacy. The function to be focused on is identified.
- Each team member privately draws one or more sketches (each on a separate sheet of paper) of how the function might be solved, passing each sketch on to the person on their right when it is finished. The sketches should not take more than five minutes or so to draw.
- Participants take the sketches passed on to them and either modify or annotate the existing one, or use it to stimulate a new sketch of their own. The amended original and/or any new sketches are then passed on to the person on their right when ready.
- After the process has been running for a suitable period and/or the group's energy is winding down, the sketches are collected by the facilitator.
- It will probably help to display all the sketches and to discuss them in turn for clarification and comment.

Brain sketching can be a very effective approach when dealing with designs, whether it is for a product or a facility of some kind. This method allows people to think visually, which is often more effective for design-related projects.

Creativity Checklists

To stimulate thinking along creative lines, the following questions, and related examples, may prove helpful. In every case, the intent is to force the value team to take a new look at the item, system, component, or action that is being studied. Einstein is quoted as saying, "The important thing is not to stop questioning."Put it to other uses

Put it to other uses
- Are there new ways to use it as it is? *Using smart phones as barcode readers.*
- What other ways could it be modified? *Fishing rods made of fiberglass imbedded in plastic.*

- What could be made from this? *Wallboard manufacturer who added a line of jigsaw puzzles.*
- How about salvaging? *Utilizing the piers of a demolished bridge as pedestals for interpretive sculpture.*
- What other uses could be added? *Telephone companies installing transcribed records to furnish the latest weather reports.*
- Could the width be increased? *Increase the median buffer on a local street to serve as a landscaped bioswale.*
- Could new ingredients be added? *Striped toothpaste having both cavity-fighting and breath-freshening ingredients.*

Make it smaller

- What if it was lower? *Trend in automobiles a few years ago.*
- What if it was narrower? *Reduce the width of a forklift so it can get down narrower aisles.*
- What if it was lighter? *Railroad cars that weigh no more than trailers.*
- What if it were more streamlined? *Tank-type vacuum cleaners.*
- What if it were condensed? *Full-size umbrellas that can fit into a purse.*
- What if part of it was eliminated? *Tubeless tires.*

Make substitutions

- Could other parts be used? *Fluid drive instead of gears on cars.*
- Could other materials be used? *Argon instead of vacuum in electric lightbulbs.*
- Could we produce it using a different process? *Stamping instead of casting.*
- Could a different power source be used? *Electricity instead of vacuum to run windshield wipers.*
- Is there another way? *Airlift that saved Berlin.*

Rearrange it

- Could the pattern be changed? *Improving traffic operations by converting an urban two-way street system to a one-way system.*
- Could the layout be revised? *Reconfigure a new college campus by consolidating buildings and reducing construction and maintenance costs.*
- Could the sequence be altered? *The use of flashbacks in movies.*
- Could the cause and effect be transposed? *Overlaying real-time traffic congestion data on an aerial photograph.*
- Could it be repackaged? *Microwave popcorn that comes in its own popping bag.*
- Could it be reorganized or regrouped? *Merging two departments to consolidate operations.*

Imitate and adapt

- What else is like this? *Studies of birds made by aircraft pioneers like Leonardo da Vinci.*
- What parallel does the past provide? *What modern fashion designers do to take yesterday's style and recast it as "retro-chic."*
- Could other processes be copied? *The cultured pearl industry, whereby nature is imitated by sticking beads into oysters so as to produce pearls.*

- What other ideas might be adaptable? *Rudolf Diesel got his engine ideas from a cigar lighter.*

Modify it

- What other shape could be used? *A buggy maker tapered the roller bearing that Leonardo da Vinci had invented 400 years before.*
- What other form could be used? *Liquid soap instead of bars of soap, or foaming hand soap instead of either.*
- Could we change the style or look? *Higher (or lower) hemlines.*
- What other color could be used? *What the television industry did to develop color TV.*
- Could we make it move differently? *The development of the V-22 Osprey tiltrotor aircraft, which can take off and land vertically like a helicopter but cruise like an airplane.*

Make it bigger

- Could we make it take longer? *Refrigerated cookie dough that can be baked at home to create the "homemade" effect.*
- Could the frequency be increased? *The doctor who originated the idea of lighter but more frequent meals for ulcer patients.*
- Could we increase its strength? *Reinforced heels and toes in hosiery.*
- Could we increase its height? *Children's safety gates to prevent taller toddlers from scaling them.*
- Could we make it go down instead of up? *Furrier who attaches his label upside down, so it can be read when the coat is over a chair.*
- Could its usual roles be switched? *Have the welders review and modify the design and engineers assemble the parts.*
- Could we make it go up instead of down? *The use of lighting fixtures that cast light up rather than directly down to create a different ambience.*
- Could it be done the opposite way? Elias Howe perfected his sewing machine by designing a needle eye at the bottom instead of at the top.

Combine it

- What about using alloys or synthetics? *Titanium or carbon-fiber bicycle frames to reduce weight.*
- What old ideas could be merged? *Window washers that combine a squeegee with a built-in hose nozzle.*
- What about considering ensembles? *For the aesthetically challenged, dress shirts are sold in boxed sets with matching neckties and handkerchiefs.*
- Can different products be marketed together? *Retailers frequently co-locate complementary items. For example, if you visit a home-improvement store, you are likely to see a display of lock sets (which are generally found in the hardware section) in the section of the store that displays doors.*
- Can different purposes be combined? *To avoid changing from one pair of glasses to another, Ben Franklin cut the lenses in two and placed them together, with the normal halves above and the reading halves below. Thus he invented bifocals.*

Stimulate Creativity: *Value Metrics*

One of the many benefits of Value Metrics is that it provides another means of stimulating creativity by placing greater emphasis on areas other than cost improvement. In the Function Phase of the Value Methodology Job Plan, the relationship among cost, performance, time, risk, and function was discussed through the use of FAST diagramming.

Typically, high-cost functions are selected as targets for team brainstorming during this phase. The work done in the Function Phase with respect to performance should have highlighted the performance, time, and/or risk critical functions, which deserve every bit of attention that is given to high-cost functions.

The components of value themselves can also serve as creativity stimulators by incorporating them into questions directed at the value team, similar to the questions presented above in conjunction with creativity checklists. For example, one might ask:

Performance
- How could we enhance the ergonomics?
- How might we tighten the turning radius?
- How could we improve lift speed?

Time
- How could we reduce delivery time?
- How can we accelerate construction
- How can we improve process time?

Cost
- How can we reduce construction costs?
- How could we reduce maintenance costs?
- How could we reduce energy costs?

Risk
- How can we avoid or mitigate threats?
- How can we enhance existing opportunities?
- How can we create new opportunities?

The important thing is that the consideration of all four of the components of value is included in the creative process as a means of augmenting the generation of ideas.

Summary

In this chapter we have discussed creativity. Creative thinking, particularly in the area of idea generation, should be used in all phases of a project's development. Creativity techniques must be aggressively applied during a value study. No specific combination of these techniques is prescribed for all VM efforts, nor is there a predetermined degree to which they should be utilized. The selection of specific

TABLE 7.1 Partial List of Ideas from Team Brainstorming Session

IDEA EVALUATION MATRIX

Attribute Legend
+ Improvement
o No change
- Degradation

Idea Rating Legend
7 = Major Value Improvement
6 = Moderate Value Improvement
5 = Minor Value Improvement
4 = Possible Value Improvement
3 = Minor Value Degradation
2 = Moderate Value Degradation
1 = Major Value Degradation
DS = Design Suggestion

Idea#	Ideas	Program Compatibility	Building Organization	Site Organization	Aesthetics	Phasability	Maintainability	Advantages	Disadvantages	Cost	Time	Risk	Rating

FUNCTION: Support Construction Technology

Idea#	Ideas
CT-1	Move construction tech. materials storage adjacent to tool storage
CT-2	Locate the office adjacent to the tools/materials storage
CT-3	Swap the locations of tools and materials storage
CT-4	Consider overhead storage for lumber
CT-5	Use racks for lumber storage inside building
CT-6	Reorganize construction tech. office to reduce number of doors
CT-7	Add sawdust collection system
CT-8	Reorganize Supermarket Building for "dirty" functions (construction, engine & materials); minimize building rehabilitation
CT-9	Demolish Supermarket Building and build new building that better fits needs
CT-10	Move restrooms to perimeter location to minimize plumbing and slab cutting
CT-11	Rehab Supermarket Building in one phase to reduce the area cost
CT-12	Leave Supermarket Building vacant and rehab as phase 2 and construct all new facilities
CT-13	Eliminate student lounge area in Supermarket Building and reincorporate into program space
CT-14	Make the Supermarket Building a new Life Sciences Building (labs)

techniques and the depth to which they are utilized is primarily a matter of judgment and varies according to the complexity of the subject under study and the time available to use them.

A multitude of opportunities will develop by applying creative ideas to a problem. Creativity sessions will be more fruitful if a multidisciplinary team is able to participate in an environment free from distractions and judgment. The quality ideas will occur as a by-product of the quantity of ideas generated. By following the guidelines for creativity provided in this chapter, there should be no problem developing the quantity of ideas necessary to achieve the quality ideas ultimately desired. Creativity techniques are used to break loose from the mental roadblocks that restrict people's creative thinking. By exercising the imagination and having the will to succeed, one may be surprised at what ideas may be developed that will revolutionize a project.

Appendix 7A: Case Study

The value team began the Speculation Phase on the morning of the second day of the study. Using printed copies of the FAST diagram as a brainstorming guide, the value specialist facilitated a team brainstorming session that lasted all morning. The ideas were brainstormed by function using a form once again projected on the screen using a multimedia projector. The value specialist had to continually remind the team not to evaluate the ideas during brainstorming, which is not something that most of us are conditioned to do.

The value team ended up generating approximately 142 ideas covering all aspects of the project. The ideas that were generated for the function "Support Construction Technology" were of particular interest as many of these dealt with different roles for the Supermarket Building. The ideas for this function are listed in Table 7.1.

CHAPTER 8

Evaluation

© Magixl 2009, www.magixl.com

It is the mark of an educated mind to be able to entertain a thought without accepting it.

—Aristotle

Aristotle was born in 384 B.C. at Stagyra, a Greek colony and seaport on the coast of Thrace. His father, Nichomachus, was court physician to King Amyntas of Macedonia, and from this began Aristotle's long association with the Macedonian Court, which considerably influenced his life.

In his eighteenth year, he left Stagyra for Athens, the intellectual center of Greece and of the civilized world. Here he became the pupil of Plato, but soon made his master aware of the remarkable penetration and reach of his intellect, for we are told that Plato spoke of Aristotle as the "Intellect of the School." He remained at Athens twenty years, during which time the only facts recorded, in addition to his studying with Plato, are that he set up a class in rhetoric, and that in so doing, he became the rival of the celebrated orator and rhetorical reader Socrates. Following the death of his mentor Plato in 347 B.C., Aristotle soon found himself employed by King Philip of Macedon, as the tutor of his young son, Alexander.

The writings of Aristotle may be said to have embraced the whole circle of knowledge of his time. Many of them are lost; of those that remain, the most important are the "Organon," or "Logic," "Rhetoric," "Poetics," and "Meteorology." The Organon is his complete development of formal reasoning, and is the basis and nearly the whole substance of syllogistic or scholastic logic. This science he almost entirely created and he may also be said to have created the basis for the natural sciences. In his great work on animals, he amassed a stock of genuine observations and introduced a method of classification, which continues to this day. His treatises on Rhetoric and Poetics were the earliest development of the Philosophy of Criticism, and continue to be studied today. The same remark is applicable to his elaborate work on Ethics.

Aristotle's convictions were so strong that they later led to oppose some of Plato's teachings. The philosophy of Aristotle differed from that of Plato on many points, especially in the fundamental doctrine termed the Theory of Ideas. The Platonic "ideas" or "forms" were conceived as real existences. Aristotle was opposed to this doctrine; his whole method was in marked contrast to that of Plato and was based on the principle that all philosophy must be founded on the observation of facts.

Aristotle serves as the archetype for critical thinking. No other philosopher can be named whose influence has been so far-reaching and so long continued. This chapter focuses on critical thinking as applied to the evaluation of ideas and some of the techniques, and unique challenges, of the Evaluation Phase.

Evaluation Phase

The purpose of the Evaluation Phase is to systematically reduce a large number of ideas to a number of concepts that appear the most promising in meeting the project's functions. The proper evaluation of the ideas requires the use of a methodical approach that will organize the critical thinking of the value team and minimize the tendency to evaluate ideas through a psychological filter or through the use of assumptions rather than facts. The key steps in the Evaluation Phase are:

- Evaluation techniques
- Enhance evaluation—*Value Metrics*
- Selecting ideas for development

Before discussing these steps in detail, however, it is first worth exploring the concepts involved in the evaluation process itself.

The Evaluation Process

The Evaluation Phase is often neglected by value practitioners because it is viewed as a rather straightforward and obvious exercise in critical thinking. Based on the discussion from Chapter 7 with respect to our inherent bias toward the use of critical thinking over creative thinking, one might be led to believe this.

In Miles's classic text on value analysis he wrote a mere two paragraphs on the "Judgment Step." His basic point is that the step should be "performed by one person, consulting with others as required."[1] Other noted practitioners and writers, such as Art Mudge, provide only limited guidance in the evaluation of ideas, primarily conducting the evaluation step through the use of a comparison of advantages and disadvantages.[2]

The fact is that the evaluation of large groups of ideas is not always an easy task—or at least, it shouldn't be! Hopefully, the value team will have invested a lot of hard work in generating ideas during the Speculation Phase and will have been successful in withholding their judgment up until this point in the process. Many participants will now be eager to share their opinions on many of the group's ideas, especially those that fall within their specific area of knowledge. It is often very easy to dismiss ideas early in the process based on a single point and much more difficult to provide the thorough evaluation that they deserve. All the creativity in the world will be useless unless the value team is willing to perform due diligence in evaluating ideas.

Cognitive Bias

It is essential to develop an understanding of how the concepts of elicitation and cognitive bias influence decision making within the context of idea evaluation. These concepts are also relevant to any type of group communication or decision-making process. Let us first examine the definitions of these two key concepts.

"Elicitation" is essentially the process whereby one draws out information from another. This process usually occurs through an iterative process of questions and answers. What is important to understand here—and what we will focus on in this chapter—is that the way in which questions are posed, or "framed," directly influences the nature of the answer or response.

"Cognitive bias" describes a distortion in the way we see reality. Cognitive bias can be thought of as a filter that alters the way in which we interpret our environment. There are a multitude of cognitive biases that can alter how we perceive the world around us and in turn affect how we make decisions based upon the mis-interpretation of information.

Cognitive bias refers to any of a wide range of observer effects identified in cognitive science and social psychology. They include very basic statistical, social attribution, and memory errors that are common to all humans. Biases can degrade the reliability of our observations and memories. Social biases, usually called attri-bution biases, affect our everyday social interactions, while biases related to prob-ability and decision making can significantly affect the very tools and techniques that have been designed to minimize such biases. Over 100 specific cognitive biases are known to exist. Imagine how many more must exist that have not yet been formally identified and studied.

There are four cognitive biases that are worth discussing that play the greatest role during the evaluation process and that may also prevent the study team from performing a thorough evaluation of the ideas. These biases center around the innate biases of the individual participants and are based upon the rules of thumb, or heuristics, that simplify the decision-making process and enable us to make quick choices in our daily lives. While these heuristics are often very helpful in dealing with an ever more complicated world, they can also create mental road-blocks that prevent objective decisions. These four biases are:

1. Anchoring Heuristic
2. Availability Heuristic

3. Confirmation Heuristic
4. Representativeness Heuristic

ANCHORING HEURISTIC In this section we are going to explore the Anchoring Heuristic. But before we begin, you will first need to participate in a brief exercise. Let us assume that you are in a room with three other people—Bob, Sarah, and Jamal. I am going to ask the four of you a question. Assume that the other three provide their answers before you do. Here is the question:

Suppose you randomly pick one of the countries represented in the United Nations. What is the probability that it will be an African nation?[3]

This very question was explored by two noted psychologists, Daniel Kahneman and Amos Tversky in 1974. They posed this exact same question to groups of individuals in a controlled environment. Before they made their estimate, they were given a random anchor that was generated by a spinning wheel that contained the numbers 0 to 100. The wheel was rigged so that half of the participants received 10 for their anchor and the other half received 65 for their anchor. They found that when "65" was the anchor, the mean result was "45." When "10" was the anchor, the mean result was "25." They identified this phenomenon as the Anchoring Heuristic.

The *Anchoring Heuristic* describes the tendency for people to explain or describe an event by fixating on the first number or evidence that they hear. After forming an initial belief, people tend to be biased against abandoning it. Referring back to the previous example, when people saw "65" they tended to anchor to that number and then adjust up or down accordingly. Adjustments based on an anchor can be inadequate if the anchor deviates significantly from reality. This suggests that you can bias people's estimates if you provide the initial anchor.

With respect to the evaluation of ideas, this heuristic describes the tendency for people to favor an initially chosen hypothesis or solution that they are not able to easily shift away from later when considering alternative ideas and concepts. The anchoring heuristic is related to the ruling theory phenomenon identified by Chamberlin in Chapter 2, "Value."

Another example of the Anchoring Heuristic plays a large role within the field of law. The interpretation of laws as they relate to present cases is generally anchored to past judicial decisions or reinforced by known case study precedents that are deemed to be similar and/or relevant to present cases. While past legal precedence is certainly an important consideration in making judicial decisions, it can create a significant bias that may overshadow facts and circumstances that might otherwise contradict legal precedence.

The anchoring heuristic can be minimized by utilizing group evaluation techniques rather than relying on individual evaluation methods. Drawing upon the experiences and perspectives of people representing different disciplines and philosophies will help to expand the discussion and keep this heuristic from eclipsing ideas that deserve further consideration.

The following strategies should be considered to minimize the influence of the anchoring heuristic during group elicitation:

- Explain the basic mechanics of the Anchoring Heuristic to the group prior to eliciting responses.
- When possible, state the "status quo" position when asking a question.

- Try to frame questions based on facts rather than assumptions.
- Utilize group evaluation techniques that are led by a neutral facilitator.

AVAILABILITY HEURISTIC   In this section we will discuss the Availability Heuristic. Choose from the following pairs after reading the following question.

What are you most likely to die from over the course of your life if you live in the United States?

- Suicide or murder?
- Fire or poisoning?
- Earthquake or bee sting?
- Accidental suffocation or drowning?

The majority of people select murders, fires, earthquakes, and drowning over suicide, poisoning, bee stings, and suffocation. This is puzzling, especially when the probability of dying from the second set of misfortunes is in most cases twice as likely. The statistics were complied by the U.S. National Safety Council and identify the probabilities of dying from the various calamities identified above (see Table 8.1).

This phenomenon is known as the Availability Heuristic. It describes the influence that cognitive visualization has on critical thinking. The more vivid an image is within our mind, the stronger the influence it has on our critical thinking. As a result, when we are faced with choices, we will tend to be biased toward the more vivid image. Murders are more vivid than suicides, and are certainly more prolific from the standpoint of the media and entertainment industries. There are far more images of graphic murders in our heads than suicides; therefore, we may be predisposed to think that murders are more frequent than suicides. Similarly, earthquakes can result in wide ranging and catastrophic damage. Bee stings, by comparison, seem rather innocuous although you are twice as likely to die from a bee sting as from an earthquake.

An important corollary finding to the availability heuristic is that people asked to imagine an outcome immediately perceive it as more likely than those that were not. And that which was vividly described is viewed as more likely than that which was provided a much duller description.

Safety is often an important performance attribute for many types of projects. It is also probably the most obvious trigger for the availability heuristic because a product, process, or facility that is perceived as "unsafe" conjures up vivid images of the consequences.

The value specialist needs to help the study team place performance attributes such as safety into proper perspective. One technique to do this is to make

TABLE 8.1   Lifetime Statistical Probabilities of Causes of Death for U.S. Residents

Cause of Death	Odds	Cause of Death	Odds
Suicide	1 in 117	Murder	1 in 210
Poisoning	1 in 161	Fire	1 in 1,192
Bee Sting	1 in 46,477	Earthquake	1 in 103,004
Suffocation	1 in 646	Drowning	1 in 1,064

statements that will appeal to the participants' logic rather than to their emotions. The following are some examples using this technique:

- "If we want this highway project to be completely safe, we should limit the speed to 5 mph or, better still, shut it down altogether." Obviously, shutting down the highway would make it safe; however, the other performance requirements would then not be met as a result. The point here is that safety is indeed an important consideration; however, it is just one aspect of performance.
- "If we want to eliminate any possibility for product liability, then we should send out a company representative to demonstrate to the consumer how to operate their new ladder." While this idea might, in concept, eliminate all potential consumer lawsuits, it would no doubt bankrupt the company offering such a service.

The following strategies should be considered to minimize the influence of the availability heuristic during group elicitation:

- Explain the basic mechanics of the Availability Heuristic to the group prior to eliciting responses. Do this by asking questions similar to the ones in the previous example.
- Try to frame questions that will appeal to logic rather than emotion.
- Be especially sensitive to emotionally charged questions and decisions, especially those that deal with safety or life and death consequences.
- Utilize group evaluation techniques that are led by a neutral facilitator.

CONFIRMATION HEURISTIC   In this discussion, we will explore the Confirmation Heuristic, also known as the Confirmation Bias. We will begin with a simple exercise to help demonstrate this heuristic in action. All of the cards in Figure 8.1 have a number on one side and a letter on the other side. Read the following statement.

If a card has a vowel on one side, then it has an even number on the other side. Assuming this statement is true, which card(s) must be turned over to see if the statement is true or false?

Think about this before proceeding to the next paragraph. Which card did you pick?

Most people easily hit upon "A" as being a necessary card to turn over. If there is an even number on the other side, then the claim is at least partially confirmed. On the other hand, if there is an odd number on the other side, then the claim is proven false.

FIGURE 8.1   Which Cards Must Be Turned over to See If the Statement Is True?

The next tendency is to turn over the "4" and see if there is a vowel on the other side. However, this really doesn't tell you anything as the claim is "If a card has a vowel on one side, then it has an even number on the other side." But finding a card with a consonant on one side and an even number on the other doesn't falsify the claim, as it doesn't say that *only* vowels have even numbers on the other side. Likewise, turning over the "D" tells you nothing, even if you do find an even number on the other side.

The correct answer is both "A" and "7" must be turned over. If only "A" is flipped over, and we find an even number on the other side, than we would have to consider "7." In order for the claim to be true, there must be a consonant on the other side. Finding a vowel would falsify the claim.

Most people are fooled by this task because of the confirmation bias. They attempt to confirm the claim, while forgetting that it is also important to try and *falsify* it. Finding a pairing of vowel and even number does nothing to support the claim; it's the failure to find a vowel with an *odd* number that confirms it.

Confirmation bias describes the tendency for people to seek evidence that supports rather than challenges their current beliefs. It occurs when people selectively notice or focus upon evidence that tends to support the things they already believe or want to be true while ignoring that evidence that would serve to disprove those beliefs or ideas. Confirmation bias plays a stronger role when it comes to those beliefs that are based upon prejudice, faith, or tradition rather than on empirical evidence.

For example, if we already believe or want to believe that someone can tell us what are pets our thinking, then we will notice when they say things that are accurate or pleasant but tend to forget things said that are simply incorrect. Another good example would be how people notice when they get a phone call from a person they were just thinking about, but don't remember how often they didn't get such a call when thinking about a person.

Similarly, studies have shown that people will often "read over" a section in a newspaper or magazine article that is in conflict with their beliefs, without being aware that they are doing it. One of the problems with the confirmation bias is that people become so dogmatic and rigid in their viewpoints that they aren't open to competing explanations or to adapting their position in light of new facts or interpretations.

The confirmation bias is best addressed by thoroughly and objectively evaluating an idea or concept that might otherwise be dismissed out of hand. Seek to invite the opinions of individuals that hold differing views. It's not unusual for participants on a study team, especially those that may already be involved on the project team, to try and look for reasons why a new way of doing something won't work. This is a perfect example of why it is wise to include team members who do not have a personal interest in the baseline concept to help provide balance in evaluating new ideas.

The following strategies should be considered in an effort to minimize the influence of the confirmation heuristic during group elicitation:

- Explain the basic mechanics of the Confirmation Heuristic to the group prior to eliciting responses.

- Be sure to gather as much data as is practical and present it to the group prior to eliciting information.
- Seek to spend an equal amount of time and effort in uncovering information that both supports and contradicts any statement.
- Utilize group evaluation techniques that are led by a neutral facilitator.

REPRESENTATIVENESS HEURISTIC   In this section we will explore the Representativeness Heuristic. We will begin with a simple exercise to help demonstrate this heuristic in action. Let me describe to you a man named Jack. Jack is 45 years old, married, and has four children. He is generally conservative, careful, and quiet. He shows no interest in political and social issues and spends most of his free time building models with his sons, reading, and solving mathematical puzzles. Based on the information provided, is Jack a lawyer or an engineer?

Imagine further that Jack is attending a conference with 99 other men. Of the total number of 100 men present, 30 are engineers and 70 are lawyers. Based on what you know about Jack, what would you estimate that the probability that Jack is one of the engineers?

If we relied upon the data in the previous paragraph, the answer would be 30 percent. Did you select a different number? If you did, your answer at least partly based upon the description of Jack. This is an example of the Representativeness Heuristic.

The use of this heuristic can, however, can systematically lead one to make poor judgments in some circumstances. Other examples include:

- The belief in runs of good and bad luck in games of chance. This particular incarnation is also known as the *gambler's fallacy.*
- People will often assume that a random sequence in a lottery (12, 19, 57, 23, 8, 31) is more likely than an arithmetic sequence of numbers (5, 6, 7, 8, 9, 10).
- If two salespeople from a large company both displayed aggressive behavior, the assumption may be that the company has established a policy of aggressive selling, and that most other salespeople from that firm will also engage in aggressive techniques.

In summary, people tend to estimate the probability of an event by how similar the event is to the population of events it came from and whether the events seem to be similar to the process that produced it.

The following strategies should be considered to minimize the influence of the representativeness heuristic during group elicitation:

- Explain the basic mechanics of the Representativeness Heuristic to the group prior to eliciting responses.
- Recognize that biases related to gender, religion, ethnicity, and social standing are all forms of the Representativeness Heuristic. They are not allowed in the workplace and, similarly, they should also be excluded from elicitation and decision-making processes.
- Raise awareness of this heuristic within the group by stating an absurd stereotype that is relevant to the group. For instance, if the group were composed of architects, you could state, "Architects don't care about what buildings cost—

they only care about what they look like." Be mindful though to avoid offensive references!

- Utilize group evaluation techniques that are led by a neutral facilitator.

The value specialist should seek to develop an understanding of these heuristics and biases and try to recognize them when they occur, as they can quickly, and unfairly, derail ideas that may otherwise prove to have merit. The representativeness heuristic is often the worst, and most unfair, of the four heuristics discussed in this chapter. In its most destructive form, this heuristic is really nothing more than prejudice based upon broad stereotypes. The value specialist must use tact in disarming this behavior.

Evaluation Techniques

There are a number of evaluation techniques that can be employed by the value specialist to evaluate the ideas generated during the Speculation Phase. The techniques that will be presented in this chapter include:

- Evaluation by Simple Rating
- Evaluation by Comparison
- Nominal Group Technique
- Evaluation Matrix—*Value Metrics*

Evaluation by Simple Rating

A relatively quick way to evaluate ideas that is commonly used by value practitioners is to identify a set of evaluation criteria, discuss the merits of the idea relative to the evaluation criteria, and then assign the idea a rating based on how well it addresses the evaluation criteria.

The use of performance attributes is ideal for use as evaluation criteria. If performance attributes are not being used for the value study, then the process of selecting evaluation criteria can be commenced by engaging in a brief brainstorming session. Start by asking, "What are the goals and objectives of this project?" Make a list of the group's answers.

For example, an information technology project that is addressing the development of a new database management software program might identify the following objectives:

- "Make the software user-friendly."
- "Make the software flexible so that it can be used for a variety of applications."
- "Make the software cost effective."

From these objectives the following evaluation criteria can be distilled:

- User-friendliness
- Flexibility
- Cost effectiveness

Each idea should then be discussed relative to the evaluation criteria and an overall l rating can then be assigned using any numeric scale preferred (1 to 3, 1 to 5, or 1 to 10 are most common). The scale should reflect overall acceptability of the idea, and each number on the scale should be defined. For example, a 1 to 3 scale might consist of numbers with corresponding values such as:

1. Unacceptable. This idea should be dropped from further consideration.
2. Shows potential. This idea should be considered only after all of the ideas rated "3" have been developed.
3. Acceptable. The idea should be developed into a value alternative.

The example in Table 8.2 shows a simple evaluation of several ideas for the forklift project's hydraulic system, which is described by the function statement *Pump Fluid*. In this case, the ideas were organized by function and discussed by the value team relative to the performance attributes that served as the evaluation criteria. In order to conserve time, the ideas are just given a simple rating.

The broader the scale, the more fidelity will be gained. Idea codes can be used to help identify and track ideas by function (e.g., *Pump Fluid* = PF-1) as they move through the evaluation and development process. This method is fairly fast but tends not to be as thorough as the techniques described below. In the example above, the rationale for the rating isn't recorded. This may handicap the team later as the reasons for the rating that is given may be forgotten or become unclear; however, it may have been the only reasonable way to evaluate the ideas given time constraints.

Evaluation by Comparison

This approach builds upon the previous technique and compares the advantages and disadvantages of an idea relative to the project's baseline concept. The value specialist should facilitate the discussion of each idea and record the advantages and disadvantages based on the evaluation criteria. From this discussion, the value team should be able to make conclusions as to which ideas merit further exploration in the Development Phase, and which ideas should be eliminated from further consideration (see Table 8.3). The ideas can be rated based on a rating scale as

TABLE 8.2   Simple Rating Evaluation Technique

Function: PUMP FLUID

Idea Code	Idea	Rating
PF-1	Hand-operated reciprocating pump	1
PF-2	Radial piston pump	2
PF-3	Gerotor (generated rotor) pump	3
PF-4	Use a gear pump from a different manufacturer	3
PF-5	Eliminate hydraulic system completely and use an electric motor	2
PF-6	Rotary vane pump	1
PF-7	Axial piston pump	2

described previously. This approach provides better documentation on the team's reasoning; however, it also requires more time.

Nominal Group Technique

The nominal group technique was originally developed as an organizational planning method by Delbecq, Van de Ven, and Gustafson in 1971.[4] This technique, with a few minor modifications, provides an effective means of prioritizing ideas through group consensus. This process includes the following steps:

- After the ideas have been captured following a creativity session, the value specialist will ask each participant to read, and elaborate on, their ideas in order to ensure everyone understands the concept. Duplicate ideas can be crossed out and the remaining ideas are numbered or assigned an idea code.
- The value specialist asks each person to write down, in a few minutes, the idea numbers or codes that seem especially important. Some people may feel only a few items are important; others may feel all items are important. The value specialist then goes down the list and records the number of people who consider each item a priority.
- Session participants are then asked to choose up to 10 ideas that they feel are the most important and rank them according to their relative importance. The

TABLE 8.3 Evaluation by Comparison

Function: CONTROL SPEED

Idea Code	Idea	Advantages	Disadvantages	Rating
CS-1	Electronic shift control	*Allows for "on the fly" shifting *Improves fuel efficiency	*Increases costs	10
CS-2	Hydrostatic hand paddles	*Allows greater sensitivity in controlling speed *Allows for visual feedback	*Increases costs *Adds complexity to hydraulic system *Concept may not be intuitive for most operators	7
CS-4	Joystick control	*Provides a unique control solution *May lend itself to a new marketing approach *Could provide for increased control if combined with an electronic shift control	*Increases costs *Concept may not be intuitive for most operators	8
CS-5	Manual shift with clutch	*Reduces costs *Allows more operator control	*Requires clutch maintenance *Less convenient for operator	3

idea they felt was most important should get at "1" down to their least important, which would get a "10." These rankings are collected from all participants, and aggregated (see Table 8.4). The lower the score, the higher the idea is ranked. Time permitting, participants should be asked why they ranked ideas the way they did.

Sometimes these results are given back to the participants in order to stimulate further discussion or to allow for the readjustment in the overall rankings assigned to the various responses. This is done only when group consensus regarding the prioritization of issues is important to the overall research or planning project. As its name suggests, the nominal group technique is composed of values provided on an individual basis, but grouped together to form a single ranking.

Enhance Evaluation—*Value Metrics*

The Evaluation Phase of the Value Methodology Job Plan is often first to be cut when time constraints arise, when a thorough, deliberative process is often what is most needed. The consideration of all four of the components of value (performance, cost, time, and risk) is paramount during this phase in order to ensure that ideas have been thoroughly evaluated.

The evaluation process should consider each idea with respect to the performance attributes. Discussions should focus on the aspects of how each individual idea would improve or degrade performance relative to the baseline concept. During this discussion, the rationale for each idea relative to performance is documented. This documentation can prove very valuable to project stakeholders, even for those ideas that are ultimately rejected, as it provides a concise but thorough discussion of key project issues. Many times, project stakeholders will want to know why an idea was not further developed into an alternative. This conscientious approach should satisfy this requirement.

Unfortunately, many promising ideas are discarded based on unfounded statements with respect to only one aspect of performance. The process described above

TABLE 8.4 Nominal Group Technique

Function: GENERATE TORQUE

Idea Code	Bill	John	Fred	Sally	Jamal	Total Votes	Ranking
GT-1	7	8	10	10	8	43	9
GT-5	8	5	4	6	3	26	5
GT-11	1	2	1	3	2	9	1
GT-16	6	9	8	7	10	40	8
GT-18	10	10	7	9	9	45	10
GT-23	2	3	3	2	1	11	2
GT-26	5	6	9	8	6	34	6
GT-29	3	1	2	1	4	11	2
GT-32	9	7	6	5	7	34	6
GT-34	4	4	5	4	5	22	4

forces participants to articulate their criticism in an organized way that addresses all aspects of performance, not just those that immediately come to mind. Additional in-depth discussion is often required before potential performance-related benefits are revealed.

The Value Metrics approach to evaluation considers performance first, followed by cost, schedule, and risk. When all of these components have been considered, a final rating is assigned to the idea. The +/o/– shorthand notation provides a simple means of expressing the improvement or degradation (or no change) of the idea relative to the baseline concept for the four components of value. Any +/– should be referenced in the advantages and disadvantages with the rationale supporting the notation. The following rating scale is suggested:

1. Major Value Degradation
2. Moderate Value Degradation
3. Design Consideration (No cost data developed)
4. Possible Value Improvement
5. Minor Value Improvement
6. Moderate Value Improvement
7. Major Value Improvement

It is recommended that the evaluation process be conducted using a multimedia projector. This will allow all of the information to be captured on the screen and provide feedback to the team so that it may be edited in real time. The Evaluation Matrix is shown in Table 8.5.

Selecting Ideas for Development

Regardless of the technique employed to evaluate the ideas, the evaluation process should have narrowed down the list of ideas considerably. The remaining ideas identified by the team for further investigation in the Development Phase should be listed by priority, based upon the outcome of the evaluation.

In some cases, further evaluation may be necessary, especially if it appears that the list of surviving ideas appears to be larger than what the value team can adequately develop in the time allotted. In cases such as this, it may be advisable to attempt to make a quick estimate of costs in order to develop a better understanding of the magnitude of savings (or cost increase) involved. Alternatively, the nominal group technique can be employed to help rank the remaining alternatives in order of importance.

Once the ideas have been listed according to their priority, they will need to be assigned to the value team members for development. It is important to emphasize that the entire team may be involved in the development of an idea into an alternative; however, it is best to assign one individual on the team to bear the responsibility that the idea is fully developed and does not fall through the cracks. This speaks to the old adage "If it's everybody's job, then it's nobody's responsibility!"

It is recommended that the value specialist request that team members select those ideas that they are most interested in developing. If there appears to be a

TABLE 8.5 Evaluation Matrix Using Value Metrics

Function: ENSURE COMFORT

Idea Code	Idea	Travel Speed	Lift Speed	Turning Radius	Drawbar Capacity	Climbing Capacity	Maintain-ability	Ergo-nomics	Advantages	Disadvantages	Cost	Time	Risk	Rating
EC-1	Include movable armrests	o	o	o	o	o	–	+	*Reduce operator fatigue *Help protect operator in case of vehicle overturning	*Increases cost *Armrests require additional mechanism to lock in place	–	o	+	6
EC-2	Include fold-away step to assist ingress/egress into operator cab	o	o	o	o	o	o	+	*Reduces chance of operator injury and/or muscle strain	*Increases cost slightly *Step needs to be designed to avoid projecting from vehicle (safety concern)	–	o	–	5
EC-3	Include 180 degree swivel seat	o	o	o	o	o	o	+	*Allows operator to get in and out of cab more easily *Seat movement should reduce operator fatigue and potential for back injuries	*Increases cost slightly *May require additional control to lock seat into one position	–	o	o	5
EC-4	Include vibration dampening floor mat	o	o	o	o	o	–	+	*Reduce operator fatigue	*Increase cost *Subject to wear and replacement	–	o	o	5

Legend: Improved: +, No Change: o, Degraded: –

Rating: 1 = Major Value Degradation, 2 = Moderate Value Degradation, 3 = Design Consideration, 4 = Possible Value Improvement, 5 = Minor Value Improvement, 6 = Moderate Value Improvement, 7 = Major Value Improvement general reluctance for team members to select ideas, then the value specialist should assign them to team members, based upon the relevance of the ideas to their respective disciplines. Once all of the ideas have been assigned, the value team will be ready to move into the Development Phase.

Summary

The evaluation of ideas requires the value team to think critically, rationally and objectively. Developing an understanding of the role that cognitive bias can play in the evaluation process is the first part in achieving this goal. The second step is to select an evaluation technique that is most suitable for the project based upon the time constraints of the study, the ability and personality of the value team, and the capacity of the value specialist to keep the team focused on providing a balanced and objective assessment of the ideas.

Appendix 8A: Case Study

The value team wrapped up the Speculation Phase by lunchtime of the second day. After lunch, the team entered the Evaluation Phase. The ideas that had been entered in the Idea Evaluation Matrix during the team brainstorming session were now evaluated on the screen.

The idea evaluation process extended into midmorning of the third day. The discussion generated during the Evaluation Phase typically takes longer than the time to generate the initial list of ideas when using the Value Metrics process and on this value study things were no different.

The Idea Evaluation Matrix for the ideas related to the function "Support Construction Technology" is provided in Table 8.6. The evaluation of the fourteen ideas identified for this function yielded three potential value alternatives and a half-dozen design suggestions. The ideas identified as design suggestions were felt to offer constructive thoughts on the design; however, they were relatively minor in nature and would likely be addressed as the design process advanced. These were presented in the report as one or two paragraph comments and were not deemed to warrant full development in the form of value alternatives.

The three ideas that warranted further analysis into development as value alternatives included:

1. *CT-8*. This idea would reorganize the Supermarket (i.e., Technology) Building by co-locating those educational programs that dealt with noisy, dirty activities (e.g., construction technology, engine repair, etc.). As a result, the criminal justice program would be shifted into the Classroom Building, while the materials engineering program would be moved into the renovated Supermarket Building. This modification would improve Program Compatibility and Building Organization.
2. *CT-9*. This idea would demolish the Supermarket Building and build a new building that would better cater to the site and the educational program. Based on the value team's cost analysis, there is no cost benefit to remodeling the

TABLE 8.6 Idea Evaluation Matrix for the Function "Support Construction Technology"

IDEA EVALUATION MATRIX

Attribute Legend
+ Improvement
o No change
– Degradation

Idea Rating Legend
7 = Major Value Improvement
6 = Moderate Value Improvement
5 = Minor Value Improvement
4 = Possible Value Improvement
3 = Minor Value Degradation
2 = Moderate Value Degradation
1 = Major Value Degradation
DS = Design Suggestion

Idea #	Ideas	Program Compatibility	Building Organization	Site Organization	Aesthetics	Phasability	Maintainability	Advantages	Disadvantages	Cost	Time	Risk	Rating
		Performance Attributes											
FUNCTION: Support Construction Technology													
CT-1	Move construction tech. materials storage adjacent to tool storage	o	+	o	o	o	o	*Allows co-monitoring of equipment and materials by one staff member		o	o	o	DS
CT-2	Locate the office adjacent to the tools/materials storage	o	–	o	o	o	o	*Improves supervision of tools	*Assumes a staff member is in the office to monitor the tools – not very practical	o	o	o	3
CT-3	Swap the locations of tools and materials storage	o	+	o	o	o	o	*Increases ease of materials delivery		o	o	o	DS
CT-4	Consider overhead storage for lumber	o	+	o	o	o	o	*Frees up more floor space for other activities	*Creates materials handling issue requiring a forklift *Creates potential safety issues	–	o	–	DS
CT-5	Use racks for lumber storage inside building	o	+	o	o	o	o	*Potentially reduces the size of the covered outdoor area	*Creates materials handling issue requiring a forklift *Creates potential safety issues	–	o	–	DS
CT-6	Reorganize construction tech. office to reduce number of doors	o	+	o	o	o	o	*Eliminates door, creates more usable space in office	*Reduces direct access	+	o	o	DS
CT-7	Add sawdust collection system	o	o	o	o	o	+	*Improve air quality *Reduce dust	*Increases equipment costs	–	o	o	DS

ID	Idea						Advantages	Disadvantages	
CT-8	Reorganize Supermarket Building for "dirty" functions (construction, engine, & materials); minimize building rehabilitation	+	+	o	+	+	*Reduces cost of renovation *Collocates like activities *Provides additional clearance for materials tech labs *Better use of existing building *Reduces need to maintain empty, future Phase 2 space	*Forces Materials Tech program into existing building versus building to suit	7
CT-9	Demolish Supermarket Building and build new building that better fits needs	+	+	+	+	+	*Allows new space to be built that is tailored to meet specific program needs *Allows site to be reconfigured and optimized by not having to work around existing building *Reduces disruptions during Phase 2 construction *Reduces O&M costs by providing all new buildings *Continuity of aesthetics will be improved as all new buildings will be constructed *Reduces risks related to rehab.	*Public may perceive demolition of usable structure as wasteful	7
CT-10	Move restrooms to perimeter location to minimize plumbing and slab cutting	o	–	o	o	o	*Reduces plumbing cost	*Less accessible location for restrooms	DS
CT-11	Rehabilitate Supermarket Building in one phase to reduce the area cost						*Combine with Idea # CT-12		
CT-12	Leave Supermarket Building vacant and build all new buildings	+	+	+	+	–	*Maximizes investment in property *Results in the construction of all new buildings *Reduces construction costs *Simplifies phasing	*Cannot provide additional site development if Supermarket Building is dedicated to District *Limits future flexibility *Requires delay of some programs until Phase 2	7
CT-13	Eliminate student lounge area in Supermarket Building and reincorporate into program space						*Combine with Idea # ET-3		
CT-14	Make the Supermarket Building a new Life Sciences Building (labs)						*Combine with Idea # CT-9		

Supermarket Building. Demolishing the building would allow the site to be better optimized, improve site circulation, and consolidate parking and drainage improvements. Further, it would allow the construction of multiple buildings that could be custom tailored to meet the specific needs of the entire educational program without having to make compromises. This would potentially result in the development of three new buildings:

- Administration Building
- Technology Building
- Life Sciences Building

This modification would improve Program Compatibility, Building Organization, and Site Organization. It would also potentially improve Phaseability by allowing new buildings to be added as needed rather than creating disruptions through the ongoing remodeling efforts of the existing spaces.

3. *CT-12.* This idea would leave the Supermarket Building vacant in Phase 1 and rehabilitate it in Phase 2. Therefore, Phase 1 would construct the Classroom and Administration Buildings while supporting the associated programs. Phase 2 would remodel the old supermarket to create the Technology Building. This approach would reduce the renovation cost of the Supermarket Building and would reduce disruptions to existing operations, thereby improving Phaseability.

These three particular ideas involved major changes to the way in which the educational program would be delivered and how the campus would be organized. This is one of the key benefits in conducting a value study early on in the design process for construction projects. Had the value study been performed later, it is unlikely that the radical changes suggested by these ideas would have rated as highly during the evaluation process due to schedule impacts and redesign costs.

Once the value team completed the evaluation process, the ideas that ranked a 4 or better were assigned to the value team members. There were 34 such ideas. These were prioritized and assigned to the value team members for development.

CHAPTER **9**

Development

© Magixl 2009, www.magixl.com

Opportunity is missed by most people because it is dressed in overalls and looks like work.

—Thomas Edison

Thomas Alva Edison (1847–1931) was born in Milan, Ohio, where he was the youngest in a family of seven. As a youth, he was employed as a telegraph operator where he developed an affinity for electricity.

In 1868, Edison patented his first invention and also learned a tough lesson. He took his electric vote-recording machine to Washington for a demonstration. He was later told that his machine was too efficient and did not allow sufficient time for negotiation and maneuvers. The lesson to be learned is that inventions are only good when they are needed. Edison would not make the same mistake again.

Three years later, he devised an improved version of the stock ticker. Offering it for sale to Gold and Stock Telegraph Company, he was reluctant to ask for the $50,000 he wanted for it, so he asked what it was worth to them. They offered him $40,000, which provided the capital for an engineering firm in Newark, New Jersey. He was only twenty-three years old at the time. During the next six years, he developed the mimeograph and improved upon the telegraph and the typewriter. He also invented wax paper.

In 1876, he focused on further expansion by creating an "invention factory." Edison said he wanted to turn out an invention every ten days. What seemed like a grandiose plan proved to be achievable, and often a patent was obtained every five days. He had a committed staff who helped produce many significant advances. One of these inventions was the carbon telephone transmitter; this device greatly improved the sound clarity of the telephone. One of Edison's personal favorites was the phonograph. The invention was a sensation and firmly established him as a major inventor.

Edison is most famous for the electric lightbulb. Though not an original Edison invention, it was he who made it practical. The problem had been the bulb's duration, or achieving prolonged periods of operation. Edison rectified this by using scorched cotton thread as a filament. It sustained light for forty straight hours. More important, he helped devise a system whereby homes and businesses could be supplied with electricity.

In his lifetime, Edison patented 1,093 inventions and earned the nickname "The Wizard of Menlo Park." He attributed much of his "genius" to hard work. Edison had many notable failures, but through perseverance and great effort, he was able to develop a prolific number of ideas into reality. Edison's life illustrates the importance of the Development Phase as part of the VM Job Plan.

Development Phase

The core of a Value Study includes the Function Analysis, Speculation, and Evaluation Phases of the job plan. At the completion of the Evaluation Phase, the value team will have identified a number of concepts that will need to be developed into possible alternatives.

The team members are responsible for preparing these recommendations, which are based upon a comparison to the project baseline concept. All recommendations are ultimately documented with written descriptions, narratives providing justification, sketches, performance assessments, calculations, and cost comparisons (both initial costs and life cycle costs if needed). These recommendations are referred to as value alternatives.

There are two steps in the Development Phase. These include:

1. Develop value alternatives
2. Review value alternatives

Develop Value Alternatives

The concepts that were short-listed during the Evaluation Phase are now developed into value alternatives. The information to be used for these value alternatives must be collected and presented in a way that will allow the project team and decision makers to easily understand the concepts involved, their justification, and their effect on cost and performance.

The value alternatives should be organized using a standardized format. Value programs and practitioners utilize a wide variety of formats for value alternatives that are based upon the type of information that is required by the decision makers of an organization to determine its acceptability. The value specialist should, therefore, ensure that whatever format will be used will contain all of the information that will be needed by the project team and/or decision makers and adjust the format of the value alternatives accordingly.

Regardless of the project type, there are certain pieces of information that any decision maker will need to have. A complete set of forms containing this basic information (see Figure 9.1) should include:

- Descriptions of baseline and alternative concepts
- Discussion and justification of the alternative concept
- Financial information (initial cost and life cycle costs, as applicable)
- Performance assessment (impacts to project scope and schedule)
- Graphical information (flow charts, diagrams, sketches, etc.)

In addition to this basic information, there may be a number of additional pieces of information that may include:

- Project management considerations
- Redesign and/or implementation costs
- Technical reviewer or stakeholder comments
- Value team member review comments

A suggested format of content to be included in the value alternatives as well as the organization of that information is presented in Figure 9.1. This format is

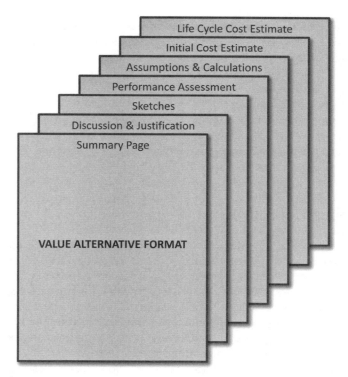

FIGURE 9.1 Value Alternative Format

intended to capture the information developed for the value alternatives through the following steps in the development process:

- Ensure technical viability
- Determine costs
- Assess performance—*Value Metrics*
- Assess risk
- Develop narratives

One interpretation of this information is suggested in the Case Study section at the end of this chapter. It must be emphasized that there are many different ways to organize and present information on value alternatives. Other examples are provided in this chapter.

If the procedures identified in this chapter are followed, the value team should be successful in developing value alternatives that will thoroughly communicate the concepts to the project team and to the decision makers. Hopefully, this information will be presented clearly and concisely enough by the value team to make the decision-making process an easy one.

Ensure Technical Viability

Assuming that all of the short-listed ideas were assigned at the end of the Evaluation Phase, the value team members will be ready to begin documenting the information that will be developed for each value alternative. The first step in this process is to ensure the technical viability of the value alternative. In other words, will it work?

Depending on the nature of the concept, technical viability may or may not be obvious. If it is not, the value team must consider this issue first, before expending any additional time on the concept. Verifying technical viability may involve different activities, for example:

- A concept involving an alternative highway alignment may require that the value team's highway design engineer lay out the geometry on a topographic map in order to ensure that the horizontal and vertical sight distances can be achieved. Will there be additional right-of-way needed? Will additional earthwork be needed? Will the alignment alter the environmental footprint? The value team will need to address all of these issues before proceeding with further development of the alternative.
- A concept involving modifications to a latch spring assembly for a screen door could involve a physical mock-up to test its performance. Will the new latch keep the screen closed while the equipment on which it is mounted is in operation? Will the latch stick? Can the new latch be produced using existing materials or will new material stock be required? The value team will need to ensure that questions such as these are answered before moving on.
- A concept involving the development of a standardized form to be used by six different city agencies to track funding requests should include a meeting with budget personnel from each agency to identify the necessary information required to process the request. Does each agency use the same terminology?

If not, can a standardized language be developed? Does each agency require the same number of approval signatures? If not, can these be consolidated and standardized? In this case, the value team will need to work directly with stakeholders to actually develop a standardized form before completing other alternative development activities.

It is important to note that the value team need only develop the concept to the level of the baseline concept. In some cases, especially for projects involving facilities, it may only be necessary to develop the concept at a preliminary level to ensure that it is fundamentally sound. In other words, it is not necessary to develop the design of a new forklift component in AutoCAD, as this is an activity that may take far more time than is available to the value team. Both the value team and project team must keep in mind that any value alternative that is ultimately accepted will need to be integrated into the project by the project team.

As the value team verifies the alternative's technical feasibility, any calculations or assumptions should be documented. These, along with any sketches, diagrams, or other graphical information will be included as part of value alternative's documentation. If it turns out that the concept is not technically viable, then the reason(s) why it will not work should be documented and the concept dropped from further consideration.

Returning to the forklift example, the value team focused on developing one of the ideas that was rated highly after the Evaluation Phase. The idea (Idea No. EC-1) was to add armrests to the operator's seat. The concept was obviously feasible; however, it required the team to consider the specifics of the idea. There are countless ways in which to add armrests to a seat.

The team began by looking at armrest assemblies on their competitor's models, several of which had been rented in order to stimulate the team's thinking. Each of the competing models approached the function differently. They examined each and then began discussing the strengths and weaknesses of each approach. Second, they considered the seat on their existing forklift model and considered whether armrests could be added to it. The team cycled several times through Speculation, Evaluation, and Development before finally settling on the approach that they would carry forward. After consulting several vendors, it was determined that the company that made the existing seat also made an armrest kit that could be fitted to the existing seat (see Figure 9.2). Later, it was learned that purchasing had been contacted about this feature by the vendor years ago but the information was never passed on to marketing or design.

The team was able to obtain the technical drawings and information on the armrest attachment and requested a price quote for the required quantities (see Figure 9.3).

Determine Costs

Once the value team feels confident that the concept will actually work, the next step will be to assess its financial impacts. Hopefully, the value team will have been provided with the project baseline's cost data prior to the value study. This cost data should serve as the basis for developing the costs for the value alternative. In some cases, the concept behind a value alternative may be so radically different

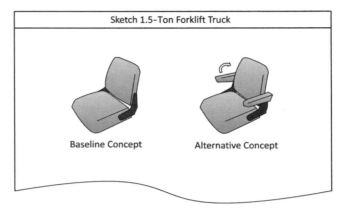

FIGURE 9.2 Value Alternative Sketch, Forklift

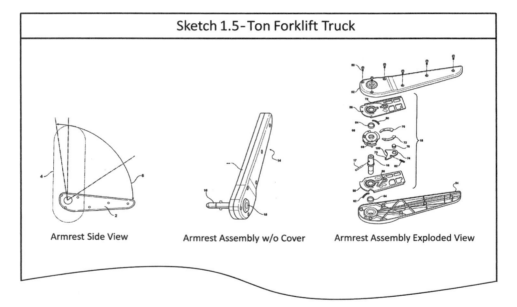

FIGURE 9.3 Value Alternative Sketch, Forklift

from the baseline concept that it will be necessary to develop a completely new cost estimate from scratch. In such cases, the value team must be careful to document where they are obtaining cost information to support the alternative. Any assumptions should be well documented and justified.

If life cycle costs will be affected by the value alternative, a life cycle analysis should be included as part of the value alternative documentation. Information pertaining to life cycle periods and discount rates should be obtained from the project team or project sponsor.

In performing cost estimates, it is always advisable that a side-by-side comparison of the baseline and the alternative costs be made in order to show which areas differ in cost. In developing the costs of the alternative concept, it is not always necessary to provide an estimate of the complete project—it is usually only necessary to include project costs that will change as a result of the implementation of the value alternative.

The value team received the price quote the next day for the armrest attachment kit. The cost worked out to be $24.50 per unit in the desired quantities. The team realized that this was the cost just for the components; it would still need to be connected to the existing seat assembly. The team calculated the time it would take to attach the armrests to the seat and came up with a loaded labor cost of $15.37, assuming it were assembled at the main assembly plant. This brought the total cost per unit to $39.87. One of the team members thought to ask the vendor's representative if they could deliver a complete seat and armrest assembly. He said they could and quoted a total price of $34.50, more than $5 less per unit than if the armrests had been assembled at the value team's assembly plant. The team also realized that this approach would also eliminate the additional production time at the plant needed to perform this assembly operation.

Assess Performance—*Value Metrics*

Once the technical feasibility and costs have been determined, the value team should have a fairly good idea whether or not the value alternative will provide an improvement in value. The next step is to assess the anticipated impacts that the value alternative will have on project performance.

Each of the performance attributes originally identified, defined, and benchmarked during the Information Phase should be reviewed with respect to the value alternative. A statement of performance should be made for each attribute and the rationale for the change (or no change) relative to the baseline noted.

A standard form can be used that includes the baseline concept's performance score and attribute weight, as well as a space to record the alternative concept's performance score. The change in performance, if any, must be assessed using the scales and parameters originally established and must be relative to the effect of the change on the entire project. An alternative may provide a dramatic improvement relative to the project element being considered; however, the overall effect upon the total project may be relatively minor or even insignificant. The rationale should relate to both; however, the performance rating must relate to the total project. This is important to understand, as the objective of the value study is to improve the total value of the project as a whole. The cumulative or synergistic effect of multiple alternative concepts on performance is discussed in Chapter 10, "Presentation." The net change in performance for the alternative concept is expressed in a percent format.

Sometimes this activity is best performed by the group as a whole. The use of a multimedia projector will allow the team to consider the performance of alternatives.

The value team next considered the impact of the armrests to the overall performance of the forklift. During the Evaluation Phase, the team had initially rated "Ergonomics" as being improved but "Maintainability" as being worse. As the team discussed the performance, it became clear that the maintenance issue was mostly related to the upholstery—they had initially expressed concerns about wear and

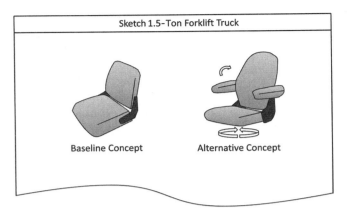

FIGURE 9.4   Value Alternative Sketch, Forklift

tear on the armrest covers. The team thought about ways to solve this problem and conceived the idea of using rigid foam in lieu of an upholstered cover. This would provide a more durable cover while still providing sufficient comfort.

The team decided to touch base with the first vendor again to see if they offered the armrests with this material. The vendor replied that they didn't have one currently available; however, he said that his company was in the process of developing a new hybrid seat and armrest assembly using a combination of rigid foam and upholstery. In fact, the vendor would be willing to negotiate a very competitive price if the team was willing to consider testing the prototype. This would require replacing both the existing seat as well as adding the armrest. The team asked if the vendor could deliver a prototype to the study site for evaluation. He said he could and the team requested a price quote as well for the required number of units (see Figure 9.4).

The seat and armrest assembly was delivered a few days later at the study site. The team began evaluating the seat and found that it had many ergonomic improvements over the existing seat in addition to having better shock absorption, more adjustment capability, and the ability to swivel 180 degrees, which was another idea that the team was planning to develop further (Idea No. EC-3). The price quote for the seat and armrest assembly in the numbers specified was $265, which was only $20 more than the current seat! The team decided to combine these two ideas into one alternative. They requested additional design data from the vendor to include in the alternative, including specifications and drawings that would allow their engineering department to modify the attachment to the chassis for the seat's new swivel mount (see Figure 9.5).

The team continued developing the performance assessment. They used a form to capture their reasoning for any changes to performance, the revised ratings using the performance scales developed during the Information Phase, and the overall change in value relative to the baseline concept (see Table 9.1). The majority of the performance attributes were not affected by this alternative; however, the significant improvement in "Ergonomics" resulted in a total overall performance improvement of about 5 percent.

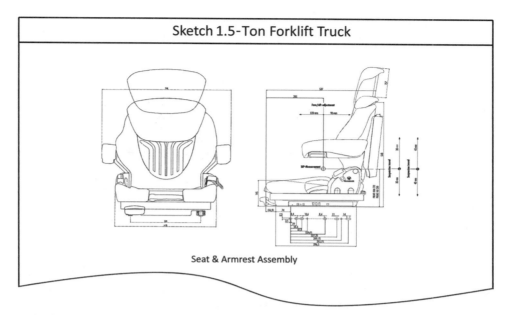

FIGURE 9.5 Value Alternative Sketch, Forklift

This continuing cycle of speculation, evaluation, and development is very typical of value studies and is essential in optimizing value. This example serves to further illustrate how the Job Plan is both cyclical and linear in its application.

Assess Risk

Consideration should be given concerning the uncertainty of the alternative and/or its effect on uncertainty inherent in the project. For each alternative, risk can be considered either qualitatively or quantitatively depending upon the level of information and time available to the value team.

Key considerations concerning risk may include:

- *Risks associated with implementing the alternative.* The value team should give some thought about the uncertainties facing the implementation of the alternative. For example, if an alternative is proposing to incorporate a new technical innovation that has never been tested, there may be a risk that the concept will not work. This could result in a loss of time and/or money and would negatively affect the project. In this case, the value team would be wise to articulate their opinion on the probability of success and the related impacts for both success and failure. If the decision makers are unaware of the risks involved with a value alternative, they may be more prone to making poor decisions.
- *The probability that the alternative will be implemented.* In some cases, the decisions related to accepting or rejecting a value alternative may involve a number of participants. The value team may want to consider articulating their

TABLE 9.1   Performance Assessment, Forklift

Performance Assessment: 1.5-ton Forklift Truck

Alternative Title:	Upgrade seat assembly				Alternative No.: 1.11	
			Ratings			
		Priorities	Baseline		Alternative	
Attribute	Rating Rationale	P	R	(PxR)	R	(PxR)
Travel Speed	No significant change.	0.208	0.700	0.146	0.700	0.146
Lift Speed	No significant change.	0.082	0.629	0.052	0.629	0.052
Turning Radius	No significant change.	0.205	0.536	0.110	0.536	0.110
Drawbar Capacity	No significant change.	0.044	0.671	0.030	0.671	0.030
Climbing Capacity	No significant change.	0.116	0.629	0.073	0.629	0.073
Ergonomics	This alternative provides a number of ergonomic enhancements including: The addition of padded, movable armrests Taller back rest with neck support Ability to swivel seat 180 degrees Tilt adjustment (−5 to +30 degrees)	0.112	0.600	0.067	0.900	0.101
Maintainability	Maintainability should be roughly comparable to the existing system due to durability of armrests.	0.234	0.600	0.140	0.600	0.140
Total Performance Score				0.617		0.651
Net Change in Performance from Baseline						+5.4%

opinion of the probability of an alternative being accepted given the process and environment in which the decision will be made. It is often the case that the probability of acceptance will decrease inversely to the number of parties involved in the decision process. Therefore, an alternative that involves only one "gatekeeper" may be less risky than one that has three. This is useful information to provide along with the alternative and may also help the value team develop strategies to improve the chances of acceptance.

- *The impact to existing project risks.* It is possible that a value alternative could either increase or decrease the probability and/or impacts of existing project risks. In fact, some alternatives are developed specifically to minimize threats or maximize opportunities on projects. The value team should discuss what effect a value alternative will have on these risks as part of the narrative.

Value alternatives may serve as risk response strategies, either intentionally or unintentionally, by design or as a by-product. It is worth considering what kind of response strategy a value alternative falls into. Generally speaking, there are four types of strategies that apply to threats (negative risks) and three that apply to opportunities (positive risks). Thought should be given on how the alternative can be employed along these lines.

The actions available to address risks are based on the following risk response strategies to deal with threats:

- *Avoidance.* The surest way to deal with a risk is to avoid it completely. There are a number of different ways to do this. One way is to modify the project scope.

  For example, assume that a particular retaining wall possesses a cost risk related to unknown geological conditions. If the retaining wall were eliminated then the risk could be avoided completely. However, the project costs may need to be increased to acquire additional real estate in order to replace the wall with an embankment. The question then is "will the cost to avoid this risk be less than its expected impact?" If the answer is yes, than this may be a good strategy to adopt. Many risks identified early on in a project's life cycle can be avoided once additional information is developed.

- *Transference.* Transferring a risk is a euphemism for "passing the buck." In other words, a risk can be passed on to another party, perhaps one that is more adept at dealing with a specific risk. Generally speaking, there is usually a price to be paid to do this. It is very common to pass on some risks to a third party such as a contractor or consultant. The success of this strategy largely depends on the third party's ability to assume and reduce the risk.

  For example, an agency charged with the construction of a subway project determines it will supply the heavy machinery needed to construct the tunnels to the contractor. The value team felt that there was a great deal of risk associated with this approach as the contractor could blame any productivity problems on the owner-supplied equipment and file a lawsuit. One strategy to deal with this risk would be to transfer it to the contractor by requiring him to furnish his own tunneling machinery. Of course, this risk transference will come at a price, but the value team's analysis indicates that the cost to do so was less than the expected impact of not doing so.

- *Mitigation.* Risk mitigation is a strategy that does not prevent a risk, but rather reduces its probability and the severity of its impact. The appropriateness of risk mitigation is often related to the time in the project's lifespan when it is considered. Often it is easier to mitigate for risks early on and more costly to do so later in the project's life cycle.

  For instance, assume that a highway project will require an extended period of heavy construction within 10 feet of several residences. If nothing is done to deal with this risk, it is likely that the affected residents will file a lawsuit, increase project costs, and more significantly, delay construction indefinitely. A mitigation response strategy for this risk would be to begin negotiations with the residents to temporarily relocate them for a period of time, thereby eliminating the chance for lengthy project delays. This particular mitigation strategy would definitely increase project costs; however, it allows for the risk by reducing its severity, especially in terms of schedule impacts.

- *Acceptance.* The last strategy is to simply accept the risk. This is a viable strategy and may be appropriate for risks that are very small, very unlikely, or very difficult to respond to using one of the previously mentioned strategies. Examples of risks where acceptance might be a good option are things like inclement weather and other naturally occurring incidents such as earthquakes and floods.

The following is a list of risk response strategies that apply to opportunities:

- *Exploit.* Opportunities possessing very strong potential benefits should be actively exploited. This is done by enhancing the probability that the opportunity will happen, or better yet, ensuring that it will happen. Often adopting this strategy will require some investment of project time and money to achieve, but if the return on investment is there, it will probably be worth it.

  For example, assume that an office building project has the opportunity to receive additional funding if it meets certain energy efficiency requirements. This opportunity can be exploited by making improvements to the building's heating, ventilation, and air conditioning (HVAC) and insulation systems. The value team should analyze the costs required to meet the requirements versus the additional funding it can receive. If the return on investment is there, the chances of getting the funding can be enhanced by spending the additional funds on the improvements.

- *Share.* Sometimes an opportunity can be capitalized on if the benefits are shared with others, as in creating a "win-win" situation. Most projects have many stakeholders with different objectives in mind. Often a little collaboration can go a long way in maximizing opportunities.

  One way to employ the "share" strategy is through a Value Incentive Clause, as discussed in Chapter 4. Basically, this contract clause establishes a profit sharing mechanism between an owner and a contractor whereby the contractor is encouraged to develop cost saving modifications to the design. Cost savings are typically split, sometimes with the owner receiving the smaller share. The U.S. Army Corps of Engineers has been using this strategy for decades, resulting in hundreds of millions of dollars in cost savings.

- *Enhance.* This strategy seeks to increase the probability of an opportunity occurring and/or the degree of the resulting benefits. Enhancement is not always a sure thing, but often it can prove to be a worthwhile approach.

  For instance, assume an opportunity is identified during a value study that indicates that there is a chance that the type of environmental document that is required for a major infrastructure project can be changed. If the type of review can be reduced from an Environmental Assessment (EA) to a Negative Declaration (ND), the schedule can be accelerated by three months. This opportunity can be enhanced if the impacts to a certain area on the project are avoided. This may require a modification to the project scope or perhaps additional analysis. Regardless, the chances of this opportunity occurring can be enhanced if specific actions are taken to do so.

It is worth evaluating multiple response strategies in dealing with risks, especially those risks that have a high expected impact. More often than not, the appropriate response is fairly self-evident. For larger projects, it is worth conducting a more comprehensive approach to developing risk response strategies by holding a Value Methodology workshop. The combination of risk analysis and VM provides a very effective means of reducing project risk. There are creative solutions available for dealing with many risks; however, time must be devoted to finding them.

If qualitative risk analysis techniques have been applied on the project, then it may be worthwhile to consider extending those same techniques to the development of the value alternatives. For example, if a probability and impact matrix has been utilized for the project as the primary risk analysis technique, then the value team should consider applying the same techniques to the value alternatives. Providing a commensurate level of analysis in line with the rest of the project will add validity to the value alternatives and provide the project team with a greater level of confidence in considering their acceptance.

If quantitative risk analysis techniques have been applied, then the value team should also consider applying them to the alternatives. If, for instance, a Monte Carlo simulation was performed for the project's risks, then the value team should consider running a parallel simulation that considers the effect of the value alternatives on project risk. Most quantitative models have the capability of analyzing risk and some can consider the effect of risk on both cost and schedule. On construction studies, it is common to run a "pre-mitigated" risk model that assesses the effect of risk to cost and schedule without the benefit of the value alternatives followed by a "post-mitigated" risk model that includes their effect. Such analysis can provide much-needed insight and a tremendous boost to the acceptance of alternatives that aid in mitigating project risk. Figure 9.6 shows a comparison of the expected values for the pre- and post-mitigated risk models with respect to cost that were used on a value study considering the construction of a highway project.

In this model, the effect of the value alternatives on existing project risks (as indicated by the curve for the post-mitigated risks) shows a significant, positive benefit. This type of information is very useful in enhancing the confidence level of decision makers faced with making project decisions. The output of the

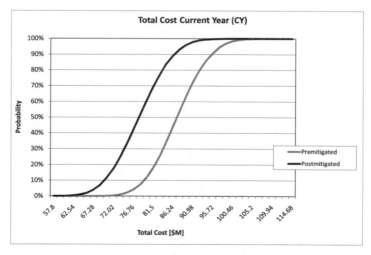

FIGURE 9.6 Probability Plot of Pre-Mitigated and Post-Mitigated Risk Scenarios for Project Cost

modeling technique shown in this example was generated using an Excel-based Monte Carlo simulation.[1]

In any event, risk should be considered at some level during the Development Phase. The level of detail will depend on the type of project, information available, time available during the value study, and the stage of the project's development.

The value team considering the new seat assembly for the forklift project discussed the potential risks associated with the concept. The biggest concern was the fact that the new seat assembly was still a prototype in development, which means that there was a chance that the concept might not perform exactly as conceived. In addition, there were modifications to the seat mounting attachment that would require some redesign. The team talked about their concerns with the vendor, who agreed to include a warranty with the seats and pay for any field repairs or replacements. This would remove a lot of the potential concern that management would likely have. The vendor had a longstanding relationship with the company and the team felt that overall, the risk of failure was very low and the degree of impact, due to the warranty by the vendor, was also very low.

Develop Narratives

The last step in finalizing the documentation for a value alternative is preparing the narratives and any additional graphical information such as sketches or diagrams. Having developed the technical concept, identified costs, and assessed performance, the value team members should now have a thorough understanding of the alternative concept. This information should now be summarized by developing a thorough narrative of the value alternative, which should include:

- A brief description of the baseline concept
- A brief description of the alternative concept
- A list of advantages and disadvantages of the alternative concept as compared to the baseline concept
- A discussion of the alternative, including a thorough description of the technical details and any further language that will provide the rationale for why the change is justified
- A summary of the alternative's financial impacts

This information should be documented on a series of forms that will allow the project team and the decision makers to review it in an organized manner.

The writing should be prepared so as to allow management personnel, who may be of a nontechnical background, to understand the basic concepts involved in the value alternative. Detailed technical information should be included to supplement this discussion so that the project team can review and verify the technical details of the value alternative.

The value team working on the forklift project, having developed the technical, cost, schedule, risk, and performance information for the seat assembly alternative, began the process of putting it altogether. They utilized a series of forms to organize the data similar to what was suggested in Figure 9.1. The executive summary page for the seat assembly alternative is shown in Figure 9.7. It summarizes the key

VALUE ALTERNATIVE EXECUTIVE SUMMARY *1.5–Ton Forklift Truck*		**AFI Industries**	
FUNCTION: Ensure Comfort		**IDEA NO.** EC-1 / EC-3	**NUMBER** 1.1
TITLE: Upgrade Seat Assembly		**PAGE NO.** 1 of 9	

BASELINE:

The current FC-150 class forklift includes a simple upholstered seat manufactured by Reliant Manufacturing Co. (Model SC-127A). This seat is fairly basic and only allows for backward/forward and up/down adjustments to the seat position to accommodate operators of different sizes.

ALTERNATIVE:

The alternative concept would utilize a new seat assembly by Reliant Manufacturing Co. (Model SC-200A) that includes several new features

1. The addition of padded, movable armrests
2. Taller back rest with neck support
3. Ability to swivel seat 180 degrees
4. Tilt adjustment (-5° to +30°)

COST IMPACT			
Unit Costs	**BASELINE**	**ALTERNATIVE**	**SAVINGS**
Material	$245.00	$265.00	-$20.00
Labor	$12.97	$14.47	-$1.50
Burden	$14.86	$16.59	-$1.73
Total	$272.83	$296.06	-$23.23
No. of Units	2,000	**Gross Savings**	-$46,460.00
Implementation Costs		-$50,000.00	
NET CHANGE			-0.2%

PERFORMANCE IMPACT	
Travel Speed	No significant change.
Lift Speed	No significant change.
Turning Radius	No significant change.
Drawbar Capacity	No significant change.
Climbing Capacity	No significant change.
Ergonomics	Offers numerous ergonomic enhancements.
Maintainability	Maintainability should be roughly comparable to the existing system.
NET CHANGE	+5.4%

SCHEDULE IMPACT
The new seat assembly will be delivered to the plan pre-assembled. The only potential impact to production time will be related to mounting the seat. Modification to the seat mounting hardware are required; however, the value team does not believe there will be a significant difference in assembly time.

RISK IMPACT

Implementation Issues

- Seat assembly is only in prototype development
- Redesign of seat mounting attachment required

PROBABILITY VH				
H				
M				
L	X			
VL				
	VL	L	M	H	VH
	IMPACT			

TOTAL VALUE IMPROVEMENT: +5%

FIGURE 9.7 Example of an Executive Summary for a Value Alternative

points of the value alternative and is supported by all of the other information developed by the team, including detailed drawings, specifications, performance assessment, cost breakdown, and vendor quotations, resulting in a nine-page document.

This value alternative resulted in a total value improvement of +5 percent when considering both performance and cost. The small additional cost of this concept was more than offset by the performance improvements identified.

A complete example of a value alternative for a construction study, with all of the forms listed in the final order in which they will appear in the written value study report, is provided in the Case Study section at the end of this chapter. These forms should be modified to suit the needs of the project under study and specific organizational requirements.

Review Value Alternatives

When all of the value alternatives have been completed, they should be reviewed by the value specialist and each of the value team members. This internal review is very important, as it will allow each team member to check for errors and ensure that narratives are complete and that the performance has been assessed properly, especially with respect to their respective disciplines.

The value team should identify any errors and/or note any suggested revisions based on their review. These edits should be incorporated into the written report when the value alternatives are eventually submitted for review.

When assessing performance for each alternative, it is often a good idea for the value specialist to conduct this as a group activity. Alternately, the value team member responsible for developing each alternative can take the first cut at it, so long as the entire value team reviews these initial ratings and has the opportunity to comment. In any event, the performance assessments should be the result of the consensus of the value team.

It is also advisable to have members of the project team, or other designated technical reviewers, to review the value alternatives midway through the Development Phase. This will allow the opportunity for a "reality check" to ensure that the value team's assumptions are correct and that there are no fatal flaws based on a cursory review.

Providing the opportunity for this midpoint review will help to provide stakeholder "buy in" prior to the exit briefing that will be held the final day of the value study. It will also reduce the potential of developing value alternatives that are technically flawed or otherwise unacceptable, thereby minimizing wasted effort and maximizing the value team's credibility.

The value specialist must be careful to avoid the temptation to throw out valid alternatives simply because they may be unpopular. The reviewers must present a credible reason for excluding a value alternative at this stage in the process to the value team, who will usually be pressed for time. This review should be more of a "reality check" review rather than a formal meeting.

If reviewers are present, their comments should be documented and included as part of the value alternative in the written report. This feedback will be valuable and will help with the future implementation of the concept should it be accepted during the Implementation Phase.

Also during the review process, the value team should consider a number of additional strategies that will facilitate the acceptance of proposed changes within an organization:

- Develop an implementation overview plan to identify key individuals or groups involved in the implementation effort.
- Review specific proposals with key managers of affected departments and solicit their support.
- Seek input regarding implementation tasks and estimated timetables.
- Highlight the overall advantages of the proposed changes to various levels of supervision *before* the final recommendations are presented to the executive group.
- Identify risks and concerns so that they may be included in the final presentation to the executive group.

Above all, be patient and thorough in your discussions. Remember to consider that the proposed changes will, in some cases, cause additional effort to achieve implementation.

Summary

The success of the Development Phase will depend greatly on the technical knowledge and experience of the value team members and the degree of effort they are able to apply in developing the documentation for the value alternatives. The value specialist will have to facilitate and manage the efforts of the value team members to ensure that all of the ideas selected for development in the Evaluation Phase are fully considered and/or developed.

Above all else, it is important that the value team fully take ownership of the concepts that they will present to the project team and to the decision makers. This requires that all of the value team members review and contribute to the development of all of the alternatives. Through teamwork and diligence, the value team, and ultimately the project, will be rewarded many times over.

Appendix 9A: Case Study

The value team spent the next two and a half days working on developing the 34 ideas that remained after the Evaluation Phase. The first step in the development process was to investigate the technical viability of these ideas and the team members began working on their assignments. This case study will focus on CT-9, which was one of the three key ideas discussed in the previous chapter.

The initial ideas immediately began to change during the development process once the team members began thinking more concretely about them. The limitations and design challenges of the ideas began to be revealed in greater detail and new opportunities began to emerge once the concepts were explored in greater depth.

Each of the three ideas (CT-8, CT-9, and CT-12) proved to be particularly challenging due to their scope. Not only did they require a complete reassessment of the project site and the layout of the buildings, but also the very nature of the educational program. Below is a discussion of CT-9, including the completed value alternative information that followed a standardized format. It is important to note that the forms presented here are but one way to organize and present the information. Practitioners should consider this only as a guide and one suggested way to develop value alternatives.

Idea No. CT-8

This idea was initially assigned to the value team's architect as it relied primarily on reorganizing the current educational program spaces. The architect, educational planner, and executive director discussed this idea, as well as the other two ideas, at great length. These discussions included an informal cycle of creative and critical thinking that ultimately solidified the basic approach to the ideas.

For CT-8, it was decided that the Administration Building (incorporating improvements from another idea that was also developed into a value alternative) and a smaller Classroom Building would be constructed and the Supermarket Building would be completely renovated all in Phase 1. Phase 2 would construct an addition to the Classroom Building to complete the project.

The resulting concept required a minor reorganization of the Supermarket Building and a major reorganization of the Classroom Building. The team members worked to ensure that the programs could be appropriately accommodated in the building spaces by developing scaled sketches and a matrix detailing program areas and locations. Once the team was satisfied that the concept was technically viable, they focused on developing cost information. The architect and cost estimator worked together to develop quantities and compare the differences from the baseline concept. In addition, it was determined that there would be the potential for life cycle cost savings as the value alternative resulted in a reduction in total building area. Much of this savings was due to a reduction in the size of the Engine Technology program, which the team determined was significantly larger than necessary. Some of the other program spaces were increased. The net result was a reduction in the total size of the facilities of about 1,200 square feet. Building operations and maintenance costs were obtained from the School District and used to develop a simple present-worth LCC analysis.

The value team focused next on assessing the performance of the value alternative. Using the performance scales and the assessment information that was developed for the baseline concept, the team discussed the performance of each attribute. These were recorded using a standardized form. The ratings were multiplied by the attributes' priorities to derive a total performance score. These were tallied and then compared against the baseline concept's total performance.

Finally, a narrative for the value alternative was written that included descriptions of the baseline and alternative concepts, a discussion of the advantages and disadvantages, a justification of the concept, and, finally, a summary of the assumptions and calculations. All of this information was organized onto standardized forms provided by the value specialist. The completed value alternative was reviewed by the team members as a group and edits were made in real time on the screen through the multimedia projector. Once all of the value alternatives for the study had been developed, they were organized as a list and assigned an alternative number.

Idea No. CT-9

The initial idea was one that was very intriguing to the value team as it turned conventional wisdom on its head by demolishing the Supermarket Building and redesigning the campus from a clean slate. The team spent a great deal of time considering the many options available to organize the program and the buildings that housed it. The elimination of constraints imposed by the building footprint of the old supermarket gave rise to numerous, previously unconsidered opportunities.

Rather than just build two new buildings, the team considered building on the concept in Idea No. CT-8 by arranging the programs so that they were organized by program type and shared common amenities. This led the team to consider a Technology Building, Life Sciences Building, and an Administration Building. Further, the team considered using a different palette of building materials for the Technology Building as well as an aesthetic that would mirror the types of industrial facilities where those activities took place. This would have the effect of reducing the building cost for these programs. The Technology Building would be located in the northeast corner of the site, where its noisier activities would be less likely to disturb the rest of the campus. Similar to Idea No. CT-8, this alternative incorporated improvement to the Administrative Building identified in another value alternative.

The value team evaluated the alternative's performance. There was a strong consensus that the educational program would be optimized through this approach. The reorganization of the spaces was a significant improvement in terms of the educational program, internal adjacencies, and circulation, resulting in an increase in both Program Compatibility and Building Organization. From the standpoint of the campus as a whole, this alternative offered a huge improvement with respect to way finding, vehicular circulation, and parking, while maintaining important view sheds. Site Organization was therefore rated very high as well. Aesthetics were much improved due to the fact that all of the buildings would be new and could be designed to complement each other architecturally. Phaseability was simplified and those programs identified for Phase 2 were located on the ends of the Phase 1 buildings. Finally, Maintainability improved slightly due to a minor reduction in overall building area.

Cost savings for this alternative were relatively high, amounting to roughly $8 million. The only disadvantage that the value team discerned was the potential negative perception the public might have concerning the demolition of the Supermarket Building. It was possible that some in the community might regard this as "government waste." This issue, however, was felt to be a small one compared to the performance and cost benefits that were identified.

Idea No. CT-12

This idea followed a similar development process to the previous two ideas. The initial idea suggested building new facilities, but leaving the Supermarket Building vacant for use as a warehouse or for some other function by the School District. Based on discussions with the new high school's principal, it was discovered that

VALUE ENGINEERING ALTERNATIVE *Technical High School*		
FUNCTION: Support Construction Technology	**IDEA NO.** CT-9	**NUMBER** 1.2
TITLE: Demolish Supermarket Building and Construct New Facilities		**PAGE NO.** 1 of 9

BASELINE CONCEPT:

The original concept would construct the following facilities in Phase 1:

- A new Administration Building that supports the Culinary Arts and Teaching Academy programs along with administrative space.
- A new Classroom Building that supports the Computer Science, Large Lab, Therapeutic Lab, Veterinary Tech., Materials Engineering, and General Classrooms programs.
- A partial renovation of the existing Supermarket Building that will support the Construction Tech. program.

Phase 2 will complete the renovations in the Supermarket Building to support the Engine Tech., Criminal Justice, and Creative Design programs.

ALTERNATIVE CONCEPT:

The alternative concept would demolish the existing Supermarket Building completely. The campus would be reorganized by function and result in the following phasing strategy for Phase 1:

- A new Administration Building that would also include the Computer Science Program and Culinary Arts.
- A new Life Sciences Building that would include Therapeutic Lab, Large Lab, Veterinary Tech., and two General Classrooms.
- The first segment of a new Technical Trades Building that would include Construction Tech. and Materials Engineering.

Phase 2 would include the following additions:

- A new Teaching Academy Building
- The second segment of the new Technical Trades Building would add the Engine Tech. and Creative Design programs and two General Classrooms.
- The Criminal Justice Program would be added to the Life Sciences Building.

ADVANTAGES:

- Enhances flexibility in matching spaces to program / campus needs
- Grouping of like programs increases ease of maintenance, way finding, and circulation
- Better facilitates sharing of program resources
- Eliminates a significant amount of internal building circulation
- Eliminates Supermarket Building phasing issues

DISADVANTAGES:

- Demolishing the Supermarket Building may be perceived negatively by the public

COST SUMMARY	Initial Cost	Present Value Subsequent Cost	Net Present Value
Baseline Concept	$ 47,803,000	$ 58,0000	$ 47,861,000
Alternative Concept	$ 39,808,000	$ 0	$ 39,808,000
Savings	$ 7,995,000	$ 0	$ 8,053,000

Performance Attribute Impacts							
Program Compatibility	Building Organization	Site Organization	Aesthetics	Phaseability	Maintain-ability	Project Schedule	Performance Change
+	+	+	+	+	0	0	+19%

FIGURE 9.8   Value Alternative Forms, Technical High School

VALUE ENGINEERING ALTERNATIVE *Technical High School*		
TITLE: Demolish Supermarket Building and Construct New Facilities	**NUMBER** 1.2	**PAGE NO.** 2 of 9

DISCUSSION / JUSTIFICATION:

The value team noted that the cost to renovate the Supermarket Building in two phases was comparable to constructing new classroom space. Further, some programs that do not benefit from the existing high-bay space in the Supermarket Building (i.e., Criminal Justice and Creative Design) are being located there in order to fill out the existing space. The presence of the Supermarket Building is also driving the site development concept to an extent.

Based on these observations, the value team wanted to explore the idea of demolishing the existing Supermarket Building and reorganizing the campus to better match building spaces to the program and to optimize the project site.

- A new Administration Building that would also include the Computer Science Program and Culinary Arts. The value team reorganized the Administration Building somewhat to combine the training and multipurpose room functions, reduce the administration office space, and enlarge the Culinary Arts kitchen. This resulted in a net building area reduction of about 1,200 SF. Please refer to VE Alt. 1.5 for details. Another 4,150 SF of space would be added to accommodate the Computer Science program.
- A new Life Sciences Building that would include Therapeutic Lab, Large Lab, Veterinary Tech., and two General Classrooms.
- The first segment of a new Technical Trades Building that would include Construction Tech. and Materials Engineering. This facility would be constructed using simplified, high-bay building system for the Technical Trades Building that would be appropriate for these functions (i.e., simplified HVAC, shed roof, composite concrete masonry / metal siding exterior, etc).

Phase 2 would include the following additions:

- A new Teaching Academy Building. This could be constructed as a separate building or possibly as an addition to the Administration Building or the Life Sciences Building.
- The second segment of the new Technical Trades Building would add the Engine Tech. and Creative Design program and two General Classrooms. The value team recommends that the Engine Tech. Lab space be reduced by 2,000 SF which could still easily accommodate spots for 12 vehicles.
- The Criminal Justice Program would be added to the Life Sciences Building.

Site development savings are addressed in other value alternatives.

It should be noted that demolishing the Supermarket Building will probably result in a negative (i.e., wasteful) way by the public. As the Supermarket Building is basically being acquired independently by the Bethel SD, they may not want to demolish the building. Consideration should be given as to how to "sell" this concept to the public.

FIGURE 9.8   (Continued)

VALUE ENGINEERING ALTERNATIVE *Technical High School*						

TITLE: Demolish Supermarket Building and Construct New Facilities				**NUMBER** 1.2	**PAGE NO.** 3 of 9

DISCUSSION / JUSTIFICATION:

Provided below is a breakdown of the programs and students served per session (assuming two per day) for each phase.

	Baseline			**Alternative**		
Program Areas	**Phase**	**Building**	**Area (SF)**	**Phase**	**Building**	**Area (SF)**
Culinary Arts	1	Admin.	8,200	1	Admin.	8,500
Teaching Academy	1	Admin.	2,400	1	New Bldg.	2,880
Materials Engineering	1	Classroom	6,250	1	Tech. Bldg.	6,250
Engine Tech.	1	Supermarket	11,655	2	Tech. Bldg.	9,655
Construction Tech.	1	Supermarket	6,800	1	Tech. Bldg.	6,800
Creative Design	2	Supermarket	2,660	2	Tech. Bldg.	2,660
Criminal Justice	2	Supermarket	3,500	2	Classroom	3,500
General Classrooms	1	Classroom	2,300	1	Classroom	2,300
General Classrooms	2	Supermarket	1,900	2	Tech. Bldg.	1,900
Therapeutic Lab	1	Classroom	2,500	1	Classroom	2,500
Veterinary Tech.	1	Classroom	1,350	1	Classroom	1,950
Computer Science	1	Classroom	4,150	1	Classroom	4,150
Large Labs	1	Classroom	2,700	1	Classroom	2,700
TOTAL			*56,365*			*55,745*
NET CHANGE						*-620*

FIGURE 9.8 (Continued)

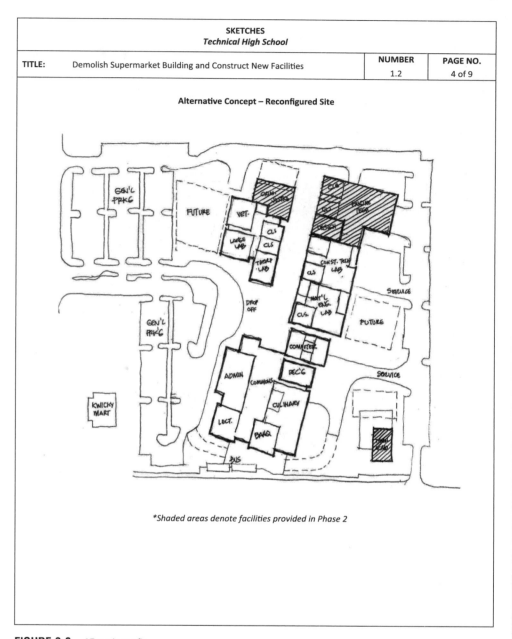

SKETCHES			
Technical High School			
TITLE: Demolish Supermarket Building and Construct New Facilities	**NUMBER** 1.2	**PAGE NO.** 4 of 9

Alternative Concept – Reconfigured Site

Shaded areas denote facilities provided in Phase 2

FIGURE 9.8 (Continued)

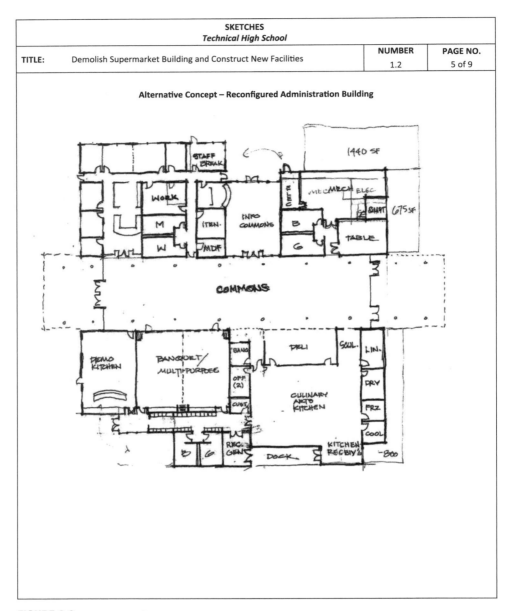

FIGURE 9.8 (Continued)

PERFORMANCE MEASURES Technical High School			
TITLE: Demolish Supermarket Building and Construct New Facilities	**NUMBER** 1.2		**PAGE NO.** 6 of 9
ATTRIBUTES and RATING RATIONALE for VALUE ALTERNATIVE	Performance	Original	Alternative
Program Compatibility	Rating	0.7	0.9
The alternative provides the optimum program compatibility because it provides the greatest flexibility in matching spaces to program / campus needs. Eliminates the need to try and match programs to existing spaces.	Weight	0.360	0.360
	Contribution	0.252	0.324
Building Organization	Rating	0.7	0.8
Organizes like programs together to enhance circulation and way finding. Eliminates a significant amount of internal building circulation. Better facilitates sharing of program resources.	Weight	0.231	0.231
	Contribution	0.162	0.185
Site Organization	Rating	0.8	0.9
Allows site circulation to be redeveloped to better address main access on 160th Avenue. Allows parking to be consolidated on the north side of the site. Reduces traffic around the entire site.	Weight	0.153	0.153
	Contribution	0.122	0.138
Aesthetics	Rating	0.75	0.80
Allows a separate Technical Trades Building to be developed that reflects a more industrial looking aesthetic. Allows improves site aesthetics with respect to building orientation and sight lines.	Weight	0.068	0.068
	Contribution	0.051	0.054
Phaseability	Rating	0.4	0.7
Eliminates phasing issues relevant to the Supermarket Building. Phase 2 Building additions can be made cleanly.	Weight	0.047	0.047
	Contribution	0.019	0.033
Maintainability	Rating	0.75	0.78
Results in a minor improvement in operations and maintenance due to the small reduction in building area.	Weight	0.141	0.141
	Contribution	0.106	0.11
Total Performance:		**0.712**	**0.844**
Net Change in Performance:			**+19%**

FIGURE 9.8   (Continued)

ASSUMPTIONS and CALCULATIONS _Technical High School_		
TITLE: Demolish Supermarket Building and Construct New Facilities	**NUMBER** 1.2	**PAGE NO.** 7 of 9

Cost Estimating Assumptions:

The value team assumed the following spaces would be included in the various buildings:

Administration Building:

- See drawing
- Computer Science Program Addition – Assumes exterior access, no interior corridors

Classroom Building:

- Restrooms – 600 SF
- Mechanical/Electrical – 500 SF
- Staff Work Area – 400 SF
- Circulation – 20% GSF

Technical Trades Building:

- Restrooms – 600 SF
- Mechanical/Electrical – 500 SF
- Circulation – 20% GSF of Creative Design and General Classrooms program spaces

Teaching Academy:

- Misc. – Assumes 20% GSF for small mechanical/electrical closet and additional restroom space.

A great deal of the reduction in interior building space is achieved by organizing some of the larger programs (i.e., Engine Tech., Materials Engineering, Construction Tech., and Computer Sciences) to have direct exterior access rather than internal corridors.

Reference contacts from four current skills centers resulted in the following data on automotive trades shop/lab space. The West Heights Technical High School houses space for six service bays, each with a lift, with approximate square footage including 7,000 square feet of classroom space (serving 40-50 students in each of the two sessions daily). The Roger Williams Technical High School houses space for 12 vehicles with six bay lifts with approximately 9,000 square feet (serving 40-50 students in each of the two sessions daily). The Connor Valley Technical High School houses space for 12 vehicles with flexible lift spaces with approximately 9,000 square feet including classroom (serving 40-50 students in each of the two sessions daily). West Sound Technical High School houses space for 4 service bays and lifts (square foot estimate not available) serving approximately 20-25 students in each of the two sessions daily.

Life Cycle Cost Assumptions:

The value team obtained LCC operations and maintenance data from the School District's facilities manager. The School District requested that a 40 year life cycle be used at a 10% discount rate in the calculations. The following values were used:

- Annual Energy (i.e., energy costs) - $3.10/SF
- Annual Maintenance (i.e., repairs, janitorial, etc.) - $6.50/SF

Per the value team's program analysis, the alternative concept will be approximately 620 SF smaller in total building area. Therefore the annual difference is:

- Annual Energy (i.e., energy costs) - $3.10/SF x 620 SF = $1,922
- Annual Maintenance (i.e., repairs, janitorial, etc.) - $6.50/SF x 620 SF = $4,030

It was assumed that all other LCC costs would otherwise be equivalent between the baseline and alternative concepts.

FIGURE 9.8   (Continued)

INITIAL COSTS							
Technical High School							

TITLE						NUMBER	PAGE NO.
Demolish Supermarket Building and Construct New Facilities						1.2	8 of 9

CONSTRUCTION ELEMENT		ORIGINAL CONCEPT			ALTERNATIVE CONCEPT		
Description	Unit	Quantity	Cost/Unit	Total	Quantity	Cost/Unit	Total
Phase 1							
Administration Building	SF	25,017	$344	$8,596,342	23,777	$344	$8,170,253
Administration Building (Teaching Academy + MP)	SF	4,400	$344	$1,511,928			$0
Administration Building (Computer Lab Addition)	SF			$0	4,150	$292	$1,212,755
Classroom Building	SF	25,348	$292	$7,407,446			$0
Life Sciences Building	SF			$0	13,140	$292	$3,839,902
Supermarket Building - Shell Upgrades	SF	35,830	$33	$1,183,465			$0
Supermarket Building - Renovations	SF	8,016	$204	$1,631,336			$0
Supermarket Building - Construction Tech. Outdoor	LS	1	$391,945	$391,945			$0
Supermarket Building - Demolition	SF				35,830	$12	$429,960
Technical Trades Building	SF			$0	14,150	$195	$2,759,250
Technical Trades Building - Outdoor	LS			$0	1	$391,945	$391,945
Site Development	LS	1	$4,756,014	$4,756,014	1	$4,756,014	$4,756,014
Off-Site Improvements	LS	1	$120,085	$120,085	1	$120,085	$120,085
Sub-Total				$25,598,561			$21,680,163
Mark-Up	41%			$10,418,614			$8,823,827
TOTAL PHASE 1				**$36,017,175**			**$30,503,990**
Phase 2							
Supermarket Building - Remaining Renovations	SF	27,814	$264	$7,335,386			$0
Life Sciences Building - Addition	SF			$0	4,200	$327	$1,371,827
Technical Trades Building - Addition	SF			$0	15,127	$218	$3,296,952
Teaching Academy	SF			$0	2,880	$327	$940,681
Site Development	LS	1	$862,068	$862,068	1	$862,068	$862,068
Sub-Total				$8,197,454			$6,471,529
Mark-Up	44%			$3,588,026			$2,832,588
TOTAL PHASE 2				**$11,785,480**			**$9,304,117**
TOTAL				$47,802,655			$39,808,107
TOTAL (Rounded)				$47,803,000			$39,808,000
						SAVINGS	$7,995,000

FIGURE 9.8 (Continued)

LIFE CYCLE COSTS - PRESENT WORTH METHOD						
Technical High School						
Title: Demolish Supermarket Building and Construct New Facilities					**Alternative No.** 1.2	**Page No.** 9 of 9
Life Cycle Period	40	Years			**BASELINE**	**ALTERNATIVE**
Discount Rate	10	%				
A.	**INITIAL COST**				$47,803,000	$39,808,000
				INITIAL COST SAVINGS:		$7,995,000
B.	**RECURRENT COSTS**					
	1. General Operations & Maintenance				$4,030	$0
	2. Energy Costs				$1,922	$0
	3. Supplies & Misc.					
				Total Annual Costs:	$5,952	$0
				PWF Factor:	9.7791	9.7791
			PRESENT WORTH OF RECURRENT COSTS:		$58,205	$0
C.	**SINGLE EXPENDITURES**	**Year**	**Amount**	**PWF' Factor**	**Present Value**	**Present Value**
	1.			1.0000	$0	$0
	2.			1.0000	$0	$0
	3.			1.0000	$0	$0
	4.			1.0000	$0	$0
	5.			1.0000	$0	$0
	6.			1.0000	$0	$0
			PRESENT VALUE OF SINGLE EXPENDITURES:		$0	$0
D.	**TOTAL RECURRENT COSTS & SINGLE EXPENDITURES (B+C)**				$58,205	$0
E.	**SALVAGE VALUE**	**Year**	**Amount**	**PWF' Factor**	**Present Value**	**Present Value**
	1.			1.0000	$0	$0
	2.			1.0000	$0	$0
F.	**TOTAL PRESENT WORTH VALUE (A+D+E)**				$47,861,205	$39,808,000
		10		**TOTAL LIFE CYCLE SAVINGS:**		$8,053,205

FIGURE 9.8   (Continued)

LIFE CYCLE COSTS - PRESENT WORTH METHOD				
Technical High School				
Title: Reorganize Supermarket Building for Technical Trades			Alternative No. 1.1	Page No. 10 of 10
Life Cycle Period 40 Years			BASELINE	ALTERNATIVE
Discount Rate 10 %				
A. INITIAL COST			$47,803,000	$42,125,000
INITIAL COST SAVINGS:				$5,678,000
B. RECURRENT COSTS				
1. General Operations & Maintenance			$7,800	$0
2. Energy Costs			$3,720	$0
3. Supplies & Misc.				
Total Annual Costs:			$11,520	$0
PWF Factor:			9.7791	9.7791
PRESENT WORTH OF RECURRENT COSTS:			$112,655	$0

C. SINGLE EXPENDITURES	Year	Amount	PWF' Factor	Present Value	Present Value
1.			1.0000	$0	$0
2.			1.0000	$0	$0
3.			1.0000	$0	$0
4.			1.0000	$0	$0
5.			1.0000	$0	$0
6.			1.0000	$0	$0
PRESENT VALUE OF SINGLE EXPENDITURES:				$0	$0
D. TOTAL RECURRENT COSTS & SINGLE EXPENDITURES (B+C)				$112,655	$0

E. SALVAGE VALUE	Year	Amount	PWF' Factor	Present Value	Present Value
1.			1.0000	$0	$0
2.			1.0000	$0	$0
F. TOTAL PRESENT WORTH VALUE (A+D+E)				$47,915,655	$42,125,000
TOTAL LIFE CYCLE SAVINGS:					$5,790,655

FIGURE 9.8 (Continued)

there were several programs that had been initially considered but dropped from consideration due to their large spatial requirements. These programs included Fire Fighting, Emergency Medical Services, and Disaster Management, which were broadly categorized as "Homeland Security" programs. These programs required large open spaces to conduct a variety of training exercises. The large, open space of the old supermarket was a perfect fit! The value team therefore modified the original idea to utilize the space for the Homeland Security programs and construct new space for the programs originally located there. The level of rehabilitation work to the Supermarket Building was dramatically decreased. To further econo-mize on the cost of the additional building area being added to the project, the team adopted the same approach to the building housing the technology programs by utilizing simplified construction more in keeping with the types of facilities where those activities are traditionally performed.

In assessing the performance impacts, the team discussed the impacts to the educational program. Although it added a significant number of educational spaces, the quality of the space was deemed to be only marginally adequate. As a result, it did rate higher than the baseline concept, but lower than Idea No. CT-9 for Program Compatibility. Similarly, it was rated higher than the baseline for Building Organization and Phaseability. In terms of Site Organization, it was felt that there was no significant change from the baseline concept's performance. In terms of the last two attributes, however, it rated lower. The minimal improvements to the Supermarket Building's interior and exterior finishes would clash with the overall campus appearance resulting in a lower rating for Aesthetics. The additional gross square footage significantly increased operations and maintenance costs, thereby resulting in a large reduction in the Maintainability rating. Interestingly, the trade-offs in performance essentially balanced out, resulting in no change. As a result, this alternative only amounted to a reduction in the initial construction costs.

CHAPTER 10

Presentation

© Magixl 2009, www.magixl.com

A fashion that does not reach the streets is not a fashion.

—Coco Chanel

The genius behind the fashion empire of House Chanel was Gabrielle Bonheur Chanel, born in 1883. Coco Chanel did not always dream of becoming a famous fashion designer. She danced, attempted to be an actress, sold hosiery, rode horses, dispensed mineral water, and worked as a cabaret singer. Coco Chanel opened her first millinery store in 1909 in Paris. The fact that Chanel was able to turn a small boutique that employed two teenage girls into one of the most profitable fashion houses of all time speaks volumes about her business acumen.

Soon she was expanding to couture, working in jersey, a first in the French fashion world. By the 1920s, her fashion house had expanded considerably, and her chemise set a fashion trend with its "little boy" look. Her relaxed fashions, short skirts, and casual styles were in sharp contrast to the corset fashions popular in the previous decades. Chanel herself dressed in clothes having a masculine aesthetic and adapted these to more comfortable clothing lines, which other women often found liberating. Coco Chanel introduced her signature cardigan jacket in 1925 and the famous "little black dress" in 1926. Her fashions had a timeless sense of style to them and proved to have tremendous staying power. They did not change perceptibly from year to year—or even from generation to generation.

Despite her tremendous impact on the fashion world, the single element that has established Chanel's legacy was not a piece of clothing but rather a perfume named after her called Chanel No. 5. It was first launched in its art deco bottle in 1923 and holds the distinction of being the first perfume to bear a designer's name.

Her fashion empire at her death brought in over $160 million dollars a year. The noted German designer Karl Lagerfeld has assumed the artistic directorship of the House of Chanel since 1954. Certainly it can be said that Chanel did an amazing amount for the development of fashion. By maintaining her incredible business sense and her uniqueness, Chanel helped create what modern fashion is considered today.

Coco Chanel was an entrepreneur who was determined to break old formulas and invent new ways of expressing herself. She serves as an archetype for the importance of selling change. Nearly single-handedly, she reinvented the role that women would play in modern society by redefining their image and successfully selling it to a worldwide market. By her death in 1971, the French couturier had long since established herself as the twentieth century's single most important arbiter of fashion. Coco Chanel illustrates the value of selling change and segues into the discussion of the Presentation Phase.

Presentation Phase

In the Presentation Phase, the value team presents specific recommendations to the project team and decision makers, in the form of value alternatives, which are intended to improve the project. Those that will be receiving the recommendations should have the authority to make the necessary decisions. The following three steps are part of this phase:

1. Assess value—Value Metrics
2. Conduct exit briefing
3. Prepare and submit written report

It must be emphasized that the objective is not merely to present the value team's findings, but to *sell* the ideas to the project team and decision makers.

Selling Change

The best ideas in the world will remain unrealized unless they can be communicated clearly and convincingly to those in a position to act on them. Those with experience in marketing, sales, and advertising no doubt understand the importance of selling new ideas and concepts. Those who are employed in technical positions, or even those in project management, may not understand the value of selling change.

Most engineers, designers, programmers, and other technical specialists will usually cringe when the subject of "selling" is brought up. Why is this? Clearly, this aversion to sales is rooted in the professional culture of dealing in facts and absolutes. In the author's experience, the image that most technical people conjure up when the topic of sales is discussed is that of the dreaded used car salesman. In their minds, selling is typically fraught with dishonesty, misrepresentation of the truth, exaggeration, and even outright fraud. These emotions and perceptions are further reinforced by the availability and representativeness heuristics discussed in Chapter 8, "Evaluation."

The value specialist will probably need to help some members of the value team overcome these mental roadblocks to selling change. The following are a number of strategies that can be employed to sell change:

- *Share the credit.* Often the project team will have vested an enormous amount of effort in developing the project's baseline concept. The important thing to recognize is that not only has time and effort been invested, but pride has too. Pride can be a major obstacle in overcoming change. If the value team has developed a concept that is particularly strong, it may be wise to demonstrate how the stakeholders and/or project team members have contributed to the development of the value alternative. If others outside the value team can feel some pride in ownership of a new concept, they will be less apt to resist it.

- *Find champions of change.* There will most likely be members within the sponsoring organization who will be advocates of change. Hopefully, these individuals will have been identified early on in the process by the value specialist. The value team must seek to include these individuals in group meetings and seek their input, especially in the exit briefing, as they can provide valuable leverage in motivating change within an organization.

- *Sell the concept of change early.* The earlier people can get involved with the value process, the more time there will be to prepare them for change. The value specialist should work with the study sponsor and project team in preparing for change. Everyone involved in the process needs to understand that the value team is simply an extension of the project team. The value team is there to help develop a better project, not to embarrass or criticize anyone, especially since they will have the advantage of hindsight that the project team did not have. The decision makers should be made to view the process as a collaborative effort.

- *Use language to communicate ideas with enthusiasm.* The value team should consider brainstorming ways of selling their most important, and potentially most valuable, concepts. Developing key catch phrases and sound bites can really help sell big ideas by creating links between words and concepts. The objective of selling an idea is to persuade others that it is a good idea and worthy of further attention. It is not to lie or misrepresent the truth. The use of a few choice words can help make ideas stick in the minds of decision makers and will encourage them to explore the alternatives developed by the value team.

- *Sell value improvement.* Keep in mind that the objective of the Value Methodology is to improve total project value, not just reduce costs. This means communicating to the project team and decision makers that the value team has been focusing on all aspects of the value equation, which include performance, time, risk, and cost. Assuming the *Value Metrics* approach has been utilized as part of the VM process, the value team will be able to show in detail how project performance will be affected by the alternatives they have developed. Selling value improvement will be much easier than merely selling cost reductions.

- *Be prepared.* All of the blood, sweat, and tears that went into developing the technical aspects of the value alternatives will pay off when the value team is hit with the tough-minded technical questions from the project team. One of the best ways to sell ideas to technical reviewers is to have developed all the facts. If a question arises concerning an issue that the value team has not addressed during the Development Phase, let everyone know that the value team will research the question and find the answer. In the zeal to sell ideas, don't be tempted to gloss over disadvantages or potential problems. The project team and decision makers will appreciate the forthrightness and honesty, which will in turn only foster trust and respect.

- *Create excitement.* Visible enthusiasm on the part of the value team will in and of itself help sell its ideas. If the value team is obviously indifferent about its work, then you can bet that everyone else will be as well. An enthusiastic attitude is infectious and will be difficult to resist if it is genuine.

- *Use graphics to convey ideas.* The use of graphic images is one of the best ways to sell ideas. Sometimes even a simple sketch or diagram can sell a concept in ways a report full of words could never achieve. When using graphics, less is more. Seek to communicate ideas visually as simply and clearly as possible.

- *Overcome visual bias.* Another important consideration in presenting graphics, especially sketches of design concepts, is to present the baseline and alternative concepts in a manner that is balanced. Usually, the level of graphic development for the baseline concept (which may be presented in a detailed technical format such as AutoCAD), while the alternative will be significantly less sophisticated (such as a hand-drawn sketch done on tracing paper). Presenting graphic data together using these two formats is a surefire way to bias the audience toward the concept that has been presented in a more detailed fashion (i.e., the baseline concept). People are going to assume that the more detailed technical graphic has been more thoroughly vetted and tend to gravitate toward certainty over uncertainty. The best way to overcome this bias is to present all concepts at the level of the lowest graphic level. For example, if the baseline has been computer drafted and an alternative has been hand sketched, then a hand-drawn representation of the baseline should be prepared and both sketches presented together. The author has found this to be an extremely effective strategy based on the experience of hundreds of technical presentations.

- *Be wary of PowerPoint.* PowerPoint is the dominant presentation development software in the world today. It has been around since the mid-1980s and has been responsible for the design and delivery of billions of presentations. That being said, it could be argued that the vast majority of these presentations have been really awful. There is a growing body of evidence to support the theory that the very nature of PowerPoint is counterproductive to both presenters and the recipients of presentations. In his landmark book on the presentation of visual data *Beautiful Evidence*, Edward R. Tufte devotes an entire chapter discussing and analyzing the cognitive structure and style of PowerPoint presentations.[1] Tufte provides a number of very compelling examples that explain how the delivery of technical information through PowerPoint can actually undermine the presentation of data. Further, the use of the "AutoContent Wizard," superfluous "chartjunk," and overuse of bullet structures often serves to confuse the message that the data is trying to make. Another noted author, Seth Godin, takes a slightly different approach to the shortcomings of PowerPoint presentations from a marketing perspective.[2] The lesson to be learned from these authors is that the structure of PowerPoint should never dictate the presentation—the content should. Use PowerPoint to sell the ideas (as recommended by Seth Godin) and use informational handouts as "leave-behinds" to present data (as recommended by Edward Tufte). The leave-behind could be a 1- to 4-page summary of important data, or it could be a full written report. Think outside of the AutoContent Wizard and pregenerated templates and focus on the most effective way to deliver the content.

- *Recognize others for their efforts.* Recognition can be more important than pay for many. The value specialist should take time to recognize the project team and other contributors for their efforts. The exit briefing provides an excellent opportunity to do this directly. Conveying a sense of graciousness will demonstrate respect for the hard work of others. This will not go unnoticed.
- *Communicate concisely.* Time is a valuable commodity, especially for executive-level management. Avoid getting into minutiae when presenting value alternatives during the exit briefing. Focus on the facts and present the concepts as concisely as possible.

Assess Value—*Value Metrics*

Following the development of the alternative concepts, the value team must next consider how they could be applied to the project in concert with one another. Typically, the value team should develop a number of potential implementation strategies (value strategies) that might be considered by the decision makers. It isn't essential to consider every possible permutation at this point, just a few that seem to be the most logical. Common themes for value strategies include:

- Best value
- Lowest cost
- Highest performance
- Shortest schedule
- Lowest risk

Other themes could revolve around competing design approaches. Often a value team will identify multiple ways to solve a problem that are mutually exclusive. The alternatives that support these separate approaches can be grouped into value strategies.

Once the value strategy or strategies have been identified, the value team should review each of the alternatives that are a part of that strategy with respect to its impact on performance. It may be that the cumulative effect of several minor performance improvements offered by various alternatives equate to a larger combined performance improvement. It may also be the case that the strengths of one alternative balance out the weaknesses of another. The focus should be on considering the aggregate, or synergistic, effect of the alternatives relevant to the project as a whole.

The most effective approach to assess the aggregate effect of multiple value alternatives combined as a cohesive strategy is to summarize the performance ratings and rationale on a single matrix. The value team can then review the ratings for each performance attribute, the reasoning supporting the rating, and arrive at a new performance rating for the value strategy as a whole.

The example presented on Table 10.1 lists four value alternatives that comprise a value strategy selected by the team. The value team transferred the individual performance assessments for each alternative onto the matrix to help them rate the total aggregate performance of the value strategy. As can be seen from the matrix, in many cases the alternatives did not change the performance as compared to the baseline concept (which is indicated by the statement "no significant change"). In this example, there are two instances where a performance attribute is affected by more than one alternative.

Maintainability is negatively affected by value alternatives 7.2 and 13.0. Alternative 7.2 affects the maintenance of the engine (a 0.10 rating drop) while alternative 13.0 requires replacement of the floor mats (a 0.03 rating drop). Since these are two different systems, it is reasonable to add these to arrive at the strategy's aggregate performance rating of 0.47 (which is the baseline rating of 0.6, minus the combined performance drops of the two alternatives, 0.13).

Ergonomics is positively affected by value alternatives 1.1 and 13.0. Both of these performance increases are related to the improving operator comfort and reducing fatigue. These are not necessarily cumulative as in the previous case with Maintainability. Both the floor mats and improved seat suspension will reduce the effect of vibration and operator fatigue. The team feels that most of the fatigue reduction will occur in the seat, and therefore the performance benefits shouldn't be 100 percent additive. Alternative 1.1 provides a 0.25 rating increase and alternative 13.0 a 0.05 rating increase. The team discusses the combined ergonomics benefits of these two alternatives and decides that together they decide to rate the total performance increase for ergonomics 0.275, which is slightly less than the sum of the individual ratings of 0.30. The team decided to count only 50 percent of the performance benefits from the floor mats in conjunction with the new seat assembly. This rationale should be noted and included in the aggregate rationale that will be used to summarize the performance of the value strategy.

Once the performance of each of the competing value strategies has been assessed using this approach, the next step is to consider the effect of the other components of value—cost, time, and risk.

In the forklift example, risk was chosen not to be considered as part of the value study; however, cost and time were. The value team developed three value strategies for consideration by management. The performance scores are derived by multiplying the aggregate performance rating by the priorities for the performance attributes as previously described in Chapter 5 (see Table 10.2). The aggregate cost and schedule scores are similarly derived (see Tables 10.3 and 10.4).

TABLE 10.1 Summary Matrix of Performance Ratings and Rationale for a Value Strategy

Value Strategy A—Performance Summary Matrix

Performance Attributes	Value Alternatives								
	1.1	Rating	4.0	Rating	7.2	Rating	13.0	Rating	Aggregate Rating
Travel Speed	No significant change.	0.70	No significant change.	0.70	Revised engine design increases top speed to just over 11 mph.	0.75	No significant change.	0.75	0.75
Lift Speed	No significant change.	0.63	The new hydraulics system increases lift speed to 130 fpm	0.72	No significant change.	0.63	No significant change.	0.63	0.72
Turning Radius	No significant change.	0.54	No significant change.	0.54	No significant change.	0.54	No significant change.	0.54	0.54
Drawbar Capacity	No significant change.	0.67	No significant change.	0.67	Increased engine horsepower increases drawbar capacity to 1,750 lbs.	0.71	No significant change.	0.71	0.71
Climbing Capacity	No significant change.	0.63	No significant change.	0.63	Increased engine horsepower increases maximum climbing grade to 43% tan q.	0.68	No significant change.	0.68	0.68

(Continued)

TABLE 10.1 (Continued)

Value Strategy A—Performance Summary Matrix

Performance Attributes	Value Alternatives								Aggregate Rating
	1.1	Rating	4.0	Rating	7.2	Rating	13.0	Rating	Rating
Ergonomics	Movable armrests will reduce operator fatigue and improve safety in the event of rollovers. Improved seat ergonomics including swivel and tilt features will improve operator comfort while improved shock absorbing suspension will reduce fatigue.	0.85	No significant change.	0.60	No significant change.	0.60	Addition of vibration dampening floor mats will reduce operator fatigue.	0.65	0.90
Maintainability	No significant change.	0.60	No significant change.	0.60	Revised engine design requires more frequent oil changes.	0.50	Floor mats subject to wear and replacement—2 year expected life	0.57	0.47

TABLE 10.2 Value Matrix Comparing Value Strategies to Baseline Concept

Performance Attributes	Priorities	Baseline Concept Rating	Baseline Concept Score	Value Strategy A Rating	Value Strategy A Score	Value Strategy B Rating	Value Strategy B Score	Value Strategy C Rating	Value Strategy C Score
	P	R	(P×R)	R	(P×R)	R	(P×R)	R	(P×R)
Travel Speed	0.208	0.700	0.146	0.750	0.128	0.700	0.146	0.850	0.177
Lift Speed	0.082	0.629	0.052	0.720	0.067	0.629	0.052	0.750	0.062
Turning Radius	0.205	0.536	0.110	0.540	0.117	0.550	0.113	0.700	0.144
Drawbar Capacity	0.044	0.671	0.030	0.710	0.032	0.671	0.030	0.750	0.033
Climbing Capacity	0.116	0.629	0.073	0.680	0.081	0.629	0.073	0.750	0.087
Ergonomics	0.112	0.600	0.067	0.900	0.084	0.950	0.106	0.700	0.078
Maintainability	0.234	0.600	0.140	0.470	0.190	0.550	0.129	0.300	0.070
Total Performance Scores			0.617		0.700		0.648		0.650

TABLE 10.3 Conversion of Strategy Costs to Relative Scores

Strategies	Total Cost	Relative Score
Baseline Concept	$15,000	0.254
Value Strategy A	$13,753	0.233
Value Strategy B	$14,235	0.241
Value Strategy C	$16,027	0.272
Total	$59,015	1.000

TABLE 10.4 Conversion of Strategy Schedules to Relative Scores

Strategies	Total Time (days)	Relative Score
Baseline Concept	42	0.255
Value Strategy A	39	0.236
Value Strategy B	40	0.242
Value Strategy C	44	0.267
Total	165	1.000

All of this data is then placed on the Value Matrix (see Table 10.5) to derive the value indices of the strategies and determine the overall potential for value improvement relative to the baseline concept. This information can also be compared graphically (see Figure 10.1).

TABLE 10.5   Value Matrix Comparing Value Strategies to the Baseline Concept

Strategies	Outputs		Inputs				Total Score	Value Index	Change in Value
	Performance Score		Cost Score		Schedule Score				
Priorities	1.0		0.8		0.2				
Baseline Concept	0.617	0.617	0.254	0.203	0.255	0.051	0.254	2.429	N/A
Value Strategy A	0.700	0.700	0.233	0.186	0.236	0.047	0.233	3.004	24%
Value Strategy B	0.648	0.648	0.241	0.193	0.242	0.048	0.241	2.689	11%
Value Strategy C	0.650	0.650	0.272	0.218	0.267	0.053	0.271	2.399	−1%

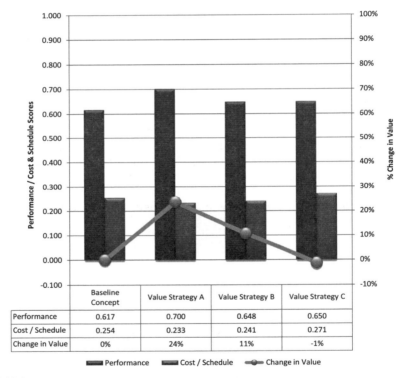

	Baseline Concept	Value Strategy A	Value Strategy B	Value Strategy C
Performance	0.617	0.700	0.648	0.650
Cost / Schedule	0.254	0.233	0.241	0.271
Change in Value	0%	24%	11%	-1%

■ Performance   ■ Cost / Schedule   ●— Change in Value

FIGURE 10.1   Comparison of Value Strategies, Forklift

Conduct Exit Briefing

Conducting an exit briefing at the conclusion of a value study is always advisable. The exit briefing provides an opportunity for the value team to directly present the value alternatives it has developed to the project team, stakeholders, and decision makers. Having a captive audience to present their hard work to while the new ideas are still fresh may be the best opportunity for the value team to sell its ideas.

The initial presentation should be for informational purposes only. It should not be a decision-making meeting. The value team may need additional time to further solidify the value alternatives following the conclusion of the value study and, in any case, the value study report will need to be written, edited and finalized. Those who will be reviewing the value team's efforts must have ample time to properly review the documentation prior to making any kind of decision regarding the acceptability of the value alternatives. This decision-making meeting will take place during the Implementation Phase, which is discussed in the following chapter.

The exit briefing should be conducted within a relatively brief time frame—60 to 90 minutes is generally a good rule. The exit briefing may be conducted using a multimedia presentation or a simple oral presentation, depending upon the resources available.

Generally, it is a good idea to wait until after the presentation to hand out the reference materials or possibly the written report, if it is completed. Disseminating materials before the presentation will distract meeting attendees from focusing on the value team's presentation, which is more about selling the alternatives then reviewing them for technical content. In fact, a good way to think about the presentation of the value study results is that there are essentially two functions being addressed by the presentation: sell change and present data

When preparing for the presentation, it is important to provide a clear and concise picture of the value alternatives by addressing such questions as why they should be implemented, who should be involved in their implementation, and the timing required. The value team must structure their presentation ahead of time if they are going to keep to the schedule. A presentation should be structured into three sections: the introduction, body and conclusion. The following is a simple outline for an exit briefing.

Introduction

In the introduction phase of the briefing, the following questions should be answered:

- What was the scope of the value study? Briefly describe the project scope and the value study scope—remember that they may not be the same.
- Who was involved? Consider not only the value team members, but also any others who have made significant contributions (e.g., other departments or community representatives involved with the study).
- What were the objectives or goals of the value study? List the objectives or the problem areas that motivated the study.
- What was the value study process? The value specialist should conduct a brief overview of the value methodology process, especially if there are members of the audience who were not present during the kick-off meeting.

Prepare the audience for the value alternatives that they will be hearing by identifying the number of proposals and the areas of the project on which they have a direct impact. This information serves as a transition into the body of the presentation.

Body

The body of the presentation contains the specific value alternatives that the team wants the decision makers to act on. Each value alternative should include a discussion of WHAT, WHY, WHEN, and WHO. These four elements are detailed below.

1. What is the alternative concept? Explain this in sufficient detail so that the concept can be clearly understood. Avoid getting too detailed, as this will tend to make the alternative confusing. Be prepared to answer questions if additional information is needed. Graphics are very beneficial in presenting the more complex ideas.
2. Why should the alternative be accepted? Describe the improvements over the baseline concept and state the impacts on project performance. Once these benefits have been clearly established, the effect on cost should be presented. Here, the impact on both initial costs and life cycle costs should be presented. It is also important that any other concerns related to the alternative be addressed at this point.
3. When can these value improvements be realized? The decision makers will want to know how long it will take for the improvements to be integrated into the project. An implementation schedule for the proposal showing the steps necessary to make the change should be prepared.
4. Who should implement the accepted alternative(s)? In most cases, with the approval of the alternatives, the involvement of the value team may end, and the implementation is assigned to the line organization or the designer. The value team should identify those individuals who may be involved in the implementation.

The value team is selling the proposals throughout the body of the presentation. Focus on identifying the important features of the proposals. Do not dwell on the present situation. Discuss other projects that may be impacted by the proposals but were out of the scope of the study.

Conclusion

After all the value alternatives have been presented, the objective is to get the decision makers to initiate action. In the conclusion of the presentation, summarize the impact of all of the alternatives and ask the decision makers to identify future implementation action. An implementation meeting should be scheduled after sufficient time has been allotted to review the value study report.

PRESENTATION CONSIDERATIONS   The selling of alternatives is often dependent on not only the facts of the study but how the facts are presented. A clear and concise presentation is much more effective than a long, wordy, detailed one. Consideration will need to be given with respect to who will be doing the presenting. This will depend greatly upon the nature of the project, the abilities of the value team members, the amount of time available to make the presentation, and the confidence of the team in both its findings and presentation skills.

If time is particularly constrained, or if much of the team does not feel confident in their presentation skills, the value specialist may want to handle the entire presentation for the purpose of clarity and consistency. Otherwise, it is always preferable to have the value team participants be directly involved in the presentation. In this case, the team members should present those value alternatives that they had the biggest role in developing and feel the most comfortable with.

The presentation can be enhanced by the following:

- Talk in a relaxed, conversational mode; do not try to make the report too formal. A relaxed mode of presentation stimulates a relaxed atmosphere, demonstrates confidence in the alternatives, and promotes good dialogue between the audience and the value team.
- Speak rapidly, but articulate clearly, leaving pauses between paragraphs. Rapid delivery has higher interest rate.
- Reveal major points to be remembered early in the presentation.
- Learn the presentation point by point, not word by word. Careful preparation and a great deal of practice are required to create a smooth, effective presentation. Mark Twain once said, "It takes three weeks to prepare a good ad-lib speech."
- Concentrate on proposed concepts; do not dwell on existing situations.
- Key on the concepts that are being presented, not the concepts that did not work out.
- Be enthusiastic about the proposals; think positively about receiving management approval.
- Use examples, visual aids, drawings, sketches, or sample parts whenever possible to help make a point.
- When questions are asked, the speaker should not feel that it is necessary to answer all of the questions personally. Questions should be responded to by the team member who is the most informed about the subject matter.
- Visual aids will only be effective if they can be seen by all. Check out the room ahead of time to see how the room arrangement can be used to its best advantage. Determine where the decision makers will be sitting with respect to the speaker and visual aids.
- If computer and or audio/visual equipment will be used, become familiar with their use and be prepared to finish the presentation through other means in the event that technical difficulties occur with the equipment.
- Check out the presentation material on the equipment to be used. Will it be clear and visible to the audience? How should the room lights be set to ensure the visuals can be seen by all? You can dim the lights, but you should not shut them completely off. The audience needs to be able to see the speaker. If the image appears washed out on the screen, dimming the lights directly over the screen generally resolves the problem.
- When using visuals, face the audience and talk to them. Often presenters tend to turn toward the visuals and talk to the screen. Feet should be pointed toward the audience and the hand closest to the screen should be used for gesturing to avoid this problem.

Prepare and Submit Value Study Report

Following the exit briefing and the conclusion of the formal value study, the value specialist may be called on to prepare the written value study report for submission to the project decision makers and/or project team. The value specialist is primarily responsible for gathering the documentation generated during the study and compiling it systematically into a report.

The Value Study Report should be organized in sections, preceded by a cover letter, a distribution list, and a table of contents. The value study report should include:

- *Executive summary.* Provides an updated overview of the project, the value alternatives, and any other the key findings and recommendations.
- *Value alternatives.* Documents the individual value alternatives.
- *Project analysis.* Summarizes the findings of the value study and includes information developed using VM techniques such as cost models, FAST diagrams, Value Matrix, and so on.
- *Project description.* Narrative of the project baseline's scope, schedule, and cost that formed the basis for the value study.
- *Idea evaluation.* List all of the ideas generated by the value team and their evaluations.
- *Value methodology process.* Summarizes the Value Methodology Job Plan, *Value Metrics* process, agenda, and participants.

Preparing a thorough value study report is essential to clearly communicate the results of the value study to the project team and decision makers as the first step in the implementation of the value alternatives.

In some cases, it may be desirable to have two iterations of the written report—a draft and a final version. In this case, the draft version need only include the executive summary and value alternatives sections. Following the implementation meeting, a final report is prepared that includes the remaining sections of the report plus an implementation section that documents the final status of the value alternatives and outlines the implementation plan, schedule, and responsibilities for each.

Summary

Success in the Presentation Phase requires that the value alternatives are effectively marketed to the decision makers. This requires attention not just to the content of the value alternatives, but on how they are presented. Recent research has found that persuasion works best when it is matched to the decision-making style used by management within an organization. One particular study concluded that almost 50 percent of all presentations are mismatched to the style of the executive decision maker:

> *"All too often, people make the mistake of focusing too much on the content of their argument and not enough on how they deliver that message. Far too many*

*decisions go the wrong way because information is presented ineffectively,"
according to the authors.*[3]

Successfully selling a value alternative to an organization involves more than
simply presenting data. It requires technical people demonstrating how a particular
change will improve project value—and doing so with passion and enthusiasm.

Appendix 10A: Case Study

The value team developed the remaining ideas, which resulted in a total of 14
value alternatives and 32 design suggestions. The value team next considered how
these alternative could be combined together to create specific strategies. The value
team had developed five major alternatives that resulted in different campus con-
figurations. After much discussion, it was decided that it made the most sense to
present four major strategies representing the different directions the project could
move toward. The four strategies, and their net effect on project cost, are summarized in Table 10.6.

Once the alternatives that would be considered in each strategy had been
identified, the next step was to consider their combined effect on cost and performance. The value specialist led the team through this process. The individual
performance assessments for each alternative within a strategy were organized on
a matrix. Each was discussed and their aggregate effect on total project performance
was then rated based on these discussions.

Provided in Table 10.7 is the Performance Summary Matrix for Strategy C. The
value team considered the performance impacts for each alternative and then
assigned an aggregate performance rating for the strategy. This process was repeated
for the other strategies.

Once the performance for each strategy was determined, the total performance
scores were calculated. This is summarized on Table 10.8.

TABLE 10.6 Summary of Value Strategies

SUMMARY OF VALUE STRATEGIES

Strategy No.	Strategy Description	Initial Cost Savings ($M)
A	Shift Phase 1 Programs to Supermarket Building (Value Alts. 1.4, 2.0—10.0)	$4.87
B	Reorganize Supermarket Building for Technical Trades (Value Alts. 1.1, 2.0—10.0)	$5.97
C	Demolish Supermarket Building and Construct New Campus (Value Alts. 1.2, 2.0—10.0)	$8.27
D	Utilize Supermarket Building for Homeland Security (Value Alts. 1.3, 2.0—10.0)	$6.07

TABLE 10.7 Development of Aggregate Performance Scores for Value Strategy

Value Strategy C—Performance Summary Matrix

Performance Attributes	Value Alternatives									
	1.2 Demolish Supermarket Building and Construct New Facilities	Rating	2.0 Reconfigure Large Support Lab to Better Support Life Sciences Programs	Rating	3.0 Relocate Teaching Academy to Southwest Corner of Site	Rating	4.0 Reconfigure Veterinary Assistant Space to Meet Program Requirements	Rating	5.0 Reconfigure Therapeutic Lab/ Classroom Area	Rating
Program Compatibility	Results in excellent program compatibility by providing the greatest flexibility in matching spaces to program/campus needs. Eliminates the need to try and match programs to existing spaces.	0.9	This alternative improves the overall program performance in relationship to the usability of the Life Sciences Lab space.	0.71	Increases the ability to deliver a comprehensive client-focused model for the Child Development Program.	0.71	Increases the ability to deliver industry-related curriculum components. Reduces the overall square footage of Materials Lab in kind, which is oversized to begin with.	0.71	Increases the ability to deliver industry-related curriculum components.	0.71
Building Organization	Organizes like programs together to enhance circulation and way finding. Eliminates a significant amount of internal building circulation. Better facilitates sharing of program resources.	0.8	No significant change.	0.7	Improves the overall building organization significantly, both internally and externally.	0.72	No significant change.	0.71	No significant change.	0.7

262

Site Organization	Allows site circulation to be redeveloped to better address main access on 160th Avenue. Allows parking to be consolidated on the north side of the site. Reduces traffic around the entire site.	0.9	No significant change.	0.8	Provides for increased student/client safety and a secure learning environment for clients. Reduces flexibility for locating future buildings. Assume a wash.	0.82	No significant change.	0.8	No significant change.	0.8
Aesthetics	Allows a separate Technical Trades Building to be developed that reflects a more industrial-looking aesthetic. Allows site aesthetics with respect to building orientation and sight lines.	0.8	No significant change.	0.75	No significant change.	0.75	No significant change.	0.75	No significant change.	0.75
Phaseability	Eliminates phasing issues relevant to the Supermarket Building. Phase 2 Building additions can be made cleanly.	0.7	No significant change.	0.4	No significant change.	0.4	No significant change.	0.4	No significant change.	0.4
Maintainability	Results in a minor improvement in operations and maintenance due to the small reduction in building area.	0.78	No significant change.	0.75	No significant change.	0.75	No significant change.	0.75	No significant change.	0.75

(Continued)

TABLE 10.7 (Continued)

Value Strategy C—Performance Summary Matrix

Value Alternatives

Performance Attributes	6.0 Consolidate Engine Tech. Program	Rating	7.0 Provide Movable Partition between General Classrooms	Rating	8.0 Consolidate Onsite Parking	Rating	9.0 Maximize Transportation Options by Improving Offsite Transportation Elements	Rating	10.0 Maximize Permeable Soils for Storm Drainage	Rating	Aggregate Rating
Program Compatibility	Better facilitates inventory management as a teaching opportunity.	0.71	Increases program flexibility in the General Classroom area to accommodate large lectures, industry partnering, large group testing, and team teaching opportunities.	0.71	No significant change.	0.7	No significant change.	0.7	No significant change.	0.7	0.95
Building Organization	No significant change.	0.7	No significant change.	0.7	No significant change.	0.7	No significant change.	0.7	No significant change.	0.7	0.82
Site Organization	No significant change.	0.8	No significant change.	0.8	Consolidates parking near the entry and will reduce circulation around the building. Provides for a more intuitive layout.	0.83	Strengthens public transportation amenities.	0.81	No significant change.	0.8	0.90
Aesthetics	No significant change.	0.75	No significant change.	0.75	No significant change.	0.75	No significant change.	0.75	No significant change.	0.75	0.80
Phasability	No significant change.	0.4	No significant change.	0.4	No significant change.	0.4	No significant change.	0.4	No significant change.	0.4	0.70
Maintainability	No significant change.	0.75	No significant change.	0.75	No significant change.	0.75	No significant change.	0.75	No significant change.	0.75	0.78

TABLE 10.8 Summary of Performance Scores for Value Strategies

Performance Attributes	Priorities	Baseline Concept		Value Strategy A		Value Strategy B		Value Strategy C		Value Strategy D	
	Priorities	Rating	Score	Rating	Score	Rating	Score	Rating	Score	Rating	Score
	P	R	(P×R)	R	(P×R)	R	(P×R)	R	(P×R)	R	(P×R)
Program Compatibility	0.360	0.700	0.252	0.550	0.198	0.800	0.288	0.950	0.342	0.900	0.324
Building Organization	0.231	0.700	0.161	0.550	0.127	0.750	0.173	0.820	0.189	0.770	0.178
Site Organization	0.153	0.800	0.123	0.800	0.123	0.840	0.129	0.900	0.138	0.840	0.129
Aesthetics	0.068	0.750	0.051	0.750	0.051	0.750	0.051	0.800	0.055	0.650	0.044
Phaseability	0.047	0.400	0.019	0.600	0.028	0.600	0.028	0.700	0.033	0.650	0.031
Maintainability	0.141	0.750	0.106	0.700	0.099	0.780	0.110	0.780	0.110	0.250	0.035
			0.712		0.625		0.779		0.866		0.740

TABLE 10.9 Conversion of Strategy Costs to Relative Scores

Strategies	Total Cost	Relative Score
Baseline Concept	47,800,000	0.224
Value Strategy A	42,930,000	0.201
Value Strategy B	41,830,000	0.196
Value Strategy C	39,530,000	0.185
Value Strategy D	41,730,000	0.195
Total	213,820,000	1.000

Next, the value team assessed the total impact on project schedule for each of the strategies. Based on an analysis of the total areas involved and construction activities (new construction versus renovation), it was determined that schedule would not vary significantly between the strategies. This was because the longest-duration activity, the construction of the Administration Building, was driving the overall critical path and this activity essentially remained constant for all the options being considered. As a result, schedule was not included in the determination of value.

The costs for the baseline concept and value strategies were calculated next and converted into a cost score (see Table 10.9).

A Value Matrix was then developed for the value study (see Figure 10.2).

Strategy A, which sought to maximize the use of the Supermarket Building in Phase 1 of the program, resulted in lower value as compared to the baseline concept despite saving nearly $5 million. This was due to a reduction in Program Compatibility and Building Organization, which were significantly compromised by trying to fit the program areas into the footprint of the Supermarket Building. Even though this resulted in an overall reduction in value relative to the baseline concept, this approach had initially been considered by the School District as a cost-cutting

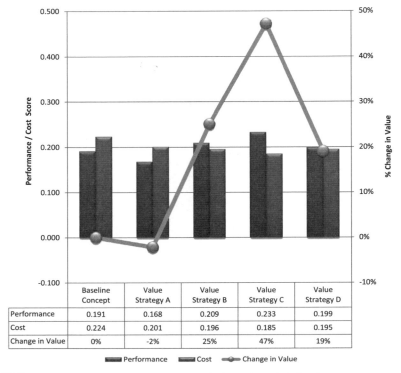

	Baseline Concept	Value Strategy A	Value Strategy B	Value Strategy C	Value Strategy D
Performance	0.191	0.168	0.209	0.233	0.199
Cost	0.224	0.201	0.196	0.185	0.195
Change in Value	0%	-2%	25%	47%	19%

■■■■ Performance   ■■■■ Cost   ●●● Change in Value

FIGURE 10.2   Comparison of Value Strategies, Technical High School

measure. The value team wanted to demonstrate that this was not a good value solution.

Strategies B, C, and D all offered significant value improvements over the baseline concept. Of these, Strategy C, which would demolish the existing Supermarket Building, offered the greatest potential for improved value. It had both the lowest cost and highest performance. The Value Matrix had revealed a powerful yet surprising comparison of options—what initially appeared to be a counterintuitive course of action, to demolish rather than renovate, proved out to be the best value alternative.

Armed with this information, the value team set about creating the presentation and developing the written report in the weeks that followed the study. The fact that the presentation had been scheduled a few weeks following the end of the study provided the team with valuable time to prepare.

The formal presentation utilized a combination of large-scale drawings; the value study report, which included all of the alternative information and supporting documentation; and a multimedia projector to highlight major points. The value specialist led the presentation and focused on introducing the team to the participants, summarizing the study process, and highlighting key issues. The value team members presented the technical information relevant to the alternatives. An informal approach was used and the team responded to questions from the audience as the presentation unfolded. The presentation culminated with a presentation of the Value Matrix, which precipitated a lively discussion.

The School District was pleasantly surprised by the results. The process, which they initially had feared would cut costs at the expense of the educational program, provided several excellent options that would significantly enhance total project value. The principal and superintendent thanked the value team for their efforts. The information in the report would be thoroughly reviewed by the district, by the state budget agency, and by the design team. An implementation meeting was schedule two weeks later to determine how the district would respond to the value alternatives.

CHAPTER 11

Implementation

© Magixl 2009, www.magixl.com

He that waits upon fortune is never sure of dinner.

—Ben Franklin

Benjamin Franklin was born in Boston on January 17, 1706. He was the tenth son of soap maker Josiah Franklin, and but one of his 17 children. In his early years, he served as an apprentice printer first in Boston and then in Philadelphia. He later went on to purchase the *Pennsylvania Gazette,* which soon became the most successful newspaper in the American colonies. He was a prolific writer and is famous for authoring *Poor Richard's Almanack,* a collection of Franklin's witty aphorisms and lively essays.

One fascinating aspect of Franklin's life was the determination and discipline he displayed in implementing changes in his life. This trait was perhaps best demonstrated during a period as a young man in which he systematically focused on improving virtuous behavior and eradicating bad habits. Specifically, Franklin would focus on one of thirteen virtues each week and methodically practice it in his daily life while keeping records of his progress.

Franklin had a strong inclination toward public service and was the catalyst for implementing many civic programs within Philadelphia. These include the "Junto," a young man's self-improvement organization; the founding of the Library Company—the nation's first subscription library; the launching of the Philosophical Society; and the foundation of the Pennsylvania Hospital to provide care to the sick and infirm. Franklin is also credited with establishing the city's first fire company.

Franklin also shone as an inventor. He is well known for some of humankind's first experiments with electricity. He invented the Franklin stove, swim fins, the glass armonica (a musical instrument), and bifocals. Franklin is also famous for his role as one of the nation's founding fathers. He is in fact credited with much of the authorship of the Declaration of Independence, which is generally overshadowed by Thomas Jefferson's role in its creation. He also served in the Second Continental Congress and served as the U.S. Ambassador to France.

Perhaps Franklin's most impressive trait was his ability to implement his ideas. He is an excellent example of the importance of following through with change. Having an idea is not enough—it must be carried out and acted upon with due diligence. Benjamin Franklin provides an excellent introduction to the importance and need for the Implementation Phase.

Implementation Phase

The Implementation Phase focuses on determining the disposition of the value alternatives and validating their effect on project value. Once the decision makers have had a chance to review the value study report and have provided their written analysis of each value alternative to the value specialist, an Implementation Meeting should be scheduled to agree upon the disposition of each value alternative. The Implementation Phase features the following steps:

- Review value alternatives
  - Improve decisions—*Value Metrics*
- Resolve value alternatives
  - Conduct implementation meeting
- Develop implementation plan
- Track and audit results

Managing Change

The Implementation Phase is all about change, as the acceptance of a value alternative by the decision makers will require the project team to integrate the associated changes into the ongoing project and may even require a systemic change within the organization to be successful. The key to dealing with the changes that occur as a result of a value study, big or small, is to competently manage them. This requires developing a basic understanding of the nature of change itself.

The Stages of Change

The capacity of individuals and organizations to cope with change varies dramatically depending on the size and nature of the change as well as an awareness of the risks associated with not accepting the change. Depending on the nature of an organization's approach to implementation, the value specialist or project manager will need to assist others in adjusting to the changes brought on by value alternatives. There are essentially four stages of change:

1. *Stage 1: Shock*. Most people interpret impending change as a threat. Much like physiological shock, the tendency is to shut down thinking, and as many other systems as possible, in order to cope with the attendant fear. Just as people need warmth and rest when in physical shock in order to initiate recovery, they need emotional support, information, and an opportunity to gather with others in order to begin recovering the shock of change.

   Coping strategy: The shock and stress of change can be minimized by building a support network in the form of a detailed implementation plan, and by providing as much information as possible with respect to the change. Upper management should provide support and, more importantly, maintain a visible level of involvement in seeing the changes through. A sense of safety can be provided by clearly communicating organizational expectations and by properly allocating time and resources to implement the change.

2. *Stage 2: Defensive retreat*. Many times, those who are most directly affected by a change will attempt to hold onto or maintain the old ways with which they are familiar. Individuals and organizations can get stuck here or return to Stage 1 as each element of the change is introduced.

   Coping strategy: Assistance can be rendered by identifying what those individuals who are resisting change are holding on to; provide insight on how to modify old behaviors in the context of the new situation; or how to simply let go of the old ways altogether if they are now inappropriate or obsolete. Identify areas of stability (i.e., things that are not changing). Provide information continually and consistently. Ask "What is risky?" and provide safety in response to the discomfort felt with risk taking.

3. *Stage 3: Acknowledgment*. This stage may include a sense of grief and sadness over what has been lost. This aspect of change may be pronounced in those that have had a major hand in the creative and/or technical development of the project's baseline concept. For these individuals, it is important to start letting go; begin to see the value of what is coming; and look for ways to make the changes successful. The project team will need to begin taking risks again in order to implement the change. This process will require additional creativity and a sense of discovery that can lead to positive team energy if well managed.

   Coping strategy: Involve people by working with them to explore options and by planning through the use of an implementation plan and schedule. The value specialist or project manager should encourage and support risk taking at this stage by pointing out ways that it will be supported by the organization. Emphasize that everyone is facing the same learning curve.

4. *Stage 4: Adaptation and change*. At this stage, the transformation is in full motion. Be prepared to establish new routines and to help others. Risk taking comes into fruition at this stage relative to changing methods, products, or whatever is called for by the change.

   Coping strategy: Stick to the implementation plan. Encourage and support risk taking, using the process and structures developed in Stage 3. Establish feedback loops so that information travels in all directions, new learning occurs, and mid-course corrections can be made when necessary.

The Forces of Change

The next step in managing change is developing an understanding of the forces involved in individual and organizational change. There are both positive and negative forces at work that tend to work at cross-purposes. These forces include positive forces and negative forces.

POSITIVE FORCES (CATALYSTS OF CHANGE)   Changes in an organization's environment, such as the introduction of new procedures, standards, or regulations, rapidly increasing competition, or unpredictable changes in the economy, may require the organization to implement new organizational structures or systems of recognition.

- The development of new products or product selection resulting from improvements in technology, changes to the competition or the industry, or unusual requirements of a new client may impact the organization.
- Changes in the workplace to employee demographics, organizational structure, management style, or employee demographics related to acquisitions or mergers may call for new forms of communication and chains of decision making.
- Reductions in productivity, product quality, customer satisfaction, commitment, or an increase in employee turnover or absenteeism may call for changes in internal relations (i.e., the relationship between different departments within an organization). Sometimes, one or two specific events outside of the organization precipitate the change.

NEGATIVE FORCES (RESISTANCE TO CHANGE)
- Resistance to change occurs when a change ignores the needs, attitudes, and beliefs of the members of an organization.
- Individuals resist change when they lack specific information about the change. This ignorance hinders them from developing an understanding of when, how, or why the change is occurring.
- Individuals may not perceive a need for change; they may feel that their organization or project is currently operating effectively and/or profitably. In such a case, change may not be voluntary or requested by organizational members.
- Members of an organization may suffer from an "us versus them" mentality that causes them to view the change agent as their enemy. These individuals may also feel inconsequential in the face of the change, especially if it is imposed by representatives from "headquarters" or by an outside entity, such as a consulting firm or regulatory agency.
- Members of an organization may view the change as a threat to the prestige and security of their manager. They may perceive the change in procedures of policies as a commentary that their manager's performance is inadequate.
- Members of an organization may perceive the change as threats to their expertise, status, or security. The introduction of a new computer system, for example, may cause some individuals to feel that they lack sufficient knowledge to perform their work duties; the revision of an organization's structure may

challenge their feelings of job security; the introduction of a new reward system may threaten their relative status within the organization.

In order for controlled, managed, and effective change to occur, the value specialist or project manager must confront each of these negative forces and strive to overcome them.

Implementing Change

The successful implementation of the changes related to value alternatives requires that the strategies outlined in the implementation plan succeed. Although careful preparation for change, including the proper documentation of the value alternatives and a sound implementation plan, increases the chances of success, it does not guarantee effective action. Implementation requires an ongoing assessment of the reactions of the project team to the change. Strategies for the successful implementation of change include:

- The use of a steering or oversight committee to monitor the change may increase the likelihood of success.
- The dynamic nature of organizational systems requires flexibility. The implementation plan must include contingency plans for unanticipated costs, potential risks, or unforeseen resistance.
- A strong commitment to the implementation plan on the part of the top management can buffer the effort from internal and external challenges and ensure that needed resources are made available to see the change through to completion.

Review and Assess Value Alternatives

The project team and decision makers will be faced with the task of reviewing and assessing the value alternatives once the value study report has been submitted. The purpose of this assessment is to provide the project stakeholders and the value team with the assurance that the alternatives contain accurate information and that the assessments are based on their merits with the current information. During the assessment of alternatives, the project manager, key project team members, technical reviewers, and external project stakeholders review the value study report and document their comments and recommendations on all value alternatives. It is not uncommon for the various reviewers of the value study report to have different positions regarding the acceptability of the value alternatives. For this reason, these comments should be collected and submitted to the value specialist so that proper preparation for the implementation meeting can be accomplished. Figure 11.1 provides an example of a form to capture the recommendations and review comments from project team members and stakeholders.

The structure of this form is fairly self-explanatory. It is an expedient way to capture comments on many alternatives and highlight issues that will affect their implementation.

Once all of the recommendation forms have been received, they should be reviewed by the value specialist and the value team. It may be desirable for the

VALUE ALTERNATIVE IMPLEMENTATION ACTION RECOMMENDATION *1.5 TON FORKLIFT TRUCK*		
Prepared by:	*Rachel Evans, Purchasing*	**Date:** *6/29/09*

Providing your disposition of this alternative denotes your recommendation to implement, based on current information. It is recognized that future conditions may change this disposition. Your comments will be discussed at the Implementation Meeting where final disposition and savings validation will be determined.

Alt #	**Alternative**
1.1	Upgrade Seat Assembly

Disposition Recommendation	**Explain, Comment and/or Discuss Rationale for Disposition Recommendation**
☒ **Agree** ☐ **Agree w/ Modifications** ☐ **Further Study Needed** ☐ **Disagree**	Purchasing has reviewed this alternative and sees no major concerns in reaching an agreement with the current vendor of the new seat assembly regarding pricing and quantities.

FIGURE 11.1   Example of a Form to Capture Stakeholder Comments

value team to meet as a group to perform this review. Alternatives that appear to have deficiencies or are found to be unacceptable for one reason or another should be discussed. It may be possible for the value team to develop workarounds or enhancements to overcome the deficiencies.

Improve Decisions—*Value Metrics*

The information developed during the value study with respect to performance and value provides the project's decision makers with additional information in considering all the options. The detailed performance rating rationale generated during the development phase will be of particular benefit in the decision-making process. The consideration of potential implementation strategies within the context of value improvement provides project stakeholders with a means for considering the contribution of performance, cost, time, and risk in achieving total value.

The project team can continue to use the Value Matrix as a means of auditing performance improvements during the implementation of the alternative concepts. A revised Value Matrix can be developed that shows the net benefits of the accepted alternative concepts.

Resolve Value Alternatives

An implementation meeting should be scheduled to develop consensus and resolve the implementation dispositions of the value alternatives. The meeting(s) include(s) pertinent value team members and the individuals with the authority to determine the alternatives' implementation decisions, the project manager, key project team members, relevant technical reviewers, and any appropriate external project stakeholders.

The meeting should be an informal working meeting to encourage the positive exchange of opinions, supporting data, and discussion. The implementation disposition for each alternative is discussed with the project manager, relevant project team members, and other project stakeholder representatives. The meeting should result in the resolution of the dispositions for every alternative, categorized by one of the following: "accepted," "conditionally accepted," or "rejected." The value team is challenged to modify rejected alternatives when it is possible that a modification could facilitate acceptance of the alternative and overcome its deficiencies.

Any alternatives noted as "conditionally accepted" should include the action required, responsibilities, and timing of the final decision. The value specialist, project manager, or value program manager (if one exists within the organization) will review the resolution of the conditionally accepted alternatives at a later date to complete the reporting on the study.

All relevant comments and dispositions during this activity should be documented by the value specialist. This documentation should also be included in the final value study report if it is included as one of the value study deliverables in the value study scope established in the Preparation Phase. A "master" implementation action form should be prepared that summarizes the comments from the reviewers.

Figure 11.2 is an example of such a form, titled Value Alternative Implementation Action. The form should obviously be modified to meet the needs of the organization. This form includes placeholders for the following information:

- *Title.* The title of the alternative as shown on the Value Alternative form.
- *Alternative no.* Alternative number as shown on the Value Alternative form.
- *Responses.* A summary of the final disposition of the alternative prepared by the project manager, value program manager, or value specialist.
- *Prepared by.* Identify who is preparing the response and date.
- *Rationale for disposition.* Provide a discussion justifying the grounds for acceptance or rejection and a brief statement of technical feasibility.
- *Implementation disposition.* Choose one of the following dispositions:
  - Accept. Acceptance of the alternative denotes the intent to implement in the given project development phase.
  - Conditionally accept. Alternative is desired but requires added technical analysis and/or stakeholder agreement before final disposition can be made.
  - Reject. Alternative is not acceptable as presented and will be dropped from further consideration.
- *Performance impacts.* Provide a discussion of the alternative's performance impacts. Elaborate on any deviations in the performance assessment from that presented by the value team.
- *Performance change.* Validate performance using the original rating scales and attribute priorities used in the value study. If any of the ratings changed, the net result should be included here.
- *Cost impacts.* Provide a discussion of the alternative's cost impacts. Identify any changes or differences from the value team's concept that affect cost.
- *Cost change.* Validate initial cost savings (or increase) in dollars.
- *Schedule/delivery impacts.* Provide a discussion of how the alternative will affect the schedule (it could be the project delivery, production time, process time, etc.).
- *Schedule change.* Identify any change in project schedule.

VALUE ALTERNATIVE IMPLEMENTATION ACTION
1.5 TON FORKLIFT TRUCK

		Alternative No.
TITLE: Upgrade seat assembly		1.1
RESPONSES	*Prepared by:* J. Tucker, Design Mgr.	*Date:* 7/18/09

Acceptance of alternatives denotes intent to implement, based on current information. It is recognized that future conditions may change this disposition. The validation of disposition and the cost and performance changes for the alternative are required to ensure that the project decision makers agree with the study results.

Rationale for Disposition	**DISPOSITION**
This alternative has been accepted for implementation into the next generation of the FC-150 class. The concept is technically feasible and has no known design issues. Acceptance is based upon total value improvement for the product.	☑ **Accept** ☐ **Conditionally Accept** ☐ **Reject**

Performance Impacts	**Performance Change**
The project team concurs with the value team's performance assessment. The new seat assembly offers significant ergonomic improvements that will make the vehicle far more attractive to customers by adding features that will reduce operator fatigue and improve safety.	+5.4%

Cost Impacts	**Cost Change**
The cost impacts will be slightly greater than initially estimated. The project team developed the necessary modifications to the seat mounting hardware which will increase slightly to accommodate the rotational movement of the seat. These additional costs are estimated to be about $2.57 per unit.	-$30.80 per unit

Schedule/Delivery Impacts	**Schedule Change**
The project team has evaluated the effect on production time and has calculated that the new seat assembly will only add about 5 minutes due to some minor changes in the mounting hardware. The associated labor and burden costs have been included in the cost change on this form.	5 min.

Risk Impacts	**Risk P&I**
There is very little risk associated with this alternative in terms of performance. From an implementation standpoint, the only uncertainties are related to final cost and production time impacts. Based on a review by the Engineering Dept., the risks related to successfully integrating the new seat assembly into the chassis are very small.	Probability / X / Impact

Other Comments	**Value Improvement**
The integration of movable arm rests to the unit will require modification of the seat assembly.	+5%

FIGURE 11.2   Example of an Implementation Action Form

- *Risk impacts.* Provide a discussion of how the alternative impacts risk. This could include the risks related to implementation, the affect of the alternative on existing project risks, or both.
- *Risk P&I.* In this example, a risk probability and impact matrix was included to summarize the implementation risks. The use of such information may change dramatically depending upon how the project is addressing risk.

- *Other comments.* Comments on other issues relating to the alternative. Note any concerns or controversial items. Identify suspense dates or action items here.
- *Value improvement.* The final effect of the value alternative on project value, expressed as a percent. This figure should incorporate any revised cost, performance and schedule data into the calculation.

This form should be modified to meet the specific needs of the project that is being studied. Different types of information will be needed for a management process project versus a construction or manufacturing project.

Develop Implementation Plan

Those alternatives that have been selected for implementation into the project will require a plan to ensure that the changes are integrated properly. An implementation plan should be developed for each value alternative that was identified as "accepted." The implementation plan will need to identify implementation responsibilities, action dates, modifications to the project schedule, and additional project development activities that may be required.

The project manager must take the lead in developing the implementation plan and be assisted by the value specialist as necessary. Modifications to the project's work breakdown structure and/or project development schedule should be developed and circulated to the project team in a timely fashion.

Some organizations, especially those with established value programs administered by a value program manager, will have already established procedures for developing implementation plans. In such cases, the project manager's efforts will be greatly reduced.

Implementation plans will vary widely and depend upon the unique nature of the changes themselves, as well as the organization involved in implementing the changes. There are, however, a number of common elements that will usually need to be considered in implementing the change. Most of these elements should have been identified in the Implementation Action form identified above. These considerations include:

- *Responsibility.* Who will be responsible for managing the changes called for in the value alternative? What authority do they have? Who will they report to? What resources will be assigned to them to assist in implementing the change?
- *Design/system integration.* How will the changes be integrated into the project? What approvals, clearances, or testing will be necessary to implement the change? Will the changes necessitate modifications to other aspects of the system or design?
- *Schedule.* How will the project schedule be impacted by implementing the change? What other projects or processes will be affected by any anticipated delays? Will critical budgeting or funding milestones be affected?
- *Implementation costs.* What will it cost the project to implement the changes? Will there be redesign or testing costs? Will there be impacts to existing supplier or consultant contracts already in place?

Track and Audit Results

It is generally the responsibility of the project manager or value program manager to track and audit the results of the value alternatives. In some cases, the value alternative will run into problems during the implementation process. It may be that unanticipated technical problems arise, or perhaps an external stakeholder will refuse to approve the change. Regardless, problems will be encountered that will need to be addressed. It is incumbent upon those monitoring the implementation process to respond proactively so that the issues can be resolved.

In many cases, numerous alternatives will have been selected for implementation. In such a situation, it is recommended that a database be developed that identifies the alternatives' information, responsible parties, latest status, and action dates. Depending upon the organizational structure of the company or agency, this may be an essential tool in ensuring that implementation is carried successfully through to completion. An example of a status report generated from such a database is provided in Figure 11.3.

Summary

The Implementation Phase is where all of the efforts of the value team will hopefully pay off. To ensure that this happens, the value specialist must be diligent in responding to problems or issues that may arise during the review process and work with the project team in developing an implementation plan.

Value Alternative Status Report	
Value Study Title	1.5 ton Forklift Truck
Alternative No.	1.1
Alternative Title	Upgrade Seat Assembly
Proposed Cost Savings	-$23.23
Proposed Performance	+5.4%
Validated Cost Savings	-$30.80
Validated Performance	+5.4%
Current Status	Under Review
Status Narrative	10 of the prototype seat units will be shipped by Reliant Manufacturing Co. on September 1. Initial production will begin the following week and any further changes that are needed will be noted and incorporated into design and production.
Status Date	8/20/2009
Project Manager	J. Withers
Value Program Manager	E. Khan

FIGURE 11.3   Value Program Status Report

The project manager will also play a critical role in the success of the implementation plan. Management involvement in the implementation process will reinforce the efforts of the project manager in seeing the changes through the project development process. Implementation is all about managing change. It is the objective of the value specialist to help others adapt to the changes that will result from a successful value study.

Appendix 11A: Case Study

The recipients of the value study report reviewed the contents over the next two weeks. During that time, the reviewers were asked to provide their comments on the value alternatives to the value team so they could better prepare for the implementation meeting. The feedback received by the value team was thoughtfully prepared and focused on the data developed by the value team rather than on opinion. The value team had done a thorough job developing the alternatives, and this paid great dividends, judging by the responses.

The general consensus was that Value Strategy C indeed offered the greatest potential for value improvement. However, the school district superintendent was concerned about how the public would react to the idea of demolishing what appeared to be a perfectly good building. His district had already been under a lot of scrutiny on recent budget requests, and the last thing he wanted to do was to provide the district's critics with ammunition to lobby for the denial of the funding increases.

The value specialist saw this as a potential roadblock to the acceptance of this strategy. Clearly, the students, the school district, and taxpayers had everything to gain if the data were considered objectively. However, the value specialist understood the difference between reality and perception in these matters. After thinking about the problem, he contacted the value program manager at the state budget agency to discuss solutions. The value program manager felt that he should arrange for a meeting with the budget director beforehand to discuss the special challenges faced by the district in considering Value Strategy C.

A few days later, the value specialist met with the value program manager and the state budget director to discuss the issue. After about ten minutes, it was clear that the state budget agency would need to reduce the risk of negative public perception. The agency's public affairs liaison was called into the meeting to discuss how the idea could be effectively sold to the public while minimizing the threat of a negative public response. The public affairs liaison recommended developing a fact sheet on the project, which would explain the reasons for the demolition of the building and how the proposed approach would result in better value to the taxpayers. The value specialist agreed to work on the fact sheet with the public affairs liaison and that they would present it during the implementation meeting to assuage the superintendent's concerns.

The day of the implementation meeting finally arrived. Most of those present at the formal presentation were in attendance. The value specialist facilitated the meeting and led the group through a discussion of each of the value alternatives. He shared the comments received from the various reviewers of the value study report. A consensus decision was made concerning each alternative, and the value specialist made notes during the meeting to capture key points of the discussion. These would later be incorporated into the final report's implementation action section. The discussion of value alternatives 1.1 to 1.4 were withheld until the end. The majority of the other alternatives was accepted and would be incorporated into the final design of the Technical High School. Each of these major alternatives was then discussed at length. It was agreed by all that, Strategy A clearly should be eliminated from further consideration. Both Strategies B and D were potentially acceptable, as they maintained the Supermarket Building and avoided the district's concerns about demolishing the Supermarket Building.

Last, they discussed Strategy C. The superintendent was very candid with the group in expressing his concerns about the demolition of the Supermarket Building. The group agreed that his concerns were valid. At this point, the state budget agency's value program manager provided the group with an overview of the events leading to the solution to this problem. He presented a copy of the project fact sheet that would inform the public of the reasoning behind the decision. In addition, he reassured the superintendent that the state budget agency would also publicly defend the district's decision. After considering the project fact sheet, the superintendent was willing to pursue Value Strategy C in light of the implementation plan that had been presented. The rest of the participants agreed that this was the best approach and it was subsequently adopted in favor of the other strategies.

The value specialist reviewed the performance ratings for Strategy C with the group and there was general concurrence with the value team's initial assessment. The meeting was adjourned and it was clear that everyone was very enthusiastic about the results.

The value specialist spent the next day formalizing the meeting minutes and completing the implementation action forms for the final value study report. He submitted the completed report to the value program manager, who would be responsible for monitoring the implementation of the accepted value alternatives.

CHAPTER 12

Value Leadership

© Magixl 2009, www.magixl.com

Leadership is the art of getting someone else to do something you want done because he wants to do it.

—Dwight D. Eisenhower

Dwight David Eisenhower was born in Texas in 1890 and grew up in Abilene, Kansas, the third of seven sons. He excelled in both academics and sports in high school, and he received an appointment to West Point. In his early army career, he excelled in staff assignments, serving under Generals John J. Pershing, Douglas MacArthur, and Walter Krueger. After Pearl Harbor, General George C. Marshall called him to Washington for a war plans assignment. He commanded the Allied Forces landing in North Africa in November 1942 and by 1944 he was the Supreme Commander of the Allied Forces in Europe.

After the war, he became president of Columbia University and then took leave to assume supreme command over the new NATO forces being assembled in 1951. Republican emissaries to his headquarters near Paris persuaded him to run for president in 1952. During his two productive terms as president, he had many significant accomplishments. With regard to foreign relations, he promoted Atoms for Peace and dealt with crises in Lebanon, Suez, Berlin, and Hungary. On the homefront, he saw Alaska and Hawaii become states, continued key social programs established during the Roosevelt Administration, and supported the process of the desegregation of public schools and the Armed Forces.

Bringing to the presidency his prestige as commanding general of the victorious forces in Europe during World War II, Dwight D. Eisenhower obtained a truce in Korea and worked incessantly during his two terms to ease the tensions of the Cold War. He pursued the moderate policies of modern republicanism, pointing out as he left office, "America is today the strongest, most influential, and most productive nation in the world."

President Eisenhower proved to be one of the greatest leaders in American history, through times of both war and peace. Much of his success can be attributed to the value he placed on his fellow citizens, which is eloquently illustrated by his famous quote "There must be no second-class citizens in this country." President Eisenhower embodied the characteristics of leadership and provides an excellent role model in this chapter's discussion of Value Leadership.

Value Leadership

The role of the value specialist is critical to the success of a value study. The most important skill set that the value specialist must possess is communication. Of critical importance is the nature in which he or she communicates—whether it is active or passive, assertive or restrained.

In thinking about the communication styles of a value specialist, it is useful to divide it into two distinct roles: leader and facilitator. Both roles are important and each is appropriate for different types of functions and activities. Communication through leadership is active and assertive. Conversely, communication through facilitation is passive and restrained. There are also many levels in between these extremes.

Leadership

There are just as many styles of leadership as there are leaders. It can further be stated that different leadership styles are appropriate for different types of situations. What style of leadership, then, is best suited for the value specialist? To answer this question, it is useful to develop a basic understanding of leadership styles through a series of leadership models. Two fundamental leadership models are fairly well recognized: the Leadership Framework model and the Managerial Grid model.

The Leadership Framework model (see Figure 12.1) indicates that leaders display leadership behaviors in one of four types of leadership styles, or "frameworks." These are the structural, the political, the symbolic, and the human resource frameworks. The effectiveness of each leadership framework is largely determined by the behavior of the leader in applying a particular leadership style within a particular setting or environment.[1]

1. *Structural framework.* Leaders who focus on strategy, implementation, adaptation, and environment best describe leaders that fit the Structural Framework approach to leadership. Leaders who are effective using the Structural approach can be best described as social architects who lead through analysis and design.

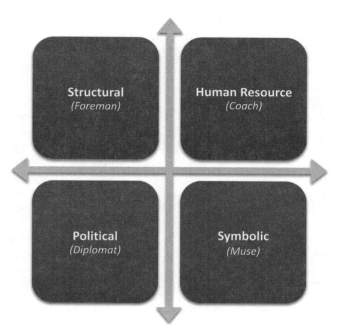

FIGURE 12.1   The Leadership Framework Model

Like a construction foreman, they manage a team within a structure. Leaders who are ineffective using this approach are generally perceived as petty and tyrannical by those working under them.

2. *Human resource framework.* Leaders who focus on individuals, communication, team empowerment, and consensus demonstrate characteristics that describe the Human Resource Framework. Leaders who are effective using the Human Resource approach act as a catalyst for empowering others that are part of their team. Indeed, the term "coach" is a fitting description for this leadership style. On the other hand, leaders who are ineffective using this approach are often perceived as being "spineless" and others will tend to walk all over them.

3. *Political framework.* Leaders who focus on power, diplomacy, and negotiation describe those that represent the Political Framework leadership approach. Leaders who are effective using the Political approach rely first upon persuasion, like a good diplomat, followed by negotiation and finally by coercion if all else fails. Successful leaders using this style rely heavily on building coalitions. Ineffectual leaders using this approach can be perceived by others as manipulative, deceiving, and even "back-stabbing."

4. *Symbolic framework.* Leaders who focus on role playing, creativity, and future outcomes best describe the Symbolic Framework approach to leadership. Leaders who are effective using the Symbolic approach find ways to harness the power of symbolism to inspire others to reach for a far-reaching vision. "Fools" and "fanatics" are terms that are often used to describe leaders who fail in following this path.

The Leadership Framework model suggests that all leaders can be put into one of these frameworks at any given point in time, depending upon their behavior. It is important to keep in mind that there are strengths and weaknesses related to each approach, and that there will be times when one approach is more appropriate than the others.

The value specialist will need to call upon all four of these frameworks to be successful. You can probably already begin to see where each of these may be appropriate in conjunction with the Value Methodology Job Plan. For instance, the value specialist might lean heavily on the Symbolic Framework during the Speculation Phase, while relying more upon the Political Framework during the Presentation Phase.

The Managerial Grid considers two dimensions (see Figure 12.2). These are "concern for people," which is plotted along the vertical axis, and "concern for production," which is plotted along the horizontal axis.[2] Both are given numerical ranges between 1 and 9 that represent the relative strength of preference for each of these two concerns. There are essentially four management (leadership) archetypes that provide reference points in describing the relevant styles.

- *Country club management.* Concern for Production = Low. Concern for People = High. This management style emphasizes personal relationships over task management. There is a great deal of reliance on goodwill and trust on the part of the manager that those working under him or her will get the job done. This approach can be effective when those on the team are self-directed and highly motivated. It can be a disastrous approach if this is not the case.
- *Impoverished management.* Concern for Production = Low. Concern for People = Low. This management style describes the executive who delegates

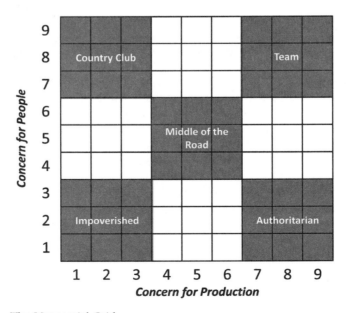

FIGURE 12.2 The Managerial Grid

his or her authority and then stays out of sight. This is without question the weakest form of leadership and is consequently the approach that is least likely to be effective.

- *Authoritarian management.* Concern for Production = High. Concern for People = Low. This management style focuses strictly on the efficient operations of a team in meeting its task and tends to be autocratic in dealing with others. Managers using this approach are generally indifferent to the people under them and do not tolerate questions or dissent. This can be an effective approach when applied to tasks that require little team communication or interaction. It is generally an inappropriate style when dealing with projects involving many stakeholders or those projects that require consensus building.
- *Team management.* Concern for Production = High. Concern for People = High. This type of leader leads by deed. He or she is focused simultaneously on both production and the people involved. The team manager (or team leader) seeks to foster an environment in which all team members can reach their highest potential through good communication and hard work.

In addition to these four archetypes, there is a fifth category into which most leaders and managers fall. These individuals show an average concern for people and production and convey a style of leadership is referred as "middle of the road."

The brevity and substantial goals of most value studies require a strong focus on production, while the human dynamics related to dealing with a multidiscipline team, as well as a collection of diverse stakeholders, require extreme sensitivity to people. The management style identified here that is most appropriate for the value specialist would be the "Team Management" archetype.

A leader must be trusted and he or she must be able to communicate effectively. The following is a number of leadership principles that foster trust and communication. A value specialist should strive to achieve them both during and after the study.

- *Know yourself and seek self-improvement.* Seeking self-improvement means continually strengthening your abilities. This can be accomplished through self-study, formal classes, and interacting with others. A value specialist is an agent of change. Expose yourself to new ideas and actively seek to incorporate what you learn into your work. Heed the words of Mahatma Gandhi: "We must become the change we want to see."
- *Be technically proficient.* As a leader, you must know your field and have a solid familiarity with the activities involved. If you are weak in certain areas then you must look for opportunities to test yourself there and develop the experience and confidence necessary to improve. Be prepared and know the details of the projects you are working on. A leader who is perceived as not understanding the project or the process he or she is in charge of will lose the faith of the team.
- *Seek responsibility and take responsibility for your actions.* Search for ways to guide your team to new heights. When things go wrong, do not blame others. Analyze the situation, take corrective action, and move on to the next challenge. There are lessons to be learned on every study. Take these lessons to heart and incorporate what has been learned.

- *Make sound and timely decisions.* The tools and techniques that have been covered in this book can be applied individually or together to improve decision making at every level. Specifically, the application of Value Metrics will keep your decisions focused on achieving value.
- *Set the example.* Be a good role model for your team. Not only must they hear what they are expected to do, but they also must see it. Demonstrate how the various activities in the job plan are performed and, when appropriate, take an active role in participating in them.
- *Know your team and look out for their well-being.* Be sensitive of others and their contributions. Recognize that their time is valuable and once spent cannot be recovered. Treat people as you would wish to be treated. Be flexible—bend but do not break.
- *Keep your team informed.* Know how to communicate with the team. Let them know what is going on outside of the study that is relevant to their performance. Keep the communication direct, clear, and concise.
- *Ensure that tasks are understood, supervised, and accomplished.* Communication is the key to this responsibility. Monitor progress and intervene when necessary to keep the team on track. This is especially important during the Development Phase when team members are working on individual assignments. Review their work frequently to make sure that they are on the right track.
- *Work as a team.* Although many a leader calls their group a team, they are not really teams; they are just a group of people doing their jobs. Team spirit requires a sense of enthusiasm and cohesion that does not happen of its own accord. It requires a leader to actively instill them through words and actions.
- *Use the full capabilities of your team.* By developing a team spirit, you will be able to employ your team to its fullest capabilities. Challenge team members to improve upon their ideas and to overcome roadblocks. During group activities, call upon everyone and ensure that they stay engaged.

Although the value specialist may not be the CEO of a company, the director of a government agency, or even a member of the organization that is sponsoring the value study, he or she will be responsible for leading the effort to create positive change on projects and within organizations by improving value. Change requires a catalyst to overcome the inertia of the status quo. The value specialist must be the catalyst for change.

Facilitation

Facilitation is an interesting word that is often misunderstood. Facilitation means "to make easier." Therefore, facilitators make things easier for people to do or to understand. In the context of a value study, facilitators make communication, change, and the various techniques involved easier. Facilitation is generally much more passive than leadership and is not as participatory in nature.

The following is one of the best definitions of a facilitator that this author has run across:

> *A facilitator is an individual who enables groups and organizations to work more effectively, to collaborate and achieve synergy. She or he is a "content-*

neutral" party who by both taking sides or expressing or advocating a point of view during the meeting, can advocate fair, open and inclusive procedures to accomplish the group's work. A facilitator can also be a learning or dialogue guide to assist a group in thinking deeply about its assumptions, beliefs, and values about its systemic processes and context.[3]

The value specialist wears the hat of facilitator on many of the activities during a value study. It is a very important role and one that has many facets. These include:

- Using the power of objectivity and credibility to help groups address issues
- Surfacing difficult issues and help others to do so
- Clarifying communication and the exchange of information between participants
- Supporting and counselling others
- Instilling a sense of calm during times of discord and conflict
- Mobilizing a group's energy and keeping it on task
- Conveying empathy to all participants to help build an environment of trust and mutual understanding
- Helping participants cope with uncertainty

To accomplish these objectives, a facilitator must apply and develop the following basic skills.

ACTIVE LISTENING   This may at first appear obvious; however, it is often the case that our listening skills are less than stellar. Active listening is different from passive listening as it requires us to be engaged with the speaker. As one author has said, "Hearing is with the ears. Listening is with the mind."[4] There are ten essential rules for active listening:

1. Stop talking. Obvious, but not always easy for some.
2. Put the speaker at ease. Create a permissive, supportive climate in which the speaker will feel free to express himself or herself.
3. Show a desire to listen. Act interested and mean it.
4. Remove distractions. External preoccupation is less likely if nothing external is present to preoccupy you.
5. Empathize. Try to experience, to some degree, the feelings that the speaker is experiencing.
6. Be patient. Give the speaker time to finish; don't interrupt.
7. Hold your temper. Don't let your emotions obstruct your thoughts.
8. Go easy on argument and criticism. Suspend judgment.
9. Ask questions. If things are still unclear when a speaker has finished, ask questions that serve to clarify the intended meanings.
10. Stop talking.

QUESTIONING   Questioning is an enormously important skill and is central to the process of eliciting information from others. The form of questioning most suitable for the techniques presented in this book is known as the Socratic Method, which is attributed to the famous Greek philosopher Socrates. Socrates originally used this approach as a means of questioning and examining ambiguous and/or abstract concepts such as morals and virtues. The Socratic Method is a *negative* method of hypotheses elimination, in that better hypotheses are found by steadily identifying and eliminating those that lead to contradictions. Although the Socratic Method is difficult and time consuming to apply directly, the general theme of using questioning to elicit information and to examine assumptions is extremely valid. One form of the Socratic Method is known as Socratic questioning.

Socratic questioning is a systematic and disciplined approach to questioning that focuses on core issues and concepts. The purpose of Socratic questioning is to delve into the heart of an issue and uncover deeper meaning by encouraging rational discourse. It encourages participants to thoroughly articulate their thoughts in a manner that forces a deeper analysis of issues and fosters a shared understanding.

In their excellent book *A Thinkers Guide to the Art of Socratic Questioning*, Paul and Elder (2006) provide a list of questions that are based on this approach.[5]

- Clarity
  - Could you elaborate further?
  - Could you give me an example?
  - Could you illustrate what you mean?
- Accuracy
  - How could we check on that?
  - How could we find out if that is true?
  - How could we verify or test that?
- Precision
  - Could you be more specific?
  - Could you give more details?
  - Could you be more exact?
- Relevance
  - How does that relate to the problem?
  - How does that bear on the question?
  - How does that help us with the issue?
- Depth
  - What factors make this a difficult problem?
  - What are some of the complexities of this question?
  - What are some of the difficulties we need to deal with?
- Breadth
  - Do we need to look at this from another perspective?
  - Do we need to consider another point of view?
  - Do we need to look at this in other ways?
- Logic
  - Does all this make sense together?
  - Does your first paragraph fit in with your last?
  - Does what you say follow from evidence?
- Significance
  - Is this the most important problem to consider?
  - Is this the central idea to focus on?
  - Which of these facts are most important?

- Fairness
  - Do I have any vested interest in this issue?
  - Am I sympathetically representing the viewpoints of others?

The application of this method of questioning is extremely effective within the context of value studies. It frames group interaction in a rational, professional manner that forces people to think critically rather than emotionally. It is an excellent approach for separating facts from bias and uncovering any hidden agendas or meaning.

USING FEEDBACK The value specialist should use feedback throughout the value study in order to make course corrections and maintain efficiency. He or she should frequently ask participants for feedback by asking questions like:

- How are we doing?
- Are we on track?
- Do you have any concerns about the process?
- What can we do better?
- Are we thoroughly addressing the issues?

The information that is received in response to these questions should be evaluated by both the value specialist and the team and incorporated in an appropriate manner.

CONFLICT HANDLING Inevitably, conflicts arise during value studies just as they do anywhere else. The value specialists must do his or her best to address conflict as they arise and deal with them appropriately.

It is best to avoid conflicts before they occur. What follow are a number of considerations that can be applied during a value study toward this end.

- Identify points of agreement
- Reformulate contributions to highlight common ideas
- Encourage people to build on others' ideas
- Test for false consensus
- Test consensus for relevance/motivation

The value specialist should try to maintain objectivity and remain neutral in the face of conflict. The best role to assume is generally that of a referee.

Leading or Facilitating?

It may be unclear as to which role the value specialist should play during a study. There are many different activities and interactions that take place throughout the VM Job Plan. Where should the value specialist lead and where should he or she facilitate? While there is no definitive answer to this question, as the context of the situation will have a major influence on which role is appropriate, there are some general guidelines worth considering.

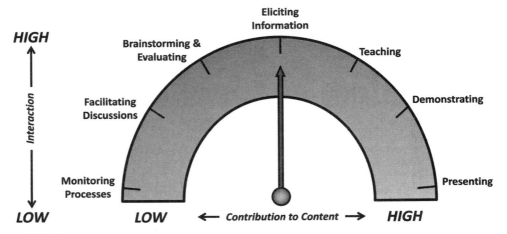

FIGURE 12.3   Facilitation Gauge

Figure 12.3 provides a facilitation gauge for value specialists. Along the horizontal axis is the value specialist's relative contribution to content. The suggested level of interaction with the group is indicated on the vertical axis. The various types of activities that the value specialist is likely to be engaged in are arrayed along the sweep of the dial. For example, the act of eliciting information during a paired comparison of performance attributes would involve a high level of interaction (mainly in the form of Socratic questioning) and a moderate contribution to content (by demonstrating how the technique works and guiding participants through the process). Another example might be during the presentation of the results of the value study. In this case, the level of interaction would be low (as communication is primarily one-way) and the contribution to content would be very high (as the content is emanating solely from the value specialist).

There are aspects of leadership and facilitation involved in virtually everything the value specialist does; it is more a question of degree. Some groups will be passive and require a higher level of leadership and direction, while others will be very active and motivated and require a greater degree of facilitation. The value specialist must gauge the personality of the group and tailor his or her interactions in a manner that will best accomplish the objectives of the value study.

Communication Dynamics

Value Methodology follows a specific Job Plan that is composed of a number of sequential steps. Maintaining good communication is essential to the flow of this process. Building on the previous discussions on leadership and facilitation, it is useful to think about how the value specialist fits into the dynamics of group communication within the context of a value study.

Figure 12.4 illustrates a model of group communication. Although this model was originally developed to demonstrate group decision-making, it also applies to the communication dynamics of a value study.[6]

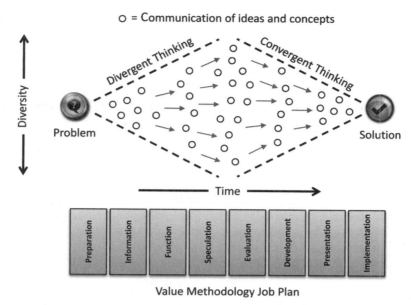

FIGURE 12.4   Dynamics of Group Communication in a Value Study

It is important to understand how the steps in the VM Job Plan relate to the dynamics of group communication. The participants of a value study are first introduced to the project's problems, issues, and objectives. The exchange of information begins, and thinking becomes divergent, which results in divergent communication. The initial presentation of project information leads to questions, which in turn leads to more questions. Thinking continues to diverge through the process of function analysis, which thinks about problems abstractly. This trend increases during creativity and team brainstorming. At about the midway point of the VM process, thinking begins to converge, as the many diverse ideas that have been generated are evaluated critically. This convergence in thinking and communication continues through the development of alternative concepts, is summarized in the Presentation Phase through reports and presentations, and culminates in deciding which alternatives to accept and reject. The result, hopefully, is improved project value.

Another way to think about the dynamics at play is that the application of Value Methodology applies creative destruction followed by critical reconstruction to improve project value. The value specialist must utilize all of his or her facilitation and leadership skills to optimize the value of every step of the Job Plan. Ultimately, effective value leadership is directly linked to good communication.

Characteristics of Value Specialists

There are a number of characteristics necessary to be successful in leading and facilitating value studies. These comprise a number of skills and temperaments that the value specialist should seek to develop.

Skills

The skills necessary to be a successful value specialist are very similar to those required to be a successful project manager. These skills include:

- *Communication.* Value specialists must be fluent in oral and written communication. They must be able to speak before large groups and articulate their thoughts clearly and concisely.
- *Organizational.* Value specialists must have strong planning and organizational skills. Both involve the ability to manage and organize large quantities of information, coordinate schedules, handle logistical considerations, put teams together, and organize meetings.
- *Financial.* Value specialists must be able to request, collect, analyze, and assemble financial information. They must be fluent with financial terminology and have a basic grasp of cost estimating relevant to the type of product or project with which they are involved.
- *Facilitation.* Facilitation, as discussed previously in this chapter, refers to the act of guiding people, either individually or in groups in order to achieve a specific objective. Value specialists must be able to do this, whether it means facilitating the evaluation of competitive bids or leading a value team through a creativity session. Not only is it necessary to possess an understanding of the application of processes and techniques, but ideally the behavioral psychology behind them.
- *Leadership.* Leadership speaks to the ability of an individual to provide strategic vision and direction, inspire confidence, and motivate others to achieve high levels of performance. For example, a value specialist will need to motivate the value team to think creatively while facilitating a brainstorming exercise. Similarly, a project manager will need to apply his or her leadership skills to keep the project team focused on the "big picture" while managing a risk response meeting. Leadership skills require practice and study regardless of the value specialist's innate charisma.
- *Problem solving.* Project managers must be able to identify, predict, resolve, and hopefully avoid, through proper planning, a variety of problems that will crop up during the project development process. Value specialists, on the other hand, must welcome and even thrive on problems, since the very nature of Value Methodology is based on creative problem solving. Both project managers and value specialists must view problems as challenges, and enthusiastically rise to meet them rather than acquiesce.

Temperaments

The value specialist must play a variety of roles in leading a value study. It is useful to draw analogies between commonly identifiable roles and the roles that the value specialist will have to play during the course of a value study. These analogies are not unlike those used in the excellent and insightful work of the noted psychologists David Keirsey and Marilyn Bates in their research on character and temperament types.[7] These diverse roles include, but are not limited to, the following:

- *General.* The value specialist is like a general. He or she must lead by example; command respect by giving respect; provide strategic vision in not losing sight of the war in the midst of the many smaller battles that will be fought; weigh risks and develop contingencies; rally the troops when morale wanes in the face of adversity; and demonstrate courage in the face of overwhelming odds.
- *Diplomat.* The value specialist is like a diplomat. He or she must create a sense of goodwill; make peace between rival factions; act as a messenger between parties; negotiate agreements; understand the political landscape; understand the value of protocol; utilize all available lines of communication; anticipate and avoid potential hostilities; and utilize tact, words, and etiquette to exert influence.
- *Manager.* The value specialist is like a manager. He or she must create plans; manage and organize time, resources, and funds; understand organizational hierarchies; respect and maintain scope, schedule, and cost; master the science of logistics; and ensure that projects are delivered on time, within budget and meet or exceed customer requirements.
- *Devil's advocate.* The value specialist is like the devil's advocate. He or she must challenge the status quo; question everything; endlessly ask the question "why?' and validate or disprove assumptions.
- *Jester.* The value specialist is like a jester and must not take himself or herself too seriously. But he or she must take the work seriously; use humor to break down barriers; create a sense of fun; instill creativity through the use of metaphor and wit; be self-deprecating; and make people feel good about themselves.
- *Salesman.* The value specialist is like a salesman. He or she must sell new ideas; persuade others of the merits of an idea; motivate others to consider change; display enthusiasm in communicating new products; create excitement; and sell change.

Value Methodology Professionals

The role of the value specialist has evolved into several unique professions and career paths since Value Methodology was established in the 1940s. Today, value practitioners serve in virtually every type of organization, large and small, public and private. Some manage value programs, while others earn a living as professional VM consultants. Many have been officially certified by the SAVE International Certification Board, while others have not. Irrespective of the organization or certification, they are all professionals involved in the improvement of value.

Professional value practitioners who have been certified by SAVE International have met an established level of mastery through training, applied experience, and testing. SAVE International recognizes three levels of certification: certified value specialist, associate value specialist, and value methodology practitioner.

Certified Value Specialist (CVS) certification represents the highest level of training and experience and recognizes those individuals whose principal career is Value Methodology. Within this certification level, there are two different classifications:

- *Value specialist.* A value specialist is an individual whose career is primarily involved in leading value studies. A professional value specialist may either operate as a part of a larger organization or as a consultant hired by an organization to conduct value studies.
- *Value program manager.* A value program manager is an individual responsible for managing a value program within an organization. It is their responsibility to identify projects for value studies, organize and manage the value studies, and to monitor the implementation of value alternatives. Value program managers may or may not be involved in conducting value studies.

Associate Value Specialist (AVS) certification recognizes those individuals who have decided to become professional value specialists but who have not yet acquired all of the experience or technical skills expected of a CVS. The AVS is a stepping-stone to becoming a CVS.

Value Methodology Practitioner (VMP) certification recognizes those individuals who have acquired the basic skills of Value Methodology, but whose careers are not principally related to VM. Value methodology practitioners often participate as value team members. They may be members of a larger organization, part of a VM department, or independent consultants hired by an organization to participate on value studies.

Related to these certification levels, VM professionals perform in essentially three roles: the value specialist, the value program manager, and the value team member.

Value Specialist

The value specialist's primary responsibility is in conducting value studies. As previously mentioned, the value specialist may work within an organization or may be a consultant who works with a variety of organizations. Value specialists who work within an organization may or may not be required to hold professional certification, depending on the organization's specific needs and requirements. Consultants, on the other hand, should always be professionally certified, as they will be working with organizations whose needs and requirements will vary widely. As such, the consulting value specialists must have a complete understanding of the Value Methodology and its many applications.

Most value specialists tend to focus in one of three areas of application—industrial, construction, or management. Industrial value specialists generally come from manufacturing backgrounds and have a solid understanding of the application of VM to industrial applications. Construction value specialists typically come from one of the design or construction disciplines and are well versed in the application of VM to facilities. Management value specialists tend to come from administrative or management backgrounds and have a good understanding of the application of VM to processes and procedures.

An increasing number of consulting value specialists have developed a high level of expertise in applying VM to all applications. These individuals generally have the highest level of understanding of VM while also possessing broad experience in the areas construction, manufacturing, and management. This pairing of knowledge and diverse experience makes for a powerful combination in leading value studies.

Value Program Manager

The value program manager will be responsible for running an organization's value program. Depending on the nature of the organization, this may include performing a variety of activities, such as:

- Maintaining up-to-date knowledge of the Value Methodology
- Identifying projects for value studies
- Selecting value team members
- Leading and coordinating value studies
- Assisting management in setting annual program goals
- Reporting regularly on progress for active value studies and projects
- Planning and conducting value training to ensure that trained personnel are available for value studies
- Conducting management orientations and briefings as appropriate to educate those in the organization regarding the value program and Value Methodology
- Working with the procurement organization to involve vendors, suppliers, and subcontractors in the program, including the development of methods and reward programs for inviting recommendations for improving value
- Tracking the implementation of accepted value alternatives to ensure the maximization of potential benefits
- Representing the organization in value improvement; contributing to the VM profession's growth through participation in technical conferences, public speaking, and so on

It is strongly recommended that value program managers achieve CVS certification, although, depending on the organization, this may not be an absolute requirement.

Value Team Member

Value team members are usually involved with VM on a part-time basis. Value team members have usually undergone formal VM training and may also hold VMP certification. Having trained and experienced value team members on a value study will greatly enhance the outcome of value studies. Value team members will already have the proper mindset and attitude required to perform the various activities involved in the VM job plan, in addition to bringing their specific technical expertise to bear on a project. Many professionals normally engaged in engineering, programming, and architecture have received formal VM training and are frequently employed as value team members, especially those who already maintain consulting practices.

Professional Standards of Conduct

Those working within professions related to Value Methodology must do so ethically, as is the case with professions in other disciplines. Maintaining a high level of professionalism and ethical behavior is of the greatest importance for anyone applying the Value Methodology. This is because value work involves the review and refinement of work developed by others. Value practitioners must therefore ensure that high standards are maintained in order to avoid discrediting the discipline and the profession.

The following Standards of Conduct is administered by SAVE International to its members and to those it certifies as value professionals:[8]

- *Uphold* the high ideals and level of personal knowledge attested by Society membership or certification, and to participate in none but honest enterprises.
- *Serve* the interests of employers and clients loyally, diligently, and honestly through worthy performance and fidelity.
- *Maintain* a broad and balanced outlook and recognize merit in the ideas and opinions of others.
- *Refrain* from any conduct or act that is discreditable to the reputation or integrity of the VM profession, and be guided in all activities by truth, accuracy, fair dealing, and good taste.
- *Promote* at every opportunity the public understanding of VM, and apply their specialized knowledge for public good.
- *Keep* informed on the latest developments in value techniques and applications, and recommend or initiate improvements to increase the effectiveness of VM.
- *Pledge* to all fellow value specialists, integrity and fair dealing, tolerance and respect, devotion to standards, and dignity of the profession.
- *Support* efforts to strengthen the profession through training and education, and help others reach personal and professional fulfillment.
- *Earn* and carefully guard their reputation for good moral character and good citizenship, recognizing that leadership is a call to service.
- *Recognize* that society membership or certification as a value specialist is not the sole claim to professional competence.

Summary

The numbers of individuals choosing careers related to Value Methodology has been increasing steadily in recent years. Value Methodology professionals can be found managing value programs for government agencies and major corporations throughout the world. We live in a time of shrinking budgets, growing competition, and ever-scarcer resources. As these economic trends continue, the role of value professionals in improving the value of goods, services, and facilities will grow more critical.

Many management improvement processes and fads have come and gone in the last century. Value Methodology has withstood the test of time as a proven means of improving value. It is one of a handful of methodologies to have been formally legislated by governments at all levels. This is because it is soundly grounded in the fundamental source of all human endeavors—the elements of cost, performance, time, risk, and function as they relate to value.

Ultimately, the successful application of Value Methodology greatly depends upon your attitude. I would like to conclude this book with a quote from noted business writer and adviser Robert R. Updegraff (1899–1977), who was perhaps most famous for his fictional character Obvious Adams. Remember it the next time an unexpected challenge arises during a value study.

Be Thankful for Your Troubles

Has it ever occurred to you to be thankful for the troubles and problems of your job?

You ought to be, because they provide at least half your pay. If it were not for the things that go wrong, the trying people you have to deal with in your work, the worries and discouragements, and the headache situations, someone could be found to handle your job for about half as much as you are being paid.

As a matter of fact, it is difficulties and discouragements that create good jobs for thousands of us.

If machines always behaved, if they turned out perfect products hour after hour, there would be no need for anybody to tend to them, and no jobs for inspectors. Nor would there be any need for repair crews of machinists, electricians, stream fitters, etc.

If the people in an organization never made mistakes, never forgot or overlooked anything, never got into each other's hair, there would be no need for managers, superintendents, department heads or foremen.

Problems make jobs. The more problems connected with a position, the better it pays. The reason you are not holding down a bigger job may be because, without realizing it, you are trying to side-step the problems of your present job instead of looking upon them for what they really are—stepping stones to promotion and better pay.

If you face the difficulties of your job squarely, and learn to handle them cheerfully and efficiently, you are likely to find yourself getting ahead surprisingly fast. For there are plenty of bigger jobs waiting for men and women who are not afraid of the troubles connected with them.

Robert R. Updegraff, "Be Thankful for Your Troubles—But Learn These 5 Helpful Rules for Ordering Them Around" (pamphlet), 1953, Executive Development Press.

Notes

Chapter 1

1. James J. O'Brien (1987), "Lawrence D. Miles Recollections, Miles Value Foundation—Excerpts Relating to the Historical Development of Value Analysis," included by permission of the Miles Value Foundation.
2. "Irrational exuberance" is a phrase excerpted from a speech made by former Federal Reserve Board Chairman Alan Greenspan to the American Enterprise Institute on December 5, 1996, commenting on the overescalated value of assets in the global market. His comments were immediately followed by a sharp downturn in stock markets worldwide.
3. E. Malmsten, E. Portanger, & C. Drazin, (2002), *Boo Hoo: A Dot Com Story*, Random House UK.
4. "CSI: Credit Crunch," *Economist*, October 18, 2007.
5. "Economist: A Helping Hand to Homeowners," Economist.com, November 10, 2008.
6. Dan Ariely (2009), *Predictably Irrational*, revised and expanded edition, New York: HarperCollins.
7. SAVE International Value Standard (2007).
8. Construction Cost Index History, Engineering News-Record, McGraw Hill (2009), How ENR Builds the Index: 200 hours of common labor at the 20-city average of common labor rates, plus 25 cwt of standard structural steel shapes at the mill price prior to 1996 and the fabricated 20-city price from 1996, plus 1.128 tons of portland cement at the 20-city price, plus 1,088 board ft of 2 × 4 lumber at the 20-city price.
9. *A Guide to the Project Management Body of Knowledge* (PMBOK Guide), 4th ed. (2008), Project Management Institute.
10. O'Brien, "Lawrence D. Miles Recollections."
11. SAVE International; information used by permission and available at http://value-eng.org/.
12. Data obtained from U.S. Army Corps of Engineers, Headquarters, October 31, 2008.
13. Data obtained from the Caltrans Value Analysis Program, Headquarters, July 7, 2009.
14. Data obtained from the City of New York, Office of Management and Budget, Technical Services Division, July 7, 2009.

Chapter 2

1. *A Guide to the Project Management Body of Knowledge* (PMBOK Guide), 4th ed. (2008), Project Management Institute.
2. Ian Hacking, (1980), "Strange Expectations," *Philosophy of Science* 47: 562–567.
3. O. Morgenstern and J. von Neumann, (2002) *Theory of Games and Economic Behavior*, Princeton University Press.
4. D. Kahnemanand A. Tversky, (1984). "Choices, Values and Frames." *American Psychologist*, 39, 341–350.
5. Lawrence D. Miles (1972) *Techniques of Value Analysis and Engineering*, 2nd ed., New York: McGraw Hill (p. 25).
6. Carlos Fallon (1990), "Value Analysis," *Value Analysis*, 2nd rev. ed., Miles Value Foundation.
7. Carlos Fallon (1965), "Value and Decision," RCA Monograph. A more accessible version of this information was presented in a technical paper by Theodore Fowler in May 2005, *Combinex*—A Method for Sound Decisions, SAVE International, Interactions.
8. David De Marle (1992), *Value: Its Measurement, Design and Management*, New York: John Wiley and Sons (pp. 16–17).
9. Miles, *Techniques of Value Analysis*, (pp. 4–5).
10. Provided here is the formal mathematical expression for Functional Value, assuming that time is treated as a resource like cost.

    V = Value
    f = Function
    P = Performance
    C = Cost
    t = Time
    α = Risk

    $$V_f(P,C,t) = \frac{P \cdot \alpha}{[(C \cdot \alpha) + (t \cdot \alpha)]} \text{ where total value is represented by:}$$

    $$V_f(P,C,t)_{total} = \frac{\sum_{n=1}^{N} P_n \cdot \alpha}{\sum_{n=1}^{N}[(C_n \cdot \alpha) + (t_n \cdot \alpha)]}$$

11. De Marle, (pp. 3-25).
12. Fallon, *Value Analysis*.
13. De Marle, (pp. 3–25).
14. SAVE International Value Standard (2007).
15. Information published on www.theacsi.org.
16. Claes G. Fornell, Sunil Mithas, Forrest Morgeson, and M. S. Krishnan. "Customer Satisfaction and Stock Price: High Returns, Low Risk" (2006) *Journal of Marketing* 70.1: 3–14.
17. John Quelch, "How General Motors Violated Your Trust," Marketing Knowhow, harvardbusiness.org, December 11, 2008.
18. Robert Cooper (1998), *Product Leadership*, Perseus Books.
19. Rosemary Fraser, Ph.D. (1972), "Dimensions and Problems of Communications," SAVE Annual Proceedings.
20. Excerpt from a transcript of a video history interview with Mr. William "Bill" Gates, Smithsonian Institution, 1993.

21. T. C. Chamberlin (1890), The method of multiple working hypotheses: *Science* (old series) v. 15, p. 92–96; reprinted 1965, v. 148, pp. 754–759.

22. Steven D. Levitt and Stephen J. Dubner (2005), *Freakonomics: A Rogue Economist Explores the Hidden Side of Everything*, William Morrow.

Chapter 3

1. Lawrence D. Miles (1972), *Techniques of Value Analysis and Engineering*, New York: McGraw Hill (pp. 53–59).

Chapter 4

1. U.S. Dept. of Transportation, FHWA (1990), "Memorandum: Purpose and Need in Environmental Documents."

2. Stephen J. Kirk (1993), *Enhancing Value in Design Decisions*, Kirk Associates.

3. C. Fallon (1986), *Value Analysis*, Triangle Press.

4. Ginger R. Adams and R. Terry Hays (1999), "The Value of Time," SAVE International Conference Paper. The content of this section is condensed from this reference.

Chapter 5

1. David Halliday (1983), "Steve Paul Jobs," *Current Biography 5*.

2. *A Guide to the Project Management Body of Knowledge* (2009), 4th ed., Project Management Institute.

3. J. J. O'Brien (1976), *Value Analysis in Design and Construction*, New York: McGraw-Hill.

4. Value Engineering Program Guide for Design & Construction (1992), General Services Administration, (pp. 7–3).

5. Steven Morton (November 2002), "Business Case for Green Design," *Building Operating Management*.

6. For the latest information on Nominal Treasury Interest Rates, the Office of Management and Budget maintains a website at www.whitehouse.gov/omb/circulars/index.html.

7. Bilial M. Ayyub (2003), *Risk Analysis in Engineering and Economics*, CRC Press.

8. Robert Johnson (1990), *The Economics of Building*, John Wiley & Sons.

9. The RBES file can be accessed via WSDOT's Estimating & Modeling page at http://www.wsdot.wa.gov/Projects/ProjectMgmt/RiskAssessment/Information. htm. The link for the RBES can be found under "Self-Modeling Tool."

10. Theodore C. Fowler (1990), *Value Analysis in Design*, New York: Van Nostrand Reinhold.

11. Thomas L. Saaty (2008), *Decision Making for Leaders*, RWS Publications.

12. Thomas L. Saaty, and Kirti Peniwati (2008), *Group Decision Making: Drawing Out and Reconciling Differences*, RWS Publications.

13. Decision Lens is commercially available at http://www.decisionlens.com/.
14. R. Stewart, M. Baza, N. Bernard (2009), *How VE and Decision Analysis Are Improving Mobility across Borders*, AASHTO Value Engineering Conference Proceedings.

Chapter 6

1. J. Kaufman and R. Woodhead(2006), *Stimulating Innovation in Products and Services*, John Wiley & Sons. The FAST Structure presented in this book is closely in line with the one presented in this reference. Jerry Kaufman has devoted most of his career to the development of FAST technique. This book is an excellent resource for those wishing to deepen their knowledge of FAST and function analysis.
2. Charles W. Bytheway (2007), *FAST Creativity and Innovation*, J. Ross Publishing.
3. T. Fowler and T. Snodgrass(1972), *Customer Oriented FAST Diagramming*, SAVE Regional Conference Proceedings, Detroit.
4. Virginia Adams (2004), "FAST Doesn't Flow." This section is condensed from a technical paper presented at the 2004 SAVE International Conference in Montreal, Quebec.
5. Kaneo Akiyama (1991), *Function Analysis: Systematic Improvement of Quality and Performance*, Productivity Press.

Chapter 7

1. Roger Von Oech (1983), *A Whack on the Side of the Head: How to Unlock Your Mind for Innovation*, New York: Warner Books.
2. Vincent Ryan Ruggiero (2002), *Becoming a Critical Thinker*, New York: Houghton Mifflin Company.
3. Robert Rosenthal and Lenore Jacobson (1992), *Pygmalion in the Classroom: Teacher Expectation and Pupils' Intellectual Development.* New York: Irvington Publishers.

Chapter 8

1. Lawrence D. Miles (1972), *Techniques of Value Analysis and Engineering*, New York: McGraw Hill (p. 58).
2. Arthur E. Mudge (1989), *Value Engineering: A Systematic Approach*, Pittsburgh: J. Pohl Associates.
3. Answer: There are currently 45 African nations out of a total of 191 member states of the United Nations. This gives a probability of about 24 percent that any one U.N member nation selected at random is located in Africa.
4. A. L. Delbecq, A. H. VandeVen, and D. H. Gustafson D. H. (1975), *Group Techniques for Program Planners*, Glenview, Illinois: Scott Foresman and Company.

Chapter 9

1. The Risk Based Estimate Self-Modeling (RBES) file can be accessed via WSDOT's Estimating and Modeling page at http://www.wsdot.wa.gov/Projects/Project Mgmt/RiskAssessment/Information.htm.

Chapter 10

1. Edward, R. Tufte (2006), *Beautiful Evidence*, Graphics Press LLC. The chapter on PowerPoint, "The Cognitive Style of PowerPoint: Pitching Out Corrupts Within,: is also available for purchase separately at the author's Web site: http://www.edwardtufte.com.
2. Seth Godin (September 2001), *Really Bad PowerPoint (and How to Avoid It)*, an e-book and companion to the author's book *The Big Red Fez*. The e-book is available at the author's Web site, http://www.sethgodin.com.
3. Based on a 2002 article, "Change the Way You Persuade," by Miller-Williams, CEO Gary A. Williams, and Chairman Robert B. Miller and published by Harvard Business School Publishing.

Chapter 12

1. Lee Bolman and T. Deal (1991), *Reframing Organizations*, San Francisco: Jossey-Bass.
2. Robert R. Blake and Jane S. Mouton (1985), *The Managerial Grid III: The Key to Leadership Excellence*, Houston: Gulf Publishing Co.
3. Sam Kaner (2007), *Facilitator's Guide to Participatory Decision-Making*, San Francisco: Jossey-Bass.
4. Keith Davis (1977), *Human Behavior at Work*, New York: McGraw Hill.
5. R. Paul, and L. Elder (2006), *A Thinker's Guide to the Art of Socratic Questioning*, Dillon Beach, CA: Foundation for Critical Thinking, Dillon Beach.
6. Kaner, *Facilitator's Guide*.
7. David Keirsey, and Marilyn Bates (1978), *Please Understand Me: Character and Temperament Types*, Prometheus Nemesis Books Co.
8. SAVE International Standards of Conduct, http://www.value-eng.org/about_standardofconduct.php.

Suggested Reading

Ariely, Dan. *Predictably Irrational*, revised and expanded edition, New York: HarperCollins, 2009.

Bytheway, Charles W. *FAST Creativity and Innovation*. Fort Lauderdale, FL: J. Ross Publishing, 2007.

De Marle, David. *Value: Its Measurement, Design and Management*. New York: John Wiley & Sons, 1992.

Fallon, Carlos. *Value Analysis*, 2nd revised edition, Miles Value Foundation, 1990; available at http://www.value-eng.org/catalog_library.php.

Godin, Seth. *Really Bad PowerPoint (and How to Avoid It)*, September 2001, e-book, available at http://www.sethgodin.com/sg/.

Kaner, Sam. *Facilitator's Guide to Participatory Decision-Making*. 2007, San Francisco: Jossey-Bass.

Kaufman, J., and R. Woodhead. *Stimulating Innovation in Products and Services*. Hoboken, NJ: John Wiley & Sons, 2006.

Kirk, Stephen J. *Enhancing Value in Design Decisions*. Detroit: Kirk Associates, 1993.

Levitt, Steven D., and Stephen J. Dubner. *Freakonomics: A Rogue Economist Explores the Hidden Side of Everything*. New York: William Morrow, 2005.

Miles, Lawrence D. *Techniques of Value Analysis and Engineering*, New York: McGraw Hill, 1972.

Paul, R., and L. Elder. *A Thinker's Guide to the Art of Socratic Questioning*. Dillon Beach, CA: Foundation for Critical Thinking, 2006.

Saaty, Thomas L. *Decision Making for Leaders*. Pittsburgh: RWS Publications, 2008.

Saaty, Thomas L., and Kirti Peniwati. *Group Decision Making: Drawing Out and Reconciling Differences*. Pittsburgh: RWS Publications, 2008.

Taleb, Nassim Nicholas. *The Black Swan*. New York: Random House, 2007.

Tufte, Edward, R. *Beautiful Evidence*. Cheshire, CT: Graphics Press LLC, 2006.

Von Oech, Roger, *A Whack on the Side of the Head: How to Unlock Your Mind for Innovation*. New York: Warner Books, 1983.

About the Author

Robert Stewart is a Certified Value Specialist and Project Management Professional who has been practicing Value Methodology (VM) for more than 20 years. During this time, he has led more than 300 value studies for clients in both the private and public sectors on a wide range of products, services, and facilities, from forklifts to multibillion-dollar transportation projects.

Stewart got his start in VM working for his grandfather's consulting firm during the summers while attending college. After receiving his BA at the University of Oregon in 1990, he went to work full time for his grandfather. During this time, he had the opportunity to learn from a number of pioneers in the discipline and was exposed to value work in design, construction, management, and manufacturing. In 1999, he joined Value Management Strategies, Inc., a consulting firm specializing in VM, project management, and risk analysis services. He became president of the firm in 2009.

Stewart has taught and lectured on VM at the University of California at Berkeley, Portland State University, and at Chung-Ang University in Seoul, South Korea. His work has been published in both Korean and Chinese. He was responsible for developing Value Metrics, a value measurement system based upon the principles of the Analytic Hierarchy Process (AHP). This system of techniques is now used by a number of public agencies as a means to evaluate the relationship of project cost and performance to value improvement.

In 2008, Stewart was nominated to serve on the board of directors for the Lawrence Delos Miles Value Foundation, a nonprofit organization dedicated to expanding the discipline of Value Methodology in higher education. In 2009, he was inducted into the SAVE International College of Fellows, which is the highest form of professional recognition in the field of Value Methodology.

Index